WORDS AGAINST WORDS

WORDS AGAINST WORDS

ON THE RHETORIC OF CARLO MICHELSTAEDTER

MALCOLM ANGELUCCI

t

Troubador
5 Weir Road
Kibworth Beauchamp
Leicester LE8 0LQ, UK
Tel: 0116 279 2277
Email: books@troubador.co.uk
Web: www.troubador.co.uk/matador

ISBN 978 1848763 975

British Library Cataloguing in Publication Data.
A catalogue record for this book is available from the British Library.

Series Editor: George Ferzoco

Dedicated to Marta Benedetti

Contents

Contents

Acknowledgements

This research has been possible thanks to a Melbourne International Research Scholarship (MIRS) and an Endeavour International Postgraduate Research Scholarship (IPRS), kindly offered by The University of Melbourne. In the course of the enquiry, the chance for a research trip to Italy was granted to me through the Emma Grollo Memorial Scholarship; without this generous financial help, the collection of the Italian bibliography and the work on the manuscripts of Carlo Michelstaedter would not have been possible. A further Dissemination Grant from the University of Technology Sydney covered the expenses for professional proof reading and editing of the book manuscript.

I would like to acknowledge gratefully first of all my PhD supervisors, who mentored and guided me during the research that forms the basis for this book. Associate Professor Stephen D. Kolsky, with his insight, patience and sympathy smoothed my journey and fostered the development of my thought; countless coffees bear witness to this great friendship. Professor Anne Freadman offered crucial support and critical attention to the theoretical aspects of my work, and her contribution and influence goes far beyond the completion of the present work. Furthermore, I wish to thank Majella Thomas for supporting me in the choice of writing in English despite my inexperience, lack of vocabulary and tendency to fall into Italian modes; her tireless proofreading and comments have been indispensable. A big thank you goes also to Cynthia Troup, for her highly professional help with the final stages of the manuscript, for her flexibility, support and friendship. For the work on the Greek sources, I am indebted to Dr Nick Nicholas, who generously offered his time and experience to guide me in the intricacies of Michelstaedter's intertextual references. In Gorizia, at the Fondo Carlo Michelstaedter of the Biblioteca Statale Isontina, the availability, professionalism and kindness of the staff and especially dottoressa Antonella Gallarotti, to whom I am particularly grateful, were of great help in my bibliographical research. In Rome, dottor Piero

Ferrante offered his important logistic help and his continuous commitment in keeping my bibliography up to date. For the many stimulating conversations, a final thank you goes to Joaquin Thomas-Mourad, Marta Thomas-Angelucci and Leda Strazzoni.

Works of Carlo Michelstaedter and abbreviations adopted in the text

Michelstaedter, Carlo. *Opere*. Edited by Gaetano Chiavacci. Firenze: Sansoni, 1958. (**O**)

Michelstaedter, Carlo. *Poesie*. Edited by Sergio Campailla. Bologna: Patron, 1974.

Michelstaedter, Carlo. *Opera Grafica e Pittorica*. Edited by Sergio Campailla. Gorizia: ICM, 1975.

Michelstaedter, Carlo. *Scritti Scolastici*. Edited by Sergio Campailla. Gorizia: ICM, 1976. (**SS**)

Michelstaedter, Carlo. *La Persuasione e la Rettorica*. Edited by Sergio Campailla. Milano: Adelphi, 1982.

Michelstaedter, Carlo. *Epistolario*. Edited by Sergio Campailla. Milano: Adelphi, 1983. (**E**)

Michelstaedter, Carlo. *Poesie*. Edited by Sergio Campailla. Milano: Adelphi, 1987. (**P**)

Michelstaedter, Carlo. *Il Dialogo della Salute e altri Dialoghi*. Edited by Sergio Campailla. Milano: Adelphi, 1988. (**DDS**)

Michelstaedter, Carlo. *La Persuasione e la Rettorica*. Edited by Sergio Campailla. Milano: Adelphi, 1995. (**PR**)

Michelstaedter, Carlo. *Il Prediletto Punto d'Appoggio della Dialettica Socratica e Altri Scritti*. Edited by Gianandrea Franchi. Milano: Mimesis, 2000. (**PPA**)

Michelstaedter, Carlo. *Parmenide ed Eraclito. Empedocle*. Milano: SE, 2003. (**PEE**)

Michelstaedter, Carlo. *Sfugge la Vita. Taccuini e Appunti*. Edited by Angela Michelis. Torino: Nino Aragno Editore, 2004.

For the English translation of passages from *La Persuasione e la Rettorica*, where possible the following edition is used:

Michelstaedter, Carlo. *Persuasion and Rhetoric*. Translated by Russel Scott Valentino, Cinzia Sartini Blum and David J. Depew. New Haven, London: Yale University Press, 2004.

Introduction

[...] dann erst kam der Tänzer.
Nicht der. Genug! Und wenn er auch so leicht tut,
er ist verkleidet und er wird ein Bürger
und geht durch seine Küche in die Wohnung.

Rainer Maria Rilke – *Duineser Elegien*

This enquiry into the work of Carlo Michelstaedter is an attempt to read a philosophical text through a framework derived from literary criticism. This general objective develops from the conviction that, from within the intricate relationship between literature and philosophy[1], it is possible to outline a method that can give an original account of both Michelstaedter's theoretical speculation and the peculiarity of his style. It is for these reasons that Michelstaedter's philosophical text, *La Persuasione e la Rettorica*, his dissertation completed in 1910, will be the centre of our research. It is within this text, in fact, that not only an original and in many ways anticipatory philosophy is developed, but also a poetic, and a consequent attempt to come to terms with it in the very process of its articulation.

In this sense, this book argues that approaching Michelstaedter's work from the angle of a stylistic reading of *La Persuasione e la Rettorica* is the preferential way to address the most problematic knots of his philosophy. Daniela Bini, in her monographic work *Carlo Michelstaedter and the Failure of Language*, outlines the risk for every interpreter of our author: «to write about him seems to defeat the purpose from the start, as "this writing about" is what he strongly rejected as the source of falsehood»[2]. Michelstaedter's attack against conceptual systematization is an implicit critique of any attempt to explain his thought through academic enquiry[3]; and yet, this critique is itself developed in a philosophical dissertation, written in an academic genre, thus presenting Michelstaedter with the paradox of having to undermine the value of the language through which the undermining itself takes place. This is the 'war with words against words' with which my enquiry is concerned. I think that many of the peculiarities of Michelstaedter's style — adoption of fictional sub-genres, multilingualism, treatment of quotations and allusions, to name a few examples — can be understood as a struggle from inside this paradox, towards its potential overcoming; if this is correct, then a research on the strategies of signification deployed in *La Persuasione e la Rettorica* is a privileged approach to address its poetic and philosophy.

In a general sense, Carlo Michelstaedter's works are the consequence of a painful knowledge of existential contingency and alienation, and the struggle to re-achieve the unity of (self) possession[4]. This existential commitment to a philosophy is the primary critical framework through which Michelstaedter's works have been read; the comparison between 'life' and 'work' often sees in the discourse on Michelstaedter's parable and final suicide a compelling intertextual and interdiscursive[5] point of departure for an interpretation of the author's philosophy and art[6]. However, this book argues that it is possible to trace this 'attempt at coherence' *inside* our author's oeuvre, thus avoiding some of the methodological problems and complications concerning the relationship between author and narrator, author and the 'I' subject of many poems, and, in the case of Michelstaedter's paintings, author and the 'self' of the self-portraits. If his philosophy defines an 'absolute' (the 'persuasion'[7] of the title), the struggle to reach it and a «via alla persuasione» (PR: 31), this 'way to persuasion' has its reflection in a particular struggle with/against language, and thus in a particular idea of the problem of signification. If this hypothesis is true, then the crucial task for us will be to outline a methodology which can give an account of the links between theory and practice and their reciprocal influences; namely, the relation of poetic and rhetoric.

This introduction is organized around few key themes. A brief historical and cultural contextualization of Michelstaedter and his work will allow us to tackle two different points: firstly, the importance of Michelstaedter's life (and final suicide) in the critical interpretation of his works, and the consequent position of this book in relation to this corpus of secondary sources; secondly, the necessary introduction to the philosophical categories of 'persuasion' and 'rhetoric' through a comparison with texts at the turn of the twentieth century that share similar preoccupations. In fact, one of the most significant achievements of critical work is not only to have revealed Michelstaedter's philosophy as an important contribution to the debate of his period, but the identification of *La Persuasione e la Rettorica* as a paradigmatic text for the interpretation of a *Zeitgeist*[8], in this sense opening the way for comparative readings of Michelstaedter in relation to a series of intertextual sources (the young Lukács, the Wittgenstein of the *Tractatus*, but also the Italian writing and thought of Slataper, Boine, Campana, and the 'vociani', to quote a few). Where direct biographical or philological links between the texts cannot be demonstrated, the affinity of themes, problems and philosophical sources offers the chance to define a framework for intertextual analysis. While the focus of this enquiry is the self-reflexivity of the text – and thus it provides an interpretation from *inside* the work – an introductory contextualization and comparison will effectively set the parameters for our discussion of *La Persuasione e la Rettorica* as the *locus* of a particular battle with/against language. In particular, the comparison between Michelstaedter's description of a 'crisis of language' and the arguments of the young Lukács, will help us to show that while Michelstaedter's theoretical analysis of the crisis is shared with many Central European intellectuals at the turn of the twentieth century, his solutions and investment in the battle 'against language' through linguistic means are his own peculiarity. This comparison will then introduce a brief discussion of the main features of Michelstaedter's philosophy and, in doing so, will outline the point of departure for the research.

0.1   Some notes on Michelstaedter's legacy

Carlo Michelstaedter left a substantial group of texts: a degree thesis in philosophy on the concepts of 'persuasion' and 'rhetoric' in Plato and Aristotle, now known as *La Persuasione e la Rettorica*[9], examples of philosophical dialogues, several poems, letters, much aphoristic prose and a large number of sketches, drawing and paintings[10]. All of these deal almost entirely with similar themes: authenticity and inauthenticity, absolute and relative, 'persuasion' and 'rhetoric'. Through various media and genres he engages in the definition of the very possibility of freedom from the contingency of time and space, and the possibility of 'pure (self) possession' outside the inadequacy of human determinations and the violence and absurdity of socio-cultural relationships. This goal implies a series of obstacles on both theoretical and pragmatic levels. The first of Michelstaedter's problems is to demonstrate the existence of this absolute, or at least its possibility, having described the human condition as contingent, perennially lacking and driven by inadequate values. He, himself a human, has to give evidence of something which is external to him, some state of absolute, emancipated understanding. In doing so, he has to find words to describe this state, and thus give an account of something that is, by definition, 'beyond' language[11]. Finally, he must give an account of the way, if there is one, in which this state can be achieved, and define the relationship between this theoretical attempt and the actual practice of this struggle towards a regained unity. Michelstaedter uses the term 'persuasion' to define his absolute, and the struggle to describe and make possible this 'persuasion' is, in extreme synthesis, the heart of the question left by our author in his papers.

But Michelstaedter left something else. He left us a life[12] and, more than that, a violent death which has itself become a narration: a further 'text' that has conditioned and often, from the very beginning of his critical fortune[13], guided and preceded any judgement on the works.

The cultural and geographical context in which Carlo Michelstaedter was born and grew up until the completion of his secondary studies in 1905 can itself give some sense of the peculiarity of his experiences, particularly if compared with the landscape of Italian literature. Born into a bourgeois, Italian speaking Jewish family in Gorizia[14] – a town on the periphery of Austro-Hungarian Empire, now part of the Italian region of Friuli Venezia Giulia – Michelstaedter could have been part of the «classe dei colti»[15], which had such importance in the cultural life of the peninsula in the years before the First World War. Or he could have beloged to the stream of intellectuals who developed their parable in conjunction with the fall of the Austro-Hungarian Empire. This is a generation that experienced the end of a possible «conciliazione dell'unità e della diversità, [...] fine che d'altronde l'Austria stessa, con le sue contraddizioni irresolubili e con la pluralità dei suoi linguaggi[16], contribuisce ad affrettare»[17]. Moreover it is a generation which lived the political, cultural and philosophical crisis both in the philosophical sense, as a crisis of language, and in the poetic sense, as a crisis of style[18]. Hence, Magris sees these writers as 'grandchildren' of Lord Chandos[19], and Hugo Von Hofmannsthal's *Letter* assumes a paradigmatic role for the explanation of an historical crisis: «Magris [...] ha sempre considerato il problema tra persuasione e rettorica un problema epocale e non solo individuale»[20]. In this sense, Michelstaedter is a child of his time, and we will see not only how much of his philosophy (and his philosophy of language) is densely populated with Central European issues, but how his reading reflects this context[21].

Yet Michelstaedter did not end up in Vienna, where he had enrolled in order to study mathematics. Instead, after matriculating, he obtained permission from his father Alberto for an educational journey to Italy and Florence to satisfy his precocious interest in art and painting, and once there he changed his plans and opted for a career at the Istituto di Studi Superiori in Florence[22]. Once in Florence he completed his exams with excellent results, but his difficulty in integrating into the 'active' cultural scene resulted in a growing sense of discontent with the rhetoric of the academy, the avant-gardes, and the town itself. Some of his letters, such as the one to Nino Paternolli dated 21st of May 1910, from Gorizia, attest to this state:

Ho vissuto quattro anni a Firenze, che è uno dei centri librari d'Italia, mi misi ripetute volte a disposizione di editori del posto, di editori d'altre città, feci loro proposte precise dopo aver scritto agli editori e agli autori esteri; offrii i miei servizi agli organizzatori di vaste pubblicazioni di cose tradotte (professori o letterati essi stessi). Tutto m'andò infruttuoso [...]. E intesi che dappertutto bisogna esser in qualche modo raccomandati o dalla fama di scrittore o dalla protezione di chi per le aderenze o la carica, o il censo, o i fatti compiuti abbia voce ad essere ascoltato. – Acquistare l'un modo o l'altro di raccomandazione per <proposito> è una cosa che io non ho mai saputo fare – né ora sono progredito in quell'arte (E: 435-6)[23].

But the letters also show that this discontent with the inhabitants of the city of his artistic dreams had begun much earlier:

Poveri fiorentini come sono caduti al basso, non hanno niente del popolo grande ed artista decaduto che per quanto guasto nel carattere nei sentimenti negl'ideali pur sempre conserva non foss'altro in un lusso sfrenato il resto di un estetismo raffinato, una certa armonia tanto nelle cose piccole come nelle grandi, una certa sapienza di vivere come l'avevano gli Ateniesi anche nei tempi della più profonda decadenza. Assolutamente i fiorentini d'ora non hanno niente dell'atticismo antico, sono piccini, gretti in tutto, limitati d'ingegno, senza sentimento né per l'arte né per alcun'altra cosa, egoisti e soprattutto falsi, hanno una certa diligenza ottusa, una laboriosità da formica che urtano i nervi (Letter to the family, 17th of January 1906. E: 86-7).

At the time, Florence was the city of the journals *Lacerba*, *Leonardo* (and later *La Voce*); Florence was the centre for a group of young scholars and artists who shaped independently, even if in complex relationships with the other experiences of the time (for example the growing influence of Benedetto Croce[24], yet to become hegemonic, and the futurist avant-gardes[25]), the figure of the Italian intellectual before the Great War. However, despite this ferment, a talented student such as Michelstaedter, who furthermore showed philosophical and literary interests (Schopenhauer, Nietzsche, Ibsen, Sorel, to quote a few) which were consistent with one of the young intellectual elite of the city, spent his tertiary career completely outside these extra-academic circles. Scipio Slataper from nearby Trieste, for example, was destined to become one of the most prominent figures of *La Voce*, performing with his seminal thesis on Ibsen and other works, the role of a 'cultural bridge' between Florence, the province and Central Europe[26]. But Michelstaedter's existential, philosophical and artistic parable develops outside such affiliations. In fact, it could be argued that the theses expressed in *La Persuasione e la Rettorica* show a radical rejection[27] of the very conception of an 'intellectual group' or movement, and put forward a position which, despite the similarity of background with the leaders of cultural debate, is diametrically opposed to their conclusions, as for example in the case of Prezzolini[28] and his work on *L'Arte di Persuadere*, published in 1907[29]. If it is difficult to accept the myth of an ascetic Carlo insulated from the influence of his context and time[30], it is true that Michelstaedter's philosophy is an advertisement, if not for solitude[31], then for individuality: «la via della persuasione non è corsa da <omnibus>» (PR: 62)[32].

In this context of rejection, deprecation and the incapability of displaying his value in an extra-academic environment, the time between the spring of 1907 and the return to Gorizia in the spring of 1908 holds at least two crucial experiences in store for Michelstaedter. In April 1907 Nadia Baraden, a Russian noble to whom Carlo was teaching Italian, committed suicide. The two had developed a strong intellectual relationship, and for Carlo the wound was deep; the violent act assumed for him the features of a powerful existential choice to which he alluded in a letter to his friend Iolanda De Blasi, dated 25th of April 1907: «Mi sento talvolta debole e piccolo e vedo con orrore il treno <trasporto animali> avvicinarsi che dovrebbe portarmi nel mondo borghesemente, trionfalmente cretino. – <No. No! Piuttosto soccombere> mi gridò una voce morente [Nadia][33]» (E: 203-4). Shortly after, a rather ingenuous attempt to formalize his relationship with Iolanda through an official proposal of engagement met strong objections from both families, and left Carlo with the necessity of a complex process of justification and submission to common social manners in front of his parents[34]. In this state, the return to Gorizia, if it was a liberation from the academic environment, proved a rockier landing place: «ti scrivo dal mio tavolo, accanto sono tutti i miei libri, sul sofà dorme papà, fumo il tabacco che mi piace, vedo i rondoni [...] attorno al castello ... ma non sono contento affatto – peggio che a Firenze perché non ho più dove desiderarmi. Concludo che è peggio il ritorno che la partenza; questa è una morte semplice, quella una doppia morte» (Letter to Gaetano Chiavacci from Gorizia, 29th of June 1909. E: 400). During the last year, the intertextual sources which would guide Carlo in the completion of his philosophical and artistic works were defined: his early infatuation with Carducci and D'Annunzio had disappeared[35] and Nietzsche and Schopenhauer were definitively 'digested', and are from this time on only indirectly alluded to in his works. What remains is a select group of people who 'said the word of persuasion'[36], and under whose influence and example the task of the thesis is undertaken: the Presocratics[37], Socrates, Ecclesiastes, Leopardi, Ibsen, Christ and Beethoven, the latter discovered in Florence through Carlo's friendship with the composer and musical critic Giannotto Bastianelli[38].

The last period in Gorizia was divided between work on the thesis, holidays in Pirano – during which Carlo cultivated a strong friendship with his sister Paula and the Cassini sisters, Argia[39] and Fulvia –, the tutoring of his cousin Emilio[40] for his matriculation exam, and the defence from the intolerance of his parents for the delay in his graduation. His letters give a flavour of these last months:

Mi accorgo sempre più con orrore che sono condannato a restar per sempre fuori dalla vita grande intensa passionale e che non avrò mai il modo di viverla in me. [...] A me non resterebbe altro che la vita violenta, errare a cavallo per la prateria e riposar la notte sotto la tenda a contar le stelle e fissar la linea chiara all'orizzonte [...] – ma navigare a vela, sulle nostre buone <brazzere> venete (Letter to Gaetano Chiavacci, 4th of August 1908. E: 331).

Ma che fai? chi sei? Sono uno che deve far la tesi. E che faccio?

penso che devo far la tesi. Lo sai come fanno i deportati inglesi nei grandi penitenziari del Regno? C'è un grande cilindro che ruota intorno all'asse longitudinale, lungo la superficie convessa corrono a giusta distanza tavole, come gradini. Su queste in lunga fila salgono i deportati da una in l'altra facendo girar il cilindro col loro peso e restando sempre fermi allo stesso posto: chi non sale è travolto di sotto. – Così io – e forse che da questa dannata fatica fra un paio di settimane verrà fuori qualche cosa che gli altri chiameranno tesi (Letter to Marino Caliterna, 11th of November 1909. E: 415).

The final weeks in the life of Carlo are a climax of alienation from social life and febrile work for the completion of his thesis; he does not follow his family for the usual summer vacation, but stays alone in the house in Gorizia, working with Emilio and dictating to him the final draft of his work. At this point in Michelstaedter's biography, speculations and hypotheses in critical literature are the most various. On the one hand, the clash between the philosophical conclusions reached by Carlo and the contradiction of the 'rhetorical' necessity of argument, demonstration and defence implied by academic writing could have been harder and harder to sustain; Muzzioli writes: «negli utimi mesi della sua vita [,] la questione è la temporalità (scrivere la tesi sulla 'persuasione' richiede tempo; costa il rinvio delle scelte di vita; allora, scrivere della 'persuasione' è non essere persuasi?) La 'persuasione' è istantanea e puntuale; o c'è o non c'è, secondo l'assolutismo parmenideo»[41]. On the other hand, it could be argued that an increasingly intense asceticism led to a drastic nervous collapse at the end of the writing experience and the 'return' to social life, as described by Campailla: «la sua vita era, senza più residui, un <fiammeggiare> in una febbre consumante, verso un'impossibile santità senza Dio»[42]. Nontheless, whatever happened in that house and in that mind, on 16th of October the thesis was awaiting only a few minor corrections, which were to be completed the following day. Carlo decided not to join the family for the birthday of his mother, and to delay giving her the small landscape he had painted as a present[43]; instead he visited Argia Cassini, asking her to play him his beloved Beethoven. The morning after, his mother walked back to the city specifically to berate her son for his absence, resulting in a harsh verbal fight which ended with Carlo throwing a tantrum. Left alone again, he communicated to Emilio that he was not needed for the usual work, and shortly after committed suicide by shooting himself with a gun previously seized from a friend. It was 17th of October 1910 and Carlo was 23 years old.

8

Michelstaedter's life was destined to become, almost overnight, a myth which would pervasively influence the literature on the author. This influence is so critical that the present volume, while not concerned primarily with biographical themes, is compelled to open with these notes; if only to give account of Carlo's critical destiny. Furthermore, the fact that Michelstaedter left 'in his drawer' a series of unpublished texts which in the century following his death would fight their way into the canon of Italian literature[44], can be used to complete the picture of the myth of a solitary achiever of a 'philosophical ascesis' culminating in suicide.

First and foremost[45], Michelstaedter left his degree thesis on the concepts of 'persuasion' and 'rhetoric' in Plato and Aristotle. This is a work which, much as it partakes of the genre 'academic writing', seems to be written against itself: here we find a philosophical argument directed against philosophy and its rhetoric, and an attempt to undermine the very core of western culture – namely science, 'science of the spirit', religion, and social organization – as inadequate and violent examples of 'rhetoric' and false objectivity that hide the tragic truth of human existence. In doing this – and in the adoption of the word 'rhetoric' there is a confirmation of this objective – Michelstaedter's degree thesis links its critique to a critique of language or, better, to an understanding of language (in its different 'genres', we would say) in its 'impossible' relationship with truth. As a result of this aim, *La Persuasione e la Rettorica* appears as a strange object indeed: a graduation thesis on Plato and Aristotle in which Plato and Aristotle are discussed only in a fictional, dismissive and tongue-in-cheek apologue, and in the appendices[46]. It is a thesis in which the Presocratics and the New Testament are the main quoted sources, without direct acknowledgement of any secondary sources contemporary to Michelstaedter[47]. Furthermore, this is a work in which, mainly because of this critical and subversive attempt, the argument is conducted through a juxtaposition of stylistic strategies and sub-genres: from a prophetic tone to a mathematical demonstration (with functions, drawings, variables and the entire range of scientific paraphernalia); from an example involving knowledge of chemistry to a folkloristic song quoted in the dialect of Veneto; from an aphorism in ancient Greek to a fictional parable. The first text to be discovered by critics, *La Persuasione e la Rettorica* seems on this level rather peculiar, and yet it can in many ways be read 'inside' the context of Central European and Italian debates. In fact, the underlying Schopenhauerian structure, the indirect connection with Nietzsche[48], the love for Ibsen and the consequent intertextual connections[49], and the rediscovery of Leopardi[50], all lead to possible and useful contextualizations. Moreover, on a stylistic level, the 'experimental' look of the text can be connected in a broad sense with the cultural climate of the time; with the experience of Futurism and *La Voce* in Italy[51], and what Harrison calls 'pre-war expressionism'[52] in Europe.

'Outside' and/or 'inside' its time: these are two of the possible interpretations of the artistic parable of Michelstaedter. Another conspicuous strand of criticism, particularly concerned with a philosophical interpretation of the author, has tendentially underlined the ways in which Michelstaedter's speculations anticipated themes of twentieth-century philosophy, locating him as a precursor[53]. This begins with idealistic readings of *La Persuasione e la Rettorica* as a poor or unsystematic example of idealism[54]; further, this interpretation is re-thought in the context of the debate on existentialism, thanks to the seminal article by Joachim Ranke, published in 1962[55]. This leads to comprehensive readings of the author in relationship with different Heideggerian themes[56], readings that conserve their strength. Following a series of Marxist interpretations[57], are more recent attempts to re-contextualize Michelstaedter through a comparison with the experience of the expressionist movement, which considers our author (who died in 1910) a precursor of themes and modes[58]. Yet arguably the most important shift in recent criticism is from a philosophical focus to a broader understanding of the author for his role in the history of literature. If this offers a range of historical interpretations, it has also the merit of bringing into focus various texts, such as poems and dialogues, which can contribute to a more complex understanding of Michelstaedter's poetic and the links between the philosophy of language and its practice through a process of academic and artistic signification. The proceedings of the conference held in Gorizia in 1987 give evidence of this interpretive shift[59]. As a consequence, the need for a stylistic reading of *La Persuasione e la Rettorica*, together with a post-structuralist sensitivity for the problems of rhetoric and signification in philosophical texts, has been recently asserted in articles by Taviani[60] and Muzzioli[61]. They underline the link between the theory of 'persuasion' and the practice of writing, defining in this area of study a new horizon of interpretation; in fact, it is in this particular field that the main aim of this book will find its space.

After this schematic introduction to the reception of Michelstaedter, it is interesting to note how, despite the importance of the major works written by our author and their influence, his biography remains crucially important for many critics, if not overshadowing the 'work', then surely influencing its interpretation. In fact, this constant interest in the tragic end of the 'young, gifted and unknown student of philosophy', seems to have been the very 'original sin' of criticism. The comparison of the texts with the discourse on Michelstaedter's life is a framework transversal to many of the approaches quoted above; the question 'why did he kill himself?' is a temptation on which we ought to spend a few words.

0.0.1 The myth of the' philosophical suicide' and its limits

In a letter to his father dated 5th of August 1910, following the completion of the first part of his thesis, Carlo writes: «ci sono dentro molte gocce del mio <sangue incontaminato>, ma non so se agli altri sembrerà acqua sporca o sudore (che è peggio)» (E:443). Two months later, the metaphorical blood becomes real, the stains of which are still visible today on the manuscripts.

The myth of the 'philosophical suicide' becomes from the very beginning a *topos*, and a jeopardizing object of interpretation. Giovanni Papini, who is merited with first drawing attention to the author shortly after his death, with an article for *Il Resto del Carlino* dated 5th of November 1910[62], inaugurates this particular 'fashion' with a clear eye on his own agenda. In fact Papini admits not to have read *La Persuasione e la Rettorica*, but speculating on some indirect sources he bets for a 'philosophical suicide', committed by Michelstaedter in a supposed coherence with his ideal. Papini's speculation seems to derive its impetus from a new generation of Italian intellectuals seeking a martyr of the ideal, and Michelstaedter's life parable, in this sense, strangely parallel to that of Otto Weininger – the author of *Sex and Character*[63], was Jewish, educated in classical studies, and committed suicide at twenty-three, following the completion of his most important work – fits the environment which surrounded the Florentine journal *La Voce*. The journal contributed in fact to the success of *Sex and Character* in Italy, and the notion of suicide as a choice of coherence thematized by Weininger is thus taken as Michestaedter's own: «è la prima volta che un suicidio per ragioni ideali e teoriche avviene nel mondo della cultura italiana ... Il dolore che ispira la sua morte non è di quelli che abbattono ma di quelli che possono inorgoglire la nazione che li comprende»[64]. The strangely 'transparent' judgement on this act carries several parallel consequences. Firstly, as Taviani pointed out, «alle beffe della rettorica non sfugge nemmeno un'opera antirettorica come quella di Michelstaedter»[65]; a work which strived for disbelonging, for self-emancipation from the militant culture and intelligentsia and advertised a human who «deve farsi da sé le gambe per camminare – e far cammino dove non c'è strada» (PR: 36) is easily digested to become a weapon for the cause. Indeed the myth of a 'Michelstaedter vociano' is still part of a tradition of literature syntheses and manuals[66].

More generally, suppositions on the motives for suicide, 'philosophical' or 'personal'[67], together with biographical readings of Michelstaedter's works, are pervasive to the point of risking some reductive judgements on the significance of the author[68]. Autobiographical readings of the *Epistolario*[69], poems and degree thesis[70], or investigations of the 'clues' that anticipate suicide[71], or interpretations of it as a 'logical consequence of a philosophical failure'[72], all run the risk of treating suicide as 'transparent', a 'given', and an umbrella that covers with a single 'sense' all the actions of a preceding human existence. Moreover, critical texts reveal a paucity of approaches that address in a comprehensive way the problems associated with the reconstruction of the author's biography from textual sources. As a result, for example, there is an absence of enquiry into the different 'masks' worn by the author in his letters according to the context, addressee, topic, agenda and period in which they were written. Moreover, this implied textual transparency is often extended to the 'I narrator' of *La Persuasione e la Rettorica*, who is posited as equivalent with Michelstaedter, where the explicit goal is, as in Kanduth, «la rivelazione dell'Io personale e poetico» of the poet[73]. I think that a further contribution to the understanding of Michelstaedter should emancipate itself from these issues[74].

This book, therefore, will not be primarily concerned with the sort of intertextual and interdiscursive problem outlined above. A different approach, starting from 'inside the text', and specifically inside the most theoretical of the texts, *La Persuasione e la Rettorica*, can offer an original contribution to the understanding of the author and further help the problematic of contextualization. However, the time spent on Michelstaedter's biography, more than a necessity for understanding the reasons behind much of the critical interest, will help to move towards a more specific point of departure for the enquiry. To locate Michelstaedter's work contextually is to enable the definition of his topics, questions and arguments in relation to his cultural milieu, and further allows some useful comparisons that permit us to delineate Michelstaedter's peculiarity and, not least, clarify the reasons behind my approach.

0.2 Paradigmatic texts: introducing 'persuasion' through Lukàcs' *Soul and Form*

Massimo Cacciari, in his interpretation of Michelstaedter, defines the importance of our author for a conceptualization of the philosophical theoretical discourse at the beginning of the twentieth century: «nel quadro non solo della cultura triestina, ma dell'intera cultura mitteleuropea dell'inizio del secolo, l'opera di Carlo Michelstaedter rappresenta uno dei poli o una delle linee di confine che tutta l'abbracciano»[75]; in fact, through the recollection of complex threads of *philotes* and *neikos*[76], Cacciari is committed to a demonstration of the paradigmatic role of three works of the period, namely Wittgenstein's *Tractatus Logico-Philosophicus*[77], György Lukàcs' *Soul and Form*[78], and Michelstaedter's *La Persuasione e la Rettorica*[79]. In line with this interpretation, I believe that tracing a few of the lines of 'friendship' and 'enmity' between Michelstaedter and the young Lukàcs – who completed his book in Florence in October 1910, the month of Michelstaedter's death – is the most effective way, in the context of this introduction, to define a series of key concepts for understanding my approach to the author.

The lines which bind *Soul and Form* and *La Persuasione e la Rettorica* cannot be found in direct intertextual references. Historically speaking, it would not have been possible for Lukács to read Michelstaedter's degree thesis, at that moment unpublished and unknown, before the publication of *Soul and Form* in 1910. Similarly there are no clues that suggest Michelstaedter had contact with Lukács[80], or that Michelstaedter had read the essays before their edition in *Soul and Form*. What makes this comparison interesting is the similar problematic, carried out through similar sources and interests: in the Greek tragic writers, Presocratic philosophy, Plato, and the more recent speculations of Schopenhauer and Nietzsche[81]. The re-actualization of the tragic will be the starting point of this discussion.

0.2.1 Life is a tragedy

«La *forma* autentica della vita è la forma tragica e la forma tragica è quella della *Leben zum Tode*, dell'esperienza del limite come momento dell'autocoscienza dell'anima, che sa di esistere ed esiste soltanto nella misura in cui è limitata»[82]; in this way Pastore interprets the categories of tragedy and authenticity in *Soul and Form*, particularly as expressed in the last essay of the text, 'The Metaphysic of Tragedy: Paul Ernst'. Tragedy is the element which 'reveals souls'[83], where «naked souls conduct here a dialogue with naked destinies»[84]. In this sense, the tragic is the rise of authenticity through the manifestation of an emancipation, in which «all the relationships of life have been suppressed so that the relationship with destiny may be created; everything atmospheric between man and object has vanished, in order that nothing should exist between them but clear, harsh mountain air of ultimate questions and ultimate answers»[85]. Here, 'the pure experience of self'[86] is defined as the pure necessity which gives «men a new memory, a new ethic and a new justice»[87]: the 'absolute'.

After outlining this 'privileged' authenticity, *Soul and Form* asks a further question: in which relationship is this 'new ethic', this absolute, this emancipation, with the possibilities implied in daily human existence? The answer defines another category, a pole of 'existence', incommensurable with the first and in an *aut aut* dialectic with it: «such a moment [of the manifestation of the tragic] is a beginning and an end. Nothing can succeed it or follow upon it, nothing can connect it with ordinary life. It is a moment; it does not signify life, it *is* life – a different life opposed to and exclusive of ordinary life»[88]. 'Ordinary existence', in a description all in negative[89], defines 'inauthenticity': a dichotomy *ordinary life (existence)/(tragedy) life*[90] equals the one between *authentic and inauthentic*.

> Life [existence] is an anarchy of light and dark: nothing is ever completely fulfilled in life [existence], nothing ever quite ends; new, confusing voices always mingle with the chorus of those that have been heard before. Everything flows, everything merges into another thing, and the mixture is uncontrolled and impure; everything is destroyed, everything is smashed, nothing ever flowers into real life. To live is to live something through to the end: but *life* [existence] means that nothing is ever fully and completely lived through to the end[91].

In this sense existence becomes the negative of pure necessity, the land of the relative and the false absolute, hidden under the mask of an individual psychology. Again, with a depiction 'in negative', the idea of a false determination of causes and 'meaning' conducted through a subjective and relative self-affirmation, is depicted:

> in ordinary life we experience ourselves only peripherally – that is, we experience our motives and our relationships. Our life ordinarily has no real necessity, but only the necessity of being empirically present, of

being entangled by a thousand threads in a thousand accidental bonds and relationships. But the basis of the whole network is accidental and meaningless; everything that is, could just as well be otherwise [...][92].

0.2.2 «Alle haben Recht – niemand ist Gerecht»

«*Alle haben Recht – niemand ist Gerecht*» (PR: 39), 'everybody has reasons, nobody is right'; this motto from *La Persuasione e la Rettorica* echoes the above quotes from *Soul and Form*. In fact, in Michelstaedter's text the concept of 'rhetoric', the absolute negative of the persuasion-rhetoric dichotomy, is primarily defined through the representation of a contingent status: an existence bound with determinate objects and conducted towards the fulfilment of determinate (finite) needs.

> Se egli è figlio delle tali cause e dei tali bisogni, non ha in sé *la ragione*; e l'affermazione della sua qualunque persona è sempre, come irrazionale, *violenta*. In qualunque modo uno chieda di continuare, parlano in lui le date necessità del suo vivere, ed egli in ciò afferma come *giusto* quello che è *giusto per lui*, nega ciò che è giusto per gli altri, ed è ingiusto verso *tutti* gli altri, avvenga o non avvenga che egli commetta ingiustizia» (PR: 40).

Two main themes are here exposed: on the one hand, the violence implied in the absurdity of the network of causal necessities, and determined ultimately by the inadequate affirmation of individuality[93]; and on the other, the detection of the very cause of this violent affirmation in the «continuare», the perpetuation of the one self. 'Perpetuation', inadequate (relative) affirmation of oneself, are then the features of the rhetorical human, always lacking (self) possession. If this 'inauthentic' state is 'rhetoric', its logical opposite is 'persuasion'. It is absolute, individual self-possession: a state which implies consciousness and full acceptance of a tragic understanding of existence[94].

A preliminary definition of Michelstaedter's 'persuaded human' can be found in the chapter of *La Persuasione e la Rettorica* on 'The Way to Persuasion': «Chi vuol avere un attimo solo *sua* la sua vita, essere un attimo solo persuaso di ciò che fa – deve impossessarsi del presente; *vedere ogni presente come l'ultimo*, come se fosse certa dopo la morte: e *nell'oscurità crearsi da sé la vita*» (PR: 33). 'Possession', the only perfect possession, is here the very possession of oneself, the solitary acceptance of a tragic destiny, of death (to see every present as if it were the last one), and through this acceptance, the achievement of self-fulfilment in *one* point[95]. In synthesis, it is the achievement of a pure present, intended as an instant of overcoming time[96]: «la *vita sarebbe* se il tempo non la allontanasse l'essere costantemente nel prossimo istante» (PR: 11). The parallel with *Soul and Form* seems appropriate at different levels: primarily, in the idea that being is not a property of all things but a value judgement passed upon things[97]; in the concept of self-possession in one point[98]; and further, in the *Leben zum Tode* connate with the appearance of the tragic[99], opposite to existence as fear of death. Or better, following the argument of *La Persuasione e la Rettorica*, this last point can be turned back to front: fear of death is the main cause for the very birth of a 'normal', inadequate, rhetoric of existence[100], a blindfold for the consciousness of the tragic.

In Michelstaedter, the agent which exhausts humans in their perennial striving for the fulfilment of never-ending and always new determinate needs, the will of life, is the god of φιλοψυχία[101]:

> nella nebbia indifferente delle cose il dio fa brillare la cosa che all'organismo è utile; e l'organismo vi contende come in quella avesse a saziare tutta la sua fame, come quella gli dovesse dar tutta la vita: l'assoluta persuasione; ma il dio sapiente spegne la luce quando l'abuso toglierebbe l'uso; e l'animale sazio solo in riguardo a quella cosa, si volge dove gli appaia un'altra luce che il dio benevolo gli accenda; ed a questa contende con tutta la sua speranza; finché ancora la luce si spegne per riaccendersi in un altro punto (PR: 16).

And the human, unable to possess her/himself in the present moment, posits her/himself as something always inexorably yet to be possessed, to be fulfilled in the future. This is existence in *La Persuasione e la Rettorica*: a perpetual absence of life, a lack, a non-life, death. In the very appearance of φιλοψυχία, 'rhetoric' is born.

0.2.3 *Towards an aporia*

«Ma gli uomini si stancano su questa via, si sentono mancare nella solitudine: la voce del dolore è troppo forte. Essi non sanno più sopportarla con tutta la loro persona. Guardano dietro a sé, guardano intorno a sé, chiedono una benda agli occhi, *chiedono di essere per qualcuno*» (PR: 53). With this 'but' «oppositivo-consequenziale»[102], which underlines the oppositions of the polarities 'persuasion' versus 'rhetoric', the second part of Michelstaedter's thesis, 'On Rhetoric', begins. With this, however, a theoretical aporia arises.

From the beginning of the text, the 'I narrator' of *La Persuasione e la Rettorica* is engaged in a striving for 'persuasion', which seems to be at the very core of his philosophical systematisation: «io salirò sulla montagna – l'altezza mi chiama, voglio averla – l'ascendo – la domino, ma la montagna come la posseggo?» (PR: 8). Yet, if this will to 'persuasion' is a will in a Schopenhauerian sense (*Wille zum Leben*), and even if will for 'persuasion' could be described in a negative sense as 'will to abandon rhetoric', would it not be inextricably linked with 'rhetoric' itself, part of it, being born from it[103]? This question can also be formulated with a focus on language: if 'persuasion' is conceived as an atemporal instant versus the linear self-perpetuation of 'rhetoric', how can a text or, better, the process of signification embody, represent or even lead to 'persuasion'? What are the links between 'persuasion' and its (unavoidably) rhetorical conceptualization? Muzzioli, 'biographizing', explains the problem in the following terms: «il tormento oscuro di Michelstaedter sta nella difficoltà di accettare la sosta forzata nel tempo penoso della pratica scrittoria. Com'è possibile che la voce della libera vita per poter parlare debba cessare di vivere, insomma, smentire se stessa?»[104]. In other words, the problem of communication of the experience of (or the need for) 'persuasion' sounds extremely close to the question asked by Klossowski of Nietzsche: «per il filosofo o per il pensatore o per il saggio in senso nietzscheano, quale sarà la forma da conferire a una tale esperienza affinché possa essere insegnata? [...] Non era forse necessario sollecitare il pensiero cosciente e dunque prendere a prestito il linguaggio della tribù (all'occorrenza quello del positivismo) e quindi riprendere la nozione di utilità e di scopo a dispetto di ogni utilità, a dispetto di ogni scopo?»[105]

0.2.4 Lukács's solution: a theory of essay writing

Following the definition of the metaphysic of the tragic form in his famous preface on *Soul and Form*, written as a letter to Leo Popper[106], Lukács directly addresses the question of essay as a form and its relationship with the problem of authenticity. In doing so, his answer to the problem defined above takes the shape of an argument on the intrinsic contradiction between 'striving' and 'writing'. Fortini, in his seminal introduction to the Italian edition of the text[107], points out that the choice of the 'essay' is conceived by Lukács as a further form that stands between 'authentic' and 'inauthentic'; it is an ahistorical «modalità privilegiata nel rapporto tra anima umana e assoluto»[108], which ultimately introduces a 'mediation' in the dichotomy life/existence, and posits the practice of essay writing «fuori dalle scelte perentorie della forma tragica»[109]. This mediation is «essa stessa un *a priori*, è il privilegiamento di una forma di vita che, pur non essendo in grado di assurgere all'autenticità della forma tragica come *Leben zum Tode*, tuttavia non ricade neppure nell'inautenticità della vita come esistenza»[110]. The *proprium* of this particular form of expression is irony, defined as «talking about something in order to say something else», and it is in this sense that Plato is «the greatest essayist who ever lived or wrote»[111]. Thus, while 'talking about something else', the essay, allows Lukács to «endow the work with the force necessary for a conceptual re-ordering of life»[112] and it becomes the form that represents the dichotomy 'authentic' versus 'inauthentic', that leads from tragedy without taking part in the dichotomy itself. In the words of Cacciari: «La verità è *l'idea* del saggio. Esso pertanto non 'fingerà' composizione, unione, ma dovrà compiutamente mostrare proprio l'insuperabile distanza che separa dalla verità – con ciò stesso *custodendone l'idea*. Il saggio [...] *mostra* la verità, ma precisamente come assenza»[113].

0.2.5 Michelstaedter's philosophy of language: an impossible battle

My approach to *La Persuasione e la Rettorica* is strictly linked with an analysis of the moments in which the text thematizes the problematic contradictions implied in its philosophy of language. I think that the analysis of those passages, together with an interpretation of the strategies for 'a way to persuasion', as they are outlined in the first part of the text, can help to demonstrate two major points: firstly, that 'inadequate' rhetorical language in Michelstaedter is intended also as an instrument that can be used in order to overcome itself, as the motto «con le parole guerra alle parole» (PR: 134) seems to programmatically advertise; secondly, that the stylistic practices of the text are consonant with the represented philosophy of language and subsequent poetic. It is as if the 'I narrator' of *La Persuasione e la Rettorica*, while defining language as the very reason for the impossibility of 'persuasion', was at the same time trying, through a particular use of that same language, to orient himself towards the impossible re-achievement of 'persuasion'. Irony, as we will see, will play a special role in this attempt, and further comparisons with Lukács will be possible[114]. However, before jumping ahead of ourselves, it is necessary to briefly outline our author's discussion on language.

In Michelstaedter, the main knot which ties the problem of inauthenticity with the dismissal of rhetoric/language lies in the mechanism of construction of values based on φιλοψυχία. Trapped in a relentless series of correlatives, that is in the contingency of relative self-determinations in and through finite objects and needs, humans

> al di sotto della relazione elementare che li vince per la loro paura della morte, [...] fingono un correlativo alla persuasione che si fingono d'avere. Un valore stabile che non si esaurisce nel giro delle relazioni particolari, ma permane di sotto fermo immutabile. Essi hanno bisogno per la loro φιλοψυχία d'attribuire valore alle cose nell'atto stesso che le cercano, e nello stesso tempo *bisogno* di dir la loro vita non essere in queste, ma di *essere libera nella persuasione e fuori da quei bisogni* (PR: 53-4).

A sort of two sided human: «egli non è più uno ma sono due: c'è un corpo, o una materia, o un fenomeno o non so cosa, e c'è un'anima, o una forma, o un'idea. E mentre il corpo vive nel basso mondo della materia, nel tempo, nello spazio, nella necessità: schiavo; l'anima vive libera nell'assoluto» (PR: 55). This invention of an absolute is indeed the 'blindfold for the eyes', a relief for the pain, a cover for the sense of the 'tragic', in the form of an illusory mask of 'persuasion', a value-mask, and one that is in constant need of a socio-cultural context for its very existence and affirmation. If, on the one side, «nel punto ch'egli mette una cosa reale fuori di sé, egli dice il sapere che hanno per lui le cose, la sua coscienza, il suo sapere – quale esso anche sia. Per la sua illusione egli dice che <è> quello che <è per lui>» (PR: 56); on the other, this reification of a relative value asks for and obtains the confirmation of the subject as existent in its relationship with other subjects and values: humans speak to each other «perché l'altro gli faccia da specchio e gli dica: <tu sei, io sono, noi siamo>; ed insieme ripetono: <noi siamo, noi siamo perché sappiamo, perché possiamo dirci le parole del sapere, della conoscenza libera e assoluta>. – *Così si stordiscono l'un l'altro*» (PR: 58). Language becomes a «velo tacitamente convenuto all'oscurità: καλλωπίσματα ὄρφνης»[115] (PR: 58).

Now the theoretical problem with which *La Persuasione e la Rettorica* is engaged can be formulated in a clear way. With the introduction of the objective search for knowledge as the very definition of a false affirmation of the self, and with the positing of language as the tool through which this false affirmation is achieved, how can a theoretical work in general, and a degree thesis in particular, have a value outside/beside the always inadequate, rhetorical definition of the evil of 'rhetoric'? Self-recognition through language posits knowledge as a surrogate for the absolute: «Il <sapere> è costituito»; «il <sapere> è per se stesso scopo della vita» (PR: 58); «così *fiorisce la rettorica accanto alla vita. Gli uomini si mettono in posizione conoscitiva e fanno il sapere. –*» (PR: 59). Starting from this point, Michelstaedter is able to dismiss, in less than a hundred pages, all the forms of systematic knowledge: from philosophy[116] to religion[117], from art[118] to science[119], until, in the chapter devoted to 'Rhetoric in Life', the whole of society is embraced as the «officina dei valori assoluti» (PR: 125), where the thread of rhetorical values introduces and assimilates every subject into the mechanism of its self-perpetuation (PR: 112). Knowledge thus becomes nothing more than a bunch of names; and «abituarsi a una parola è come prendere un vizio» (PR: 59).

0.2.6   What to do with the aporia

At this point in our discussion, the synthetic formulation of Michelstaedter's aporia offered by Massimo Cacciari should not sound obscure: «dover-volere la vita vera, non poterla che volere, e non poterla avere volendola – di quest'aporia vive la ricerca di Michelstaedter, e Michelstaedter ne è perfettamente consapevole»[120]. Furthermore, this will is immersed in the intrinsically determinate nature of language: «inautentico, alla radice, per Michelstaedter non è una forma del linguaggio (quella del 'si', del Man, dell'impersonale: il linguaggio presupposto, ereditato, già-detto), ma la costituzione stessa del linguaggio in quanto tale [...]. Il linguaggio non può servire a significare – non può non risultare gravitazionalmente attratto ad 'altro' da sé»[121].

If this view of Michelstaedter's thought is correct, a theoretical and philosophical enquiry could easily stop at this point. Bini, for example, reaches this conclusion when focusing her analysis on the logical aporia of 'persuasion'. After correctly defining «the impossibility of achieving Persuasione»[122], she identifies 'death' as the only logical option for the 'absolute' without a determinate language: the logical opposite of contingent existence. Bini links this with Michelstaedter's biography, and the suicide becomes a 'logical consequence' of the philosophical speculation[123]: «In Chapter 3, where he tries to show the 'route to Persuasion', his fatal destiny becomes evident»[124], and thus Michelstaedter becomes a «a victim of honest thought»[125]. Not only the text, but the author's tragedy itself are reduced to their aporia: the consciousness of the logical contradiction, for logic's sake, should, in its arising, bring the incoherent life to an end.

With a stronger focus on the problem of textual production, this is also the result of Pieri's interpretation: «l'eco del suo suicidio sfonda il muro di silenzio che lo studente pensa di erigere intorno alla sua 'tesi di laurea'. Neppure il suicidio è riuscito ad interrompere il costruttivo rapporto della storia col testo. La morte dell'autore reale non impedisce allo scrittore di comunicare al lettore di ieri e di oggi la verità della 'persuasione'»[126] – as if the struggle for 'persuasion' was conducted through a sort of 'writing and hiding', unaware of the intertextual nature of the text. The present introduction, on the contrary, underlines how the problem of the relational nature of language is a constitutive theme of Michelstaedter's text, and not a sudden surprise or point of arrival which imposes, in its being the statement of a failure, the drastic decision to end one's existence. Harrison, as acknowledged above[127], pushes the critique a step further with his contextualization of Michelstaedter inside the cultural landscape of expressionism and the 'problem of form', a move which leads to a discussion of style and strategies of representation[128]. In this sense, a focus on the style of the philosophical argument is what could be called a critical approach that works 'inside' the aporia.

It is strange how the most striking features of *La Persuasione e la Rettorica* are often taken for granted; we are facing a text which is officially conceived as a degree thesis, yet it does not look like a thesis at all. We meet a narrator who often recurs to prophetic tones[129]; who develops his argument through a multiplicity of languages (ancient Greek, German, Veneto dialect), sub-genres (apologues, dialogues, fictional examples, parodies, and so on), and an extremely small number of referred sources (often, oddly enough, coming from the Presocratic fragments and the New Testament) and mostly embodied as aphorisms. At the same time, there is an almost complete absence of second hand sources, and a diffuse exploitation of different linguistic registers and technical jargons, from chemistry to mathematics, and from physics to law. In the 'Appendici Critiche', we finally find the two authors who should have been the object of the thesis, Plato and Aristotle, fully discussed. But, at the same time we encounter a dialogue between a man and his foot, a parable involving a bored tyrant and, again, mathematics[130]. This poses the question of style in urgent terms: why write in this way? What has this way of writing to do with the philosophy with which it is concerned and inextricably entangled?

0.3   A matter of style[131]
Asking the question of style means placing the accent on what Cacciari defines as «ricerca». Michelstaedter's enquiry consciously 'lives' inside the

contradiction embodied in the necessity of 'wanting persuasion' and because of this act of will, thwarting the very possibility of obtaining it. Moreover, the means of representing 'persuasion' coincide with the means of its pursuit. A positive definition of 'persuasion' implies an argument on the linguistic possibility of an adequate utterance and the definition of its features.

Two very recent and brief articles by Taviani and Muzzioli suggest the possibility of reviving and actualizing the studies on Michelstaedter starting from a literary and stylistic point of view. Muzzioli, one of the few critics to have addressed the past stylistic features of Michelstaedter's texts[132], in his recent contribution defines 'persuasion' in terms of a linguistic practice: «la persuasione è un dialogo. Magari uno strano tipo di dialogo. [...] Un'ermeneutica negativa, insomma, la quale prevede che gli uomini non si capiscano (ciascuno interpreta l'altro secondo il vantaggio della propria rassicurazione), ma che tuttavia si pone la comprensione come valore da raggiungere attraverso il suo contrario, ossia rompendo continuamente l'accordo comunicativo (<negare l'apparente valore>)»[133]. This is nothing more than an attempt at the definition of a poetic. Taviani also, in her attempt at re-actualizing our author, reads «*La Persuasione e la Rettorica* come un libro di poetica e non esclusivamente di filosofia [...] basato sulla degradazione della lingua e sulla perdita di fiducia del linguaggio; di una poetica anti-classicistica di rottura delle forme in un testo che anticipa il gran filone avanguardistico della letteratura europea e pone i prolegomeni ad una poetica dell'espressionismo»[134], the striving for 'persuasion' is seen «più che una realizzazione in pieno, [...] come una scommessa – persistente, lacerante, continua – contro la deriva del significato»[135]. In this sense, it seems that Taviani defines a link between the actual production of the text and its philosophical project: the 'way to persuasion' is signified through a style that shows a level of coherence with the poetic of the text.

According to these two critics, in *La Persuasione e la Rettorica*, poetic and style need to be considered on the same level. This is, in synthesis, the perspective that will be at the basis of the present research. The brevity and the approach of the articles by Taviani and Muzzioli suggest a point of departure for further research, the first step of which should be a broader review of what we are calling the 'poetic of persuasion', in order to bring to light its diversity and the complexity of its mechanisms. The 'negative hermeneutic' – a theme very close to Taviani since her monograph of 2002[136] – is a good point of departure, yet it carries the danger of reducing the ambiguities of the different definitions of 'persuasion' as deployed in the text.

Within this framework, a second line of enquiry will be the development of an analysis of the style of the text that accurately avoids too tempting, easy and reductive parallels, such as the assumption of a perfect interchangeability between Michelstaedter the author and the 'I narrator' of the text, and between the narratorial practice and the poetic of the text[137]. *La Persuasione e la Rettorica*, in its quest for the impossible (PR: 43), and despite its aporia, can be considered a battlefield in which different strategies for overcoming the problem of rhetorical language are employed, and fail. The challenge here is to trace the routes of these failures in relationship with the poetic of 'persuasion' to which they refer; it will test the coherence between what the text professes and what it delivers, in order to map the position of *La Persuasione e la Rettorica* with regard to itself[138]. This aim obviously has the further goal of underlining the complexity of the concept of 'persuasion', rather than insisting on univocal interpretation characteristic of much of the strictly 'philosophically oriented' criticism. This necessity should appear clear at this point. If the text is not itself written from the point of view of 'persuasion', then the representation of this state is necessarily burdened with all the problems of 'rhetoric'.

In order to begin this journey toward mapping the attempts at definition, their incoherences and overlaps, a preliminary working definition of 'persuasion' should be introduced, as the springboard for the enquiry that follows.

0.4   Reading the 'way to persuasion': dialogic, monologic

La Persuasione e la Rettorica generally defines 'persuasion' in negative terms. Indeed, the pages dedicated to the description of the 'persuaded human' are a constellation of negations (my underlining):

> Egli [the 'persuaded human'] non può prender la persona di questi bisogni come sufficiente [...]: egli non può affermar se stesso nell'affermazione di quelli [...]: egli non può muoversi a differenza della cose che sono perché egli ne abbia bisogno: non c'è pane per lui, non c'è acqua, non c'è letto, non c'è famiglia, non c'è patria, non c'è dio [...]. No, egli deve *permanere*, non andar dietro a quelli fingendoseli fermi [...]: Egli deve *resister* senza posa alla corrente della sua propria illusione (PR: 34).

The 'persuaded human' «non s'accontenta» (ibid.), and this takes the form of a 'resistance', of 'always saying no' to inadequate affirmation of himself.

The explicit description of the whole mechanism of this 'resistance' (signified) as negation can be found shortly after in the text (PR: 40-2), and is expressed through the mathematical formula of the hyperbole, which is worth discussing in some depth.

0.4.1 «Iperbolica è la via della persuasione» (PR: 40)

The 'way to persuasion' is represented as a hyperbole, not only in a rhetorical, but a mathematical sense. If on the asymptote 'y' there is the line[139] of justice, of 'persuasion', and on the line of the 'x' what humans ask for themselves, «i diritti che credono di avere» (PR: 41), then the 'way to persuasion' is hyperbolic: «come per piccola che sia la distanza d'un punto dell'iperbole dall'asintoto, infinitamente deve prolungarsi la curva per giungere al contatto, così per poco che l'uomo vivendo chieda come giusto per sé, infinito gli resta il dovere verso la giustizia» (PR: 40-1). In this sense the way ('up', being the 'y' asymptote oriented vertically) to 'persuasion' implies for the subject a negation of what is considered right for oneself; in other words, it is covered through a constant negation of an inadequate (relative, egoistic) affirmation of oneself. It is the process of always saying no, in an infinite activity: «il diritto di vivere non si paga con un lavoro finito, ma con un'infinita attività» (PR: 41).

This definition has obvious repercussions on the level of language, and in chapter 1 we will discuss how this idea is bound up with a certain understanding of Socratic dialectic. In this sense, given that the narrator of Michelstaedter's text, its 'I', is in some ways engaged in a project towards 'persuasion', his attempt can be read as an undermining of rhetorical and ideological positions, conducted through a series of stylistic strategies: not only science or philosophy have to be shown as inadequate, but also their rhetoric, their language. This is one of the possible interpretations of the distance which divides both the multiplicity of registers of La Persuasione e la Rettorica and its logic of argumentation from the umbrella of the 'degree thesis' under which the work is initially conceived; it is in this sense, that the motto «con le parole guerra alle parole» (PR: 134) at the opening of the 'Appendici Critiche'[140] can be understood.

0.4.2 Is the word of 'persuasion' monologic?

The hyperbolic understanding of 'persuasion' opens to some further questions on the limits of the undermining process. Firstly, the text defines the necessity of an infinite undermining activity, because only in that infinite point will the curve touch the line of 'persuasion'. What does this mean in terms of the practice of negation itself? Shouldn't the subject undermine his own activity, negate the will to persuasion, 'say no' to the same project of 'saying no'? Michelstaedter seems to affirm this in a letter to his sister[141], while expressing, in rather romantic terms, his understanding of Beethoven as a 'persuaded', a 'genius', and his feelings after the experience of the famous *Ninth Symphony*:

> Pensa che dopo aver scritto quasi tutto [... Beethoven] stette per 10 anni senza scrivere una nota. Il silenzio della persona arrivata all'ultimo dolore: della nullità del proprio dolore [...]. L'uomo arrivato quasi alla vita universale – e che ha perduto ogni coscienza individuale. In lui vive e soffre ogni cosa nell'universo. E quando, chi sa per quale misterioso incidente, si risveglia alla vita pare davvero che per la sua bocca tutto l'universo con tutte le sue forze si levi dal dolore a un'ultima illusione orgiastica di vita libera (E: 383-4).

The 'nothingness of his own pain': is this the last moment before the leap towards absolute? And how can this been uttered? Is it a 'silent knowledge', alinguistic (if this could be conceived), and thus far from the battles of *La Persuasione e la Rettorica*? But, if this is true, why the thesis? These are the questions from which we will start our enquiry.

The quote regarding Beethoven, however, offers something more to an introductory definition of the concept of 'persuasion'. In fact, because of a 'mysterious accident', Beethoven's re-awakening to language takes the form of a speech uttered by 'all the universe', in a last 'orgiastic illusion'. If the term 'illusion' still mantains the sense of an 'impossibility'[142], even at this limit-state, of 'telling the persuasion', it is nonetheless clear that this 'positive' utterance is conceived as an overcoming of the process of negation: here, the human 'at the limit', does not say no but speaks as if he were the entire universe. Again, the problem will be to define the relation between such an understanding of the language of 'persuasion' and the stylistic practice of the text. And can a prophetic style in *La Persuasione e la Rettorica*, for example, be considered as a 'translation' of this conceptualization, so that «anche i ciechi vedranno» (PR: 43)? And how can such an attempt as translation be developed beside more clearly satirical and parodic critiques of the inadequacy of human habits, ideas, and social organization? Two partially contradictory ideas of 'persuaded language' seem to constitute the poetic of the text.

Perhaps this analysis exceeds our introductory aims, and we should end by stressing our point of departure: a stylistic analysis committed to interpret the text as a field in which different attempts to fulfil the poetic of 'persuasion' are conducted. The ultimate hope is that, through a mapping of the failures to achieve the absolute language of 'persuasion', we could say something more about Michelstaedter's philosophy, something focused on its complexity, its contradictions and its different layers, as opposed to a reductive constriction into a supposed coherence.

Notes

1. Given that some of my concluding interpretations will be developed with reference to the works of Paul De Man, for an introduction to the problems inherent in the interdisciplinary relationships between literary criticism and philosopy, see: Rodolphe Gasché, 'Deconstruction as Criticism,' *Glyph*, no. 6 (1979), and the discussion on Derrida and De Man by Suzanne Gearhart, 'Philosophy Before Literature: Deconstruction, Historicity, and the Work of Paul De Man,' *Diacritics* 13, no. 4 (1983). For the adoption of a literary framework in the analysis of philosophical texts that is close to my approach, and particularly the discussion of the relationship between philosophical and literary genres and their interrelation in a text, and for the recourse to narratorial analysis, see: Jonathan Rée, *Philosophical Tales: An Essay on Philosophy and Literature* (London, New York: Methuen, 1987); see also: Berel Lang, *The Anatomy of Philosophical Style: Literary Philosophy and the Philosophy of Literature* (Oxford, Cambridge: Blackwell, 1990); Warner Martin, *Philosophical Finesse: Studies in the Art of Rational Persuasion* (Oxford, New York: Clarendon and Oxford University Press, 1989).

2. Daniela Bini, *Carlo Michelstaedter and the Failure of Language* (Gainesville: University Press of Florida, 1992): 31. Over recent decades, many exhaustive literary reviews of Michelstaedter's critical works have been published; the most recent was in 2002 and since then updated. See: Licia Semeraro, *Lo Svuotamento del Futuro. Note su Michelstaedter* (Lecce: Milella, 1986); Sergio Campailla, 'Le Prime Interpretazioni di Michelstaedter (1910-1916),' *Cultura e Scuola*, no. 114 (1990); Sergio Campailla, *Quaderno Bibliografico su Carlo Michelstaedter* (Genova: Università degli Studi, 1976); Francesco Muzzioli, *Michelstaedter* (Lecce: Milella, 1987); Giovanna Taviani, *Michelstaedter* (Palermo: Palumbo, 2002); Nicola Merola, ed., *Ricerche sul Moderno* (Soveria Mannelli: Rubettino, 2005).

3. Bini (Bini, *Carlo Michelstaedter and the Failure of Language*) quotes alternative attempts at re-creating Michelstaedter through other genres, for example the play by Devtag: Antonio Devtag, *Michelstaedter. La Grande Trasgressione* (Piccolo Teatro 'Città di Gorizia', December 9-10, 1981). I would add Magris' novel *Un Altro Mare*: a fictional tale loosely based on the biography of Michelstaedter's closest friend Enrico Mreule, through which Michelstaedter's themes are evoked: Claudio Magris, *Un Altro Mare* (Milano: Garzanti, 2003). This analysis of Michelstaedter's philosophy of language will indirectly show the problems that these choices, if considered as attempts at coherence with Michelstaedter's speculation, raise.

4. The means and the sources adopted in order to develop this speculation, exhibit strong similarities with the experiences of other European intellectuals of the first decade of the twentieth century, as for example argued by Thomas Harrison, who uses the term 'pre-war expressionism' to describe the cultural climate in which Michelstaedter can be

contextualized. See: Thomas Harrison, 1910. *The Emancipation of Dissonance* (Berkeley, Los Angeles, London: University of California Press, 1996).

5. According to the distinction made by Cesare Segre and discussed in Massimo Bonafin, 'Appunti sull'Intertestualità Parodica,' in *Intertestualità*, ed. Massimo Bonafin (Genova: Il Melangolo, 1986).

6. The origin and history of this approach will be discussed later in this introduction. For the most accurate biography of Michelstaedter, see: Sergio Campailla, *A Ferri Corti con la Vita* (Gorizia: Arti Grafiche Campestrini, 1981) In this text as well, perhaps because of a popular and wider implied audience, it is possible to find a clear parallel between life of the author and his works and read the latter as a direct expression of that singular existential struggle, and cause of the final crisis.

7. 'Persuasion' and 'rhetoric', as we are about to introduce, assume in Michelstaedter's work a peculiar philsophical meaning, distinct from a normal understanding of the terms in classical rhetoric. Therefore, to avoid confusion, when intended in Michelstaedter's sense, these terms will be put in inverted commas.

8. For example, Michelstaedter is Harrison's point of departure and *trait d'union* in his quoted text on pre-war expressionism: Harrison, 1910. *The Emancipation of Dissonance*. The explicit statement of the idea that sees *La Persuasione e la Rettorica* as carrying a paradigmatic value derives from: Massimo Cacciari, 'Interpretazione di Michelstaedter,' *Rivista di Estetica* XXVI, no. 22 (1986).

9. Since the first publication (1913) by Michelstaedter's friend Vladimiro Arangio Ruiz.

10. Since its foundation in 1973, the Fondo Carlo Michelstaedter of the Biblioteca Statale Isontina in Gorizia has been dedicated to the collection of the manuscripts and the autographs of the author. For the most detailed description of the 'fondo', see Antonella Gallarotti, 'Ricordare Attraverso la Carta: Carlo Michelstaedter,' in *La Speranza: Attraverso l'Ebraismo Goriziano* (Monfalcone: Edizioni della Laguna, 1991).

11. I am using the term 'beyond' and not 'outside', in anticipation of the point that follows. In fact, my argument in this thesis will address the fact that despite 'persuasion' being defined as an 'impossibility', *La Persuasione e la Rettorica* sketches an ethic 'on the way to persuasion' which has much to do with language and the rejection of inadequate (linguistic) affirmations of truth.

12. As acknowledged, the most exhaustive biography on Michelstaedter, using the letters, legacy, and accounts of the few witnesses still alive at the time of the research is: Campailla, *A Ferri Corti con la Vita*. For an interesting introduction to the major works of Michelstaedter, contextualized chronologically, see Taviani, *Michelstaedter*: 11-38. A fictionalized and romanticized biography is: Alessandro Arbo, *Carlo Michelstaedter* (Pordenone, Padova: Studio Tesi, 1997). For the short synopsis in this introduction I will follow these references and the letters collected in the Epistolario. For a brief account in English of the life of the author, see the introduction to the English edition of *La Persuasione e la Rettorica*: David J. Depew, Russel Scott Valentino, and Cinzia Sartini Blum, 'Introduction: Carlo Michelstaedter's Persuasion and Rhetoric,' in *Persuasion and Rhetoric* (New Haven, London: Yale University Press, 2004): IX-XI.

13. As discussed in: Campailla, 'Le Prime Interpretazioni di Michelstaedter (1910-1916)'.

14. The father Alberto, a man with a certain literary ambition (he was the president of the town's 'Gabinetto di lettura'), was the director of the city branch of an important insurance company. The grandfather Reggio (on the paternal side), had been the rabbi of the community; while his aunt, Carolina Luzzato covered the role of director of the local newspaper: 'Il Corriere Friulano'. It was in this newspaper that the only three articles

published by Carlo during his life appeared: *Reminescenze dei Funerali di Carducci. Impressioni. La Veglia della Salma*, 22nd of February 1907: 1; 'Più che l'Amore' di Gabriele D'Annunzio al Teatro di Società, 6th of May 1908: 1-2; *Tolstoj*, 18th of September 1908. «Bisogna d'altronde ricordare che, come risulta dalle lettere del 26 febbraio e del 4 marzo 1907, il primo dei tre articoli altro non è che 'quanto v'era di stampabile' di una precedente lettera dell'autore alla famiglia che la zia fece uscire sul suo giornale all'insaputa del nipote». M. G. Giordano, 'Il Pensiero e l'Arte di Carlo Michelstaedter,' in *Sotto il Segno di Michelstaedter*, ed. T. Iermanno (Cosenza: Edizioni Periferia, 1994). Taviani also quotes another article, under the name 'uno a nome di molti', published in 'Il Gazzettino Popolare' on the 29th of April 1910 with the title *Ancora lo Stabat Mater di Pergolesi*. Taviani, *Michelstaedter*: 192.

15. The definition is borrowed from: Lucia Strappini, Claudia Micocci, and Alberto Abruzzese, eds., *La Classe dei Colti. Intellettuali e Società nel Primo Novecento Italiano* (Bari: Laterza, 1970).

16. This plurality is also a peculiarity of Michelstaedter. As a student of the *Staatgymnasium*, German was the main language of his education, however Italian was the language of Michelstaedter in the home environment, with a colloquial use of the Veneto dialect, as many of his letters show. Added to this bilingualism is his fluent knowledge of ancient Greek, consolidated at the time of high school; to the extent that Carlo is able to write fluently in ancient Greek, take notes, and compose prose. *La Persuasione e la Rettorica* is evidence of this multilingualism, and effectively exploits it for reasons that I will try to underline in the following chapters.

17. Claudio Magris, *L'Anello di Clarisse* (Torino: Einaudi, 1984).

18. In fact, the term of comparison for Magris is the 'grande stile', and his work can be read as the mapping of the reactions against it.

19. For the interpretation of this work by Magris: Magris, *L'Anello di Clarisse*: 32-62.

20. Giovanna Taviani, 'Attualità di Michelstaedter,' in *Ricerche sul Moderno. Terza Serie*, ed. Nicola Merola (Soveria Mannelli: Rubbettino, 2005): 321.

21. On this topic, see also the approach of Camerino, in: Giuseppe Antonio Camerino, 'L'Impossibile Cura della Vita e della Società. Affinità di Michelstaedter con Svevo e la Cultura Absburgica,' in *Dialoghi Intorno a Michelstaedter*, ed. Sergio Campailla (Gorizia: Biblioteca Statale Isontina, 1987). This article is contained also in: Giuseppe Antonio Camerino, *La Persuasione e i Simboli*. Michelstaedter e Slataper (Milano: Istituto Propaganda Libraria, 1993).

22. For a hisory of the Istituto di Studi Superiori in the context of the Florentine social and cultural milieu, see: Walter Adamson, *Avant-garde Florence: From Modernism to Fascism* (Cambridge, Mass.: Harvard University Press, 1993).

23. Two attempts can be identified: a letter to Henri Lavedan written in the year 1907, with a proposal of translation (E: 172); and a letter to Benedetto Croce in which a proposal for a translation of Schopenhauer is formalized. See E: 147.

24. The bibliography on the Florentine journals and intellectuals of the first decade of the twentieth century is incredibly wide, and it is not within the scope of this work to give an account of it. However, on the topic of the relationship with Benedetto Croce, see: Alberto Asor Rosa, 'La Cultura a Firenze nel Primo Novecento,' in *Intellettuali di Frontiera. Triestini a Firenze* (1900-1950), ed. Roberto Pertici (Firenze: Olschki, 1985).

25. On this topic, see for example: Livio Ligi, *Il Teatro in Rivolta. Futurismo, Grottesco, Pirandello e Pirandellismo* (Milano: Mursia, 1976), particularly the chapters devoted to the study of the theatre of Filippo Tommaso Marinetti.

26. On this topic, of great interest is: Antonio Abruzzese, *Svevo, Slatsper, Michelstaedter: Lo Stile e il Viaggio* (Venezia: Marsilio, 1979). See in particular the first chapter: 'Da Trieste a Firenze. Lavoro e Tradizione Letteraria'.

27. Giovanna Taviani recounts this process of rejection through a series of quotes from letters and notes of the author, in: Taviani, *Michelstaedter*: 31-2, to which I refer for further readings.

28. «Esiste un nesso tra l'argomento delle due opere? Probabilmente non lo sapremo mai. Certo, però, *La Persuasione e la Rettorica* ha tutta l'aria di essere una risposta a *L'Arte di Persuadere del Sofista*, a partire dall'uso profondamente diverso, anzi contrapposto, che Michelstaedter fa del concetto stesso di <persuasione>». This is as far as a critic gets in the definition of a textual parallel between the two texts, in Alberto Asor Rosa, 'Introduzione. Ritratto dell'Intellettuale da Giovane,' in *L'Arte di Persuadere*, ed. Giuseppe Prezzolini (Napoli: Liguori, 1991): 22. On this topic, see also: Alberto Asor Rosa, ''La Persuasione e la Rettorica' di Carlo Michelstaedter,' in *Letteratura Italiana-Le Opere. Volume Quarto, Il Novecento. 1. L'età Della Crisi*, ed. Alberto. Asor Rosa (Torino: Einaudi, 1995). The theme is also touched upon in Taviani, *Michelstaedter*: 32-3. This is not the place to provide an exhaustive discussion of the topic; what can be said is that a close intertextual analysis does not support this hypothesis. More general considerations, such as the survey of Michelstaedter's known library of sources, and the explicit mentioning of the origin of his interest in the problem of 'persuasion' in a letter to his father (E: 321) support the idea of the extraneousness of *L'Arte di Persuadere* to the horizon of *La Persuasione e la Rettorica*.

29. Now republished: *Giuseppe Prezzolini, L'Arte di Persuadere*, ed. Alberto Asor Rosa (Napoli: Liguori, 1991).

30. Yet appealing, see for example: Maria Adelaide Raschini, *Carlo Michelstaedter* (Milano: Marzorati, 1965).

31. It is too early for a discussion on this terminological distinction. However, given the fact that the 'way to persuasion' of the subject is a personal, individual way, one of the latest critical contributions which interprets this 'way' as unravelling in a communicative relationship with an 'other', and thus not in solitude, is to be found in: Francesco Muzzioli, 'L'Antagonismo di Michelstaedter,' in *Ricerche sul Moderno. Terza Edizione*, ed. Nicola Merola (Soveria Mannelli: Rubettino, 2005).

32. Here Michelstaedter plays with the latin omnibus = everybody and the Italian omnibus = bus. Thus stressing the rarity, exclusivity and individuality of the path. On this, see Bini, *Carlo Michelstaedter and the Failure of Language*: 37-8.

33. This is confirmed in the following letter: «Quando le parlavo delle parole di una morta, non parlavo per metafora» (Letter to Iolanda Be Blasi, dated by the family between 25th of April and 2nd of May, E: 205).

34. See in particular E: 211-26.

35. Emblematic in the case of D'Annunzio is the dismissal in the article *'Più che l'Amore' di Gabriele D'Annunzio al Teatro di Società*, now partially reprinted in O: 645-9: «Gabriele D'Annunzio non l'ha vista la situazione filosofica, non l'ha dominata. Egli ha assorbito le idee ultramontane sommariamente ed ha dato loro uno svolgimento rettorico, che non ha alcuna profondità, che scivola e sorvola come un pallone sgonfio» (O: 645).

36. «Quanto io dico è stato detto tante volte» (PR: 3) is the sentence that introduces the list of the 'positive examples' and sources exploited in *La Persuasione e la Rettorica*.

37. Particularly Parmenides, Heraclitus, Empedocles. For the relationship between Michelstaedter and these sources, see: Giorgio Brianese, 'Michelstaedter e Greci. Appunti per un Confronto,' *Studi Goriziani* 72 (1990). For the understanding of Parmenides and

Heraclitus as sources for the theory of an absolute 'unity' before and against determinate differentiation, see Bini, *Carlo Michelstaedter and the Failure of Language*, but also the comments in the introduction to the English translation of La Persuasione: David J. Depew, Russel Scott Valentino, and Cinzia Sartini Blum, 'Introduction. Carlo Michelstaedter's Persuasion and Rhetoric,' in Persuasion and Rhetoric (New Haven, London: Yale University Press, 2004): XVIII-IX.

38. For the role of Beethoven in Michelstaedter's texts and unpublished notes, see: Alessandro Arbo, 'La Persuasione Beethoveniana. Riflessioni su un Tema di Carlo Michelstaedter,' *Studi Latini e Italiani*, no. 3 (1989): 247-61. Of particular interest in this article is the contextualization of «il mito dell'universalità beethoveniana» as something «assimilato spontaneamente dalla generazione di studiosi di area mitteleuropea che visse a ridosso dei due secoli» (ibid.: 250). The link between Michelstaedter and the cultural milieu of Central Europe has, to my recollection, never been studied through the figure of Beethoven. More in general, a study of Michelstaedter's aesthetic in relation with the theoretical speculation of Bastianelli could potentially be of great interest, but exceeds the objects and goals of our project. See: Giannotto Bastianelli, *La Musica Pura, Commentari Musicali e Altri Scritti*, ed. Miriam Omodeo Donadoni (Firenze: Leo S. Olschki Editore, 1974).

39. To whom Carlo will dedicate his series of poems *A Senia*, one of his best in this genre. Now in P: 85-96.

40. He will be one of the main 'hands' who copies the final text of Carlo's thesis, and will be faithful to the memory of his cousin by editing the first complete edition of *La Persuasione e la Rettorica* in 1922 for Vallecchi (the very first edition for Formaggini, edited in 1913 by Vladimiro Arangio-Ruiz, was published without the 'Appendici Critiche').

41. Muzzioli, 'L'Antagonismo di Michelstaedter': 314.

42. Campailla, *A Ferri Corti con la Vita*: 139. This is an interpretation which echoes intertextually some passages of *La Persuasione e la Rettorica* and other notes by Michelstaedter, such as the one on the margin of his edition of *Indische Sprüche*: «La lampada si spegne per mancanza d'olio – io mi spensi per traboccante sovrabbondanza» (see Campailla, ibid.: 139; see also the same quote in PR: 39). The topos of the coherence between 'life' and 'art' is here strongly advertised.

43. «E sotto avverso ciel, luce più chiara» quotes the caption of the painting, maybe as sign of mission accomplished. Now the painting is exhibited in the museum of the Synagogue of Gorizia. See the reproduction in: Antonella Gallarotti, ed., *L'Immagine Irraggiungibile. Dipinti e Disegni di Carlo Michelstaedter* (Gorizia: Edizioni della Laguna, 1992): 42.

44. Mostly for the value of *La Persuasione e la Rettorica*; see for example: Giulio Ferroni, *Storia della Letteratura Italiana. Il Novecento* (Torino: Einaudi, 1991): 98-100. The absence of Michelstaedter from important anthologies of poetry such as: Pier Vincenzo Mengaldo, ed., *Poeti Italiani del Novecento* (Milano: Mondadori, 1978), is also emblematic.

45. 'Foremost' as argued by Raschini in her: Maria Adelaide Raschini, 'Rilettura di Michelstaedter,' in *Dialoghi Intorno a Michelstaedter*, ed. Sergio Campailla (Gorizia: Biblioteca Statale Isontina, 1987). The thesis here is that *La Persuasione e la Rettorica* has a crucial role in determining the importance of the author. This judgement is indirectly and implicitly acknowledged in the choice of having *La Persuasione e la Rettorica* as the main object of my analysis.

46. The question of the role of the 'Appendici Critiche' is still open: are they part of the main text, or do they have to be considered as the fulfilment of a basic academic requirement, in order for the thesis to be accepted by the university commission? This point, which exceeds the goals of our introduction, I will come bck to in chapter 4. However, for some comments

the topic see: Asor Rosa, "La Persuasione e la Rettorica' di Carlo Michelstaedter,'; see also the 'Introduction' by Campailla to his first edition of *La Persuasione e la Rettorica*, edited with the excision of the 'Appendici'. Carlo Michelstaedter, *La Persuasione e la Rettorica*, ed. Sergio Campailla (Milano: Adelphi, 1982).

47. In our first chapter we will discuss the only exception.

48. On this point see: Giorgio Brianese, *L'Arco e il Destino. Interpretazione di Michelstaedter* (Abano Terme (Padova): Aldo Francisi Editore, 1985).

49. See: Sergio Campailla, 'Michelstaedter Lettore di Ibsen,' *Lettere Italiane* XXVI, no. 1 (1974).

50. See: Sergio Campailla, 'Postille Leopardiane di Michelstaedter,' *Studi e Problemi di Critica Testuale,* no. 7 (1973). The thesis, on a theoretical level, is also discussed in Massimo Cacciari, 'Leopardi Platonicus?,' *Con-tratto* I, no. 1 (1992). For a general interpretation of the importance of Leopardi as an intertextual source in twentieth century Italian literature, see for example: Carlo Bo, *L'Eredità di Leopardi e Altri Saggi* (Firenze: Vallecchi, 1964); Antonella Bellucci and Andrea Cortellessa, eds., *Quel Libro Senza Eguali. Le Operette Morali e il Novecento Italiano* (Roma: Bulzoni, 2000).

51. A comparison, it is worth stressing, based only on the general interest for stylistic and rhetorical re-definition developed by the different avant-gardes. We have outlined above in this introduction both the extraneity and the critique of Michelstaedter in regard to these emerging groups.

52. Harrison, 1910. *The Emancipation of Dissonance*.

53. The idea that the literature on Michelstaedter is a reiterate philosophical re-contextualization of the author inside the contemporary debate of the various decades of the last century, with moments of stronger revival in coincidence with editions or re-editions of the author's texts, is the thesis of the accurate review by Giovanna Taviani, to which I refer for further readings: Taviani, *Michelstaedter*: 111-78.

54. See: Giovanni Gentile, 'Recensione a Carlo Michelstaedter, *La Persuasione e la Rettorica*,' *La Critica* XX, no. 4 (1922).

55. Joachim Ranke, 'Il Pensiero di Carlo Michelstaedter. Un Contributo allo Studio dell'Esistenzialismo Italiano,' *Giornale Critico della Filosofia Italiana*, no. 4 (1962).

56. Particularly the theme of the *Leben zum Tode*, as discussed in: Giorgio Brianese, 'Essere per il Nulla. Note su Michelstaedter e Heidegger,' *Studi Goriziani* LIX (1984), and the interpretation of the Presocratics, as poignantly acknowledged in the introduction to the English edition of *La Persuasione e la Rettorica*: Russel Scott Valentino, Cinzia Sartini Blum, and David J. Depew, 'Introduction: Carlo Michelstaedter's Persuasione and Rhetoric,' in *Persuasion and Rhetoric* (New Haven and London: Yale University Press, 2004). Another contemporary reading of this topic can be found in: Claudio La Rocca, 'Esistenzialismo e Nichilismo. Luporini e Michelstaedter,' *Belfagor* LIV, no. 322 (1999). Also Raschini devotes the concluding part of her research to a discussion of Michelstaedter in comparison with various streams of existentialism: Maria Adelaide Raschini, *Michelstaedter* (Venezia: Marsilio, 2000).

57. Above all see: Marco Cerruti, *Michelstaedter* (Milano: Mursia, 1967).

58. As for example in Harrison, *1910. The Emancipation of Dissonance*; for expressionist interpretations of Michelstaedter's art, see also: Fulvio Monai, 'Michelstaedter Anticipatore in Arte dell'Espressionismo,' in *Dialoghi Intorno a Michelstaedter*, ed. Sergio Campailla (Gorizia: Biblioteca Statale Isontina, 1987); Daniela Bini, 'L'Autenticità del Segno,' in *L'Immagine Irraggiungibile. Dipinti e Disegni di Carlo Michelstaedter*, ed. Antonella Gallarotti (Gorizia: Edizioni della Laguna, 1992).

59. Silvio Cumpeta and Angela Michelis, eds., *Eredità di Carlo Michelstaedter* (Udine: Forum, 2002).

60. Taviani, 'Attualità di Michelstaedter'.

61. Muzzioli, 'L'Antagonismo di Michelstaedter'.

62. Now readable as Giovanni Papini, 'Un Suicidio Metafisico,' in *Tutte le Opere* (Milano: Mondadori, 1961).

63. Otto Weininger, *Sex and Character* (New York: AMS Press, 1975).

64. Papini, quoted in Campailla, 'Le Prime Interpretazioni di Michelstaedter (1910-1916)': 20. On the reception of Weininger in Italy, see: Alberto Cavaglion, *Otto Weiningr in Italia* (Roma: Carucci Editore, 1982).

65. Taviani, *Michelstaedter*: 114.

66. Muzzioli addresses this point in: Francesco Muzzioli, 'Il Vociano Michelstaedter,' *Alfabeta*, no. 57 (1984). See, as an example of this 'misunderstanding', the reading of Michelstaedter as an 'asystematic idealist' in Gentile, 'Recensione a Carlo Michelstaedter, La Persuasione e la Rettorica'.

67. Joachim Ranke is the first critic who consistently dismissed both the idea of 'philosophical suicide', and the adoption of suicide as a interpretive paradigm. See: Ranke, 'Il Pensiero di Carlo Michelstaedter. Un Contributo allo Studio dell'Esistenzialismo Italiano'.

68. For a reading of the theme of 'death' in Michelstaedter's works that dismisses the hypothesis of 'philosophical suicide', see the sixth chapter of: Nicola Cinquetti, *Michelstaedter. Il Nulla e la Folle Speranza* (Padova: Messaggero, 2002): 85-96.

69. As, for example, Campailla, *A Ferri Corti con la Vita*; and to a wide extent Aurelio Benevento, 'L'<Epistolario> di Michelstaedter,' *Esperienze letterarie* XV, no. 4 (1990).

70. As widely expressed in Muzzioli, *Michelstaedter*. For the degree thesis, see for example: Cristina Benussi, 'La Persuasione e la Rettorica: Autobiografia e Scrittura,' in *Eredità di Carlo Michelstaedter*, ed. Silvio Cumpeta and Angela Michelis (Udine: Forum, 2002).

71. As in Campailla, *A Ferri Corti con la Vita*, or in Lucile Garcia Pignide, who ends her article with the sentence: «La Persuasione? Ecco dunque l'immortalità, l'illuminazione narcisistica senza la separazione dei sessi, senza il tempo, le sue frustrazioni e i suoi rischi di castrazione, con l'illusione di rapporti totali al mondo e – in realtà – nulli, visto che il mondo altri non è che il doppio fatale, spazio della distruzione: il suicidio»: see Lucile Garcia Pignide, 'Michelstaedter: Un Punto di Vista Psicanalitico,' in *Eredità di Carlo Michelstaedter*, ed. Silvio Cumpeta and Angela Michelis (Udine: Forum, 2002): 140.

72. As for example in Daniela Bini, 'Michelstaedter tra 'Persuasione' e 'Rettorica',' *Italica* 63, no. 4 (1986).

73. Erika Kanduth, 'Dal Tu all'Io nella Poesia di Carlo Michelstaedter,' in *Eredità di Carlo Michelstaedter*, ed. Silvio Cumpeta and Angela Michelis (Udine: Forum, 2002): 125.

74. Even if derived from a theoretical discussion. For example Taviani, who in her monograph was so consistent in the critique of this habit, in her latest article affirms: «La morte è l'atto conclusivo di chi fu veramente persuaso, sembra avere detto fino ad ora la critica. Oggi forse la frase può essere capovolta: la morte è l'atto conclusivo di chi rinunciò a fare del proprio pensiero un'arma critica di costruzione e demolizione presso gli uomini. Di chi, insomma, non riuscì mai a persuadersi»; see Taviani, 'Attualità di Michelstaedter': 321.

75. Cacciari, 'Interpretazione di Michelstaedter': 21.

76. Ibid.

77. Ludwig Wittgenstein, *Tractatus Logico-Philosophicus e Quaderni 1914-16*, trans. Amedeo G. Conte (Torino: Einaudi, 1995).

78. Georg Lukács, *Soul and Form*, trans. Anna Bostock (London: Merlin Press, 1974).

79. «Tre opere, io credo, emergono in questo contesto come opere limite, capaci di 'orientarne' la complessiva interpretazione: *L'Anima e le Forme* del giovane Lukács, uscito a Budapest nel 1910 e in traduzione tedesca a Berlino l'anno dopo; *La Persuasione e la Rettorica di Michelstaedter,* le cui appendici critiche furono terminate il 16 ottobre del 1910, il giorno prima del suicidio; il *Tractatus* di Wittgenstein, terminato, come è noto, a Vienna nel 1918, a pubblicato soltanto nel '22 (lo stesso anno della prima edizione completa della Persuasione), ma le cui idee fondamentali appaiono già definite intorno al 1912-1913. Gli stessi anni dei primi libri di Kafka». (Cacciari, 'Interpretazione di Michelstaedter': 22).

80. It is known that Lukács wrote the introduction to *Soul and Form* in Florence in October 1910, however, his stay in the Tuscan city does not coincide with Michelstaedter's.

81. Nietzsche's *Birth of the Tragedy* is an obvious predecessor in the analysis of ancient Greek thought and its exploitation of contemporary philosophy. However, Cacciari points out that the particular idea of 'persuasion' in Michelstaedter, with its suspension of contingency of time and space in a singular point, an 'instant', has close resemblances with the Nietzsche of the *Unfashionable Observations*; in any case, again before the theorization of the 'eternal return' (see: Cacciari, 'Interpretazione di Michelstaedter': 34). This understanding will be crucial in our interpretation. As we will see, such an interpretation can be referred to the concept of 'authenticity' discussed in *Soul and Form*. For the discussion of the *Unfashionable Observations* in regard with Michelstaedter's speculations, see for example: Muzzioli, *Michelstaedter*.

82. Federico Pastore, *La Conoscenza come Azione. Saggi su Lukács* (Milano: Marzorati, 1980): 40. The use of the Heideggerian definition is extended by Pastore to the interpretation of Michelstaedter, locating him in the stream of literature criticism that sees Michelstaedter as a precursor of existentialism. The comparison is controversial, particularly with regard to the concept of 'existence as project', which seems alien to *La Persuasione e la Rettorica*. This controversy, however, does not touch the concept of *Leben zum Tode*, which I assume as a correct interpretation.

83. Lukács, *Soul and Form*: 155.

84. Ibid.

85. Ibid.

86. Ibid.: 156.

87. Ibid.: 157.

88. Ibid.: 158.

89. «Life is the most unreal and unliving of all conceivable existences; one can describe it only negatively» (ibid.: 153).

90. The English translation does not underline the dichotomy by using the two different terms 'existence' and 'life', as the Italian does (see György Lukács, *L'Anima e le Forme*, trans. Sergio Bologna (Milano: SE, 2002)). I will assume this useful distinction and, from now on, existence will be intended as 'daily life' in opposition to 'authentic life'.

91. Lukács, *Soul and Form*: 152-3.

92. Ibid.: 157.

93. «*È inadeguata affermazione di individualità: la rettorica*» (PR: 57). This is one of the most concise definitions of 'rhetoric' to be found in the whole text.

94. On the adialectical relationship between 'rhetoric' and 'persuasion', and the consequent critique from an idealist point of view, see: Raschini, *Michelstaedter*: 143.

95. See: Daniela Marcheschi, 'La Persuasione o il Dileguare dell'Illusione del Tempo. Note a Carlo Michelstaedter,' *Letteratura Italiana Contemporanea*, no. 10 (1983); Raschini, *Michelstaedter*: 159.

96. And thus far from the Nietzschean idea of eternal return. On this, see above.

97. Lukács, *Soul and Form*: 156.

98. «This is the metaphysical reason for the concentration of drama in time, of the condition of unity of time. It is born of the desire to come as close as possible to the timelessness of this moment which yet is the whole of life (Unity of place is the natural symbol of such sudden standing still in the midst of the continual change of ordinary life, and is therefore a technically necessary condition of dramatic form-giving)»; see ibid.: 158.

99. «For tragedy, death – the frontier as such – is always immanent reality, inseparably connected with every tragic event»; «the experiencing of the frontier between life and death is the awakening of the soul to consciousness or self-conscoiusness» (ibid.: 161), while «real, ordinary life never reaches the frontier; it knows death only as something frightening»; see Lukács, *Soul and Form*: 160-1.

100. The point in which the incapability to sustain the pain of facing one's own mortality is posed as the cause of 'rhetoric', is where one of the main differences between Michelstaedter and Lukács emerges. Faith in the possibility of the subject of reaching 'persuasion' through an act of will, or better, through a constant struggle of her/his will, is the key ethic of the first author, but absent in the second. What this implies for Lukács, and his later understanding of forms as 'historical', I will briefly discuss later in this introduction.

101. «Amore alla vita, viltà» (PR: 17).

102. A stylistic constant in *La Persuasione e la Rettorica*. See: Asor Rosa, "La Persuasione e la Rettorica' di Carlo Michelstaedter': 294. In O: 708-10, Michelstaedter discusses «delle particelle avversative», arguing that «l'uomo per affermare come <suo> un pensiero *non ha altro mezzo* che quello d'opporlo al pensiero degli altri» (O: 710). This opposition, in *La Persuasione e la Rettorica,* develops into a negative dialectic, the philosophical value of which, our enquiry is devoted to demonstrating.

103. This is one of the theses in Brianese, *L'Arco e il Destino. Interpretazione di Michelstaedter.*

104. Muzzioli, *Michelstaedter*: 51.

105. Pierre Klossowski, *Nietzsche, il Politeismo e la Parodia* (Milano: SE, 1999): 37-8. This article could only be retrieved in Italian. Klossowski's argument on masks, parody and eternal return would be an interesting point of departure for a comparison with our author.

106. Lukács, *Soul and Form*: 1.

107. Seminal at least for the comparison with Michelstaedter. This text can now be found in Lukács, *L'Anima e le Forme*: 273-77.

108. Ibid.: 273.

109. Ibid.: 274.

110. Pastore, *La Conoscenza come Azione. Saggi su Lukács*: 44-5.

111. Lukács, *Soul and Form*: 1.

112. Ibid.

113. Cacciari, 'Interpretazione di Michelstaedter': 24.

114. A double idea of irony will emerge from the enquiry. The first will be discussed with regard to the strategies for undermining ideological positions (chapter 2); the second, closer to Cacciari's reading of Lukács, will be the result of the interpretation of the negative dialectic deployed in *La Persuasione e la Rettorica* and the consequent self-undermining. This self-negation as an inadequate attempt is at the same time the way, ironically, to signify what beyond this inadequacy lays (chapter 5).

115. While καλλωπίσματα ὄρφνης is a platonic term (see *Gorgias*, 492 c. My source for Plato's works is: Platone, *Tutti gli Scritti*, ed. Giovanni Reale (Milano: Rusconi, 1997). For

the quote from *Gorgias*: 902), it seems clear how much the figure of 'veil' has in common with the Schopenhauerian 'veil of Maya'. This is finally clear in the pages where Michelstaedter describes the states of sudden consciousness of the human condition: dreams, fear, states of panic (PR: 22).

116. «Il *valore*, la *realtà* è la via: la macchina che muove i concetti: *l'attività filosofica*. Ma se pensare vuol dire *agitare concetti,* che appena *per questa attività* devono *divenire conoscenza*: io sono sempre vuoto nel presente e la cura del futuro dove io fingo il mio scopo *mi toglie tutto il mio essere. Cogito = non entia coagito, ergo non sum*» (PR: 61).

117. «I primi Cristiani facevano il segno del pesce e si credevano salvi; avessero fatto più pesci e sarebbero stati salvi davvero, ché in ciò avrebbero riconosciuto che Cristo ha salvato se stesso poiché della sua vita mortale ha saputo creare il dio: l'individuo; ma che nessuno è salvato da lui che non segua la sua vita: ma seguire non è imitare [...]» (PR: 62). For the first Christians, "Ἰησῦς Χριστὸς Θεοῦ Ὑὸς Σωτήρ, 'Jesus Christ of-God Son the Saviour', notoriously forms the acronym ΙΧΘΣ, 'Fish', and subsequently becomes an iconic symbol; in Michelstaedter: "'Ἰησῦς Χριστὸς Θεοῦ Ὑὸς Σωτήρ Ἑαυτοῦ Σωτήρ", 'Jesus Christ of-God Son of-Himself Saviour', forms ΙΧΘΥΕΣ, 'Fishes'. See Campailla's note in PR: 316-17.

118. «Così gli artisti impotenti che cercano <l'impressione> mettendosi e rimettendosi nelle posizioni note, che come la cercano così non l'hanno, ma hanno solo la propria volontà di averla e sfruttano invano nella pietosa rettorica il loro prezioso organismo dalle sensazioni raffinate» (PR: 64-5).

119. «Eppure se <oggettività> vuol dire <oggettività>, vedere oggettivamente non ha senso perché deve avere un soggetto o è l'estrema coscienza di chi è *uno con le cose, ha* in sé tutte le cose: ἐν συνεχές, il *persuaso*: il dio» (PR: 77). A further link with Parmenides' 'one and indivisible'.

120. Massimo Cacciari, 'La Lotta 'su' Platone,' in *Eredità di Carlo Michelstaedter,* ed. Silvio Cumpeta and Angela Michelis (Udine: Forum, 2002): 104.

121. Cacciari, 'Interpretazione di Michelstaedter': 27.

122. Daniela Bini, 'Carlo Michelstaedter: the Tragedy of Thought,' *Differentia: Review of Italian Thought,* no. 2 (1988): 187.

123. However, in the horizon of 'persuasion', as Bini points out as well, suicide is obviously an analogous logical mistake. Michelstaedter's rewriting of the end of his *Dialogo della Salute*, for example, is a well known example of this point; see: DDS: 84-6. The same is stated in one of Michelstaedter's most accomplished poetic achievements, *I Figli del Mare* (P: 79-84). Logically speaking, it is clear how every representation and definition of death is inexorably corrupted by its being conceived from a relative point of view (on this topic, the discussion of which exceeds the goals of our thesis, see at least: Maurice Blanchot, *The Literary Space* (Lincoln: University of Nebraska Press, 1982), particularly chapter IV: 67-88). The same order of problems, as we will address in our fifth chapter, arises for the possibility of a positive definition of 'persuasion'.

124. Bini, 'Carlo Michelstaedter: the Tragedy of Thought'.

125. Ibid.: 193.

126. Piero Pieri, 'Per una Dialettica Storica del Silenzio. La 'Vergogna' del Filosofo e l'Autoinganno dello Scrittore,' in *Eredità di Carlo Michelstaedter,* ed. Silvio Cumpeta and Angela Michelis (Udine: Forum, 2002): 235.

127. See the quoted Harrison, *1910. The Emancipation of Dissonance.*

128. Furthermore, as we will see below in our fifth chapter, Harrison will interpret the absolute of 'persuasion' in a wider sense than the limiting concept of 'death', namely as something that by definition lies outside the subject-object distinction, with consequences that will be

coherent with our conclusion on the stylistic achievements of the text.

129. On this basis, and because of an acknowledgement of the use of different sub-genres in the text, two early dismissals of Michelstaedter's project are conducted. See: Giacomo Debenedetti, 'Michelstaedter,' in *Saggi* (Milano: Mondadori, 1999); Emilio Cecchi, *Taccuini*, vol. VI (Milano: Mondadori, 1976).

130. For an introductory presentation of some of the different sub-genres in *La Persuasione e la Rettorica*, see: Aurelio Benevento, "*La Persuasione e la Rettorica*' di Michelstaedter e la 'Concretezza Artistica',' Otto/Novecento XV, no. 1 (1991).

131. In order to minimize misunderstanding, I shall avoid the term 'rhetoric' when referring to the style of argumentation in *La Persuasione e la Rettorica*; Michelstaedter's category of 'rhetoric' is obviously charged with different philosophical meanings, and my use would surely generate some problems. Throughout this enquiry, I will adopt the term 'style', intended in a broad sense as 'strategies of signification'; my chapter 1 will be the place in which, after the demonstration of the self-reflexivity of the text, a methodology of stylistic interpretation will be outlined.

132. See: Muzzioli, *Michelstaedter*.

133. Muzzioli, 'L'Antagonismo di Michelstaedter': 314.

134. Taviani, 'Attualità di Michelstaedter': 320.

135. Ibid.: 321.

136. Taviani, *Michelstaedter*.

137. As seems implied in Taviani's recent article.

138. This approach is close to De Man's reading of Rilke, in Paul De Man, *Allegories of Reading* (New Haven, London: Yale University Press, 1979).

139. In Italian the word for straight line is 'retta', also meaning 'righteous'. Together with the double use of 'hyperbole' in the different contexts of mathematical and rhetorical language, this is an example of Michelstaedter's exploitation of 'pluri-lingualism'.

140. For a general discussion of Michelstaedter's reasons for writing a degree thesis, in obvious logical contradiction with the dismissal of academic rhetoric, see for example: Asor Rosa, "La Persuasione e la Rettorica' di Carlo Michelstaedter'; Muzzioli, *Michelstaedter*.

141. Letter to Paula Michelstaedter, 30th of May 1909.

142. This term also offers a link with Leopardi's poetic and, more in general, with an understanding of artistic language inside a romantic aesthetic. We will address this point throughout the present volume, particularly in chapters 2, 4 and 5.

CHAPTER ONE

Strategies of Commitment

Das Fleisch des Heiligen auf glühendem Rost hinschmilzt.

Georg Trakl

Our introduction outlined an hypothesis which defines the basis of our approach to Michelstaedter's work. It suggests that Michelstaedter's investment in language is a weapon on the way to 'persuasion', and that *La Persuasione e la Rettorica* is one of the main 'fields' in which the battle between 'persuasion' and 'rhetoric' takes place. The objective of this first chapter is double: firstly, to demonstrate this hypothesis through close reading, and, secondly, to outline a coherent strategy of enquiry based on these results.

1.1   In the beginning was the preface

At the Fondo Carlo Michelstaedter of the Biblioteca Statale Isontina in Gorizia, amongst the manuscripts collected under the label 'Appunti Preparatori', and not ascribed to specific sections of any of Michelstaedter's major works (*La Persuasione e la Rettorica*; *Il Dialogo della Salute*), one can find three small notebook pages with the autograph draft of a 'preface'[1]. This hidden paratext could be easily overlooked (and indeed it hasn't yet been published)[2], but it is important in itself, and in relation to a more famous paratext, the preface restored by Campailla in his edition of *La Persuasione e la Rettorica* for Adelphi. The latter text, present in the autograph manuscript of the thesis (A), and crossed out from the final copy (C) prepared for the Istituto di Studi Superiori, is accepted by Campailla with the following justification: «per la prima volta è stata anche accolta nel testo la prefazione, di eccezionale importanza, che si legge in A e che non risulta ricopiata, mentre trasmette il messaggio di Michelstaedter in una testamentaria sintesi»[3], stressing in this way a unity between the message of the paratext and the work to which it refers[4]. Campailla's words are somehow prophetic – given that since the publication of his edition, the presence and the 'exceptional importance' of the preface has been taken for granted – to the extent that one of the most widely read studies of Michelstaedter[5] conducts its argument on the «motivazioni tutte esteriori» of the thesis by drawing heavily on the preface.

In our context, the question is simple: if the restored preface is of 'exceptional importance', why was it crossed out? In what ways was it more unacceptable than the thesis itself? These questions lead to a discussion on the possible philosophical reasons behind the rejection. The crucial point here is to understand if, and to which extent, the dismissal of the entire project of writing *La Persuasione e la Rettorica* present in the second preface is a reason for deletion of the paratext. In other words, our interpretation of the two paratexts is conceived in order to test the hypothesis that Michelstaedter is committed to (academic/philosophical) writing as a step on the hyperbolic way.

1.1.1 The first preface

Prefazione[6]

[1 RECTO] [Come] Da un' [padre] arringa d'uova nascono molte[i] [figli] [arringhe], e da ognuna[o] [dei] delle molte[i] [figli] arringhe nate dalla arringa madre altre[i] molte [figli] arringhe e da ognuna[o] di queste[i] molte[i] [figli] arringhe nate da ognuna[o] delle[i] molte arringhe nate dalla proto-arringa altre molte arringhe …

Così per <u>un</u> solo[a] [parola] 'verbo' sfuggito[a] [al primo uomo s]al Creatore senza ch'egli sia riuscito a mettergli dentro tutto il contenuto tutto il senso evidente concreto e persuasivo per tutti altre molte parole sono nate per spiegare ciò che il verbo non annunziava [a dare] per dare la persuasione ch'esso non dava, ma ognuna di questa parole [1 VERSO] essendo figlia della prima si comportava come questa e nessuna aveva tutto il contenuto e [ognu] la forza [mancava] della persuasione [assoluta]. – Così per [supplire] dare [la forza persuasiva di] ciò che ognuna d'esse voleva ma non dava nacquero per ognuna molte nuove parole e ognuna delle nuove [manca de] è fatta a sembianza della prima e manca della persuasione <u>ed</u> è causa ad infinite altre infinitamente.

Forse come nell'arringa riguardo alle arringhe questa era nel 'verbo di Dio' l'intenzione: crescete e moltiplicatevi.

[2 RECTO] Certo la persuasione è il fine d'ogni parola umana – e l'impossibilità della persuasione è causa che gli uomini parlano ancora, [parlano] e senza fine parleranno. –

Ché se il primo verbo l'avesse convinto Adamo [non avrebbe] sarebbe morto muto e non si sarebbe curato né d'Eva né del serpente né dell'albero della scienza. Ma volendo la felicità che il *verbo* non era riuscito a convincerlo [essere] trovarsi soltanto nel paradiso [2 VERSO] lo perdette per sempre e generò uomini e parole senza fine. – ([in nota] Quest'ultime aumentarono tanto che gli uomini vi Annegarono tutti e si salvò dal diluvio universale solo Noè perché lui … Era sobrio; – ma più la)

Ed è perciò che noi uomini siamo qui ora alla caccia della felicità come c'insegnò il nostro antenato travagliandoci l'un l'altro con miriadi di parole che cercando invano [colla persuasione] la felicità [ci allontanano sempre più] della persuasione [ci annegano] (3 RECTO) ci rendono sempre più infelici e sempre meno persuasi. –

Nel mare senza confini del nuovo diluvio questo che segue è la mia liberazione.

––––––––––––––––-

In principio erat verbum.

… Quando questa prima parola sfuggì al creatore non ben ponderata né faro Della ragion persuasiva egli si pentì amaramente ma 'voce dal sen fuggita, disse, più richiamar non vale' e si mise a osservare quello che andava a succedere.

[3 VERSO] Se il primo uomo si fosse persuaso non sarebbe stato il primo uomo ma l'ultimo [poiché ci] sarebbe stato nessuno dopo di lui.

Se il *verbo* l'avesse persuaso non si direbbe 'in principio erat verbum' ma
lui Sarebbe ancora uno immobile e nessuno fiaterebbe

In the context of an analysis of the relationship between singularity and
multiplicity – introduced through the example of the herrings and the play on
the double meaning of 'herring' (in the spelling variant 'arringa') and
'harangue' ('arringa'), and further specified in the second term of the simile,
where the Creator is seen as a single origin of the infinite chain of words – the
ironic inverse exegesis of Genesis 1,2 and John's Gospel 1,1 that constitutes
this first preface addresses both the question of the possibility of a non-
contingent, a-rhetorical utterance and, in a final self-reflexive turn, the position
of the text itself with regard to this possibility. In this sense, the philosophical
problem is immediately presented as a problem of language, thus entirely
justifying the adoption and original re-appropriation of a vocabulary derived
from classical rhetoric[7]. In doing so, it is not explicitly presented as an
argument on poetics, oriented towards the definition of an adequate mode of
signification; rather, it exclusively points towards the inadequacy of the entire
enterprise of signification. The story of the Creator and his 'mistake'
exemplifies language as intrinsically post-lapsarian: the proto-herring is not
qualitatively distinguished from the others to which it gives birth, and the word
of the Creator is 'creating' to the extent to which it is already an incomplete
utterance, a 'creative' error that generates multiplicity from unity.

This 'lapse' of the Creator is both evidence of a particular stage of the
development of Michelstaedter's speculation, and offers the chance to outline
a useful framework for the interpretation of the second, restored preface and
the contextualization of the paratexts inside the philosophical enterprise of *La
Persuasione e la Rettorica* in general. Firstly, *in principio erat verbum*:
Michelstaedter adopts here the Latin *vulgata*[8], thus keeping coherence with the
Italian word 'verbo' and explicitly stressing the irony of the passage, against the
use of *logos*. This is even more crucial, if considered in the light of
Michelstaedter's fluency in ancient Greek and the positive investment in this
language throughout *La Persuasione e la Rettorica*, which some critics have
ventured to identify as a sort of 'atemporal' means of communication between
'persuaded' souls[9]. The lapse, the 'word', is not opposed to a pre-existing pre-
lapsarian adequate utterance, there is no hint here of an edenic language; the
opposite of the post-lapsarian word is only silence: the word is 'the first' and,

were it 'persuaded/persuading', it would have been the last («ché se *il primo verbo* l'avesse convinto Adamo *sarebbe muto*» [my emphasis]). Seemingly, this is enough, at this stage of the development of his argument on 'persuasion', for Michelstaedter to argue the opposite: that if there is a state of 'persuasion', this state is beyond language, it is silent[10].

In this context, where the inadequacy of human language and the absolute otherness of 'persuasion' are defined, the passage introduces a further point, alluding to the link between the problem of language and will: as much as the impossibility of 'persuasion' is the engine for the infinite perpetuation of 'rhetoric', it is also giving birth to an always frustrated will to recover 'persuasion': «*volendo* la felicità che il verbo non era riuscito a convincerlo trovarsi soltanto nel paradiso lo perdette per sempre» (my emphasis). This is coherent with Cacciari's definition of Michelstaedter's aporia. In this sense, will is at the same time the consequence and perpetuating engine of what the paratext sees as the post-lapsarian contingent nature of Adam and (his) language.

The first preface is more than a confirmation of this awareness. The positive project of 'liberation' («quanto segue è la mia liberazione») introduced in the passage, in its working against, yet well inside linguistic contingency (the 'something' which follows) strengthens a link between text and paratext, adding a dimension to *La Persuasione e la Rettorica* as the field in which a 'way to persuasion' is attempted.

The paratext exemplifies – as does the hyperbole in the body of the text – the incongruence between a liberation and the absolute distance that separates its achievement, with every word moving away and not towards the original silence; and yet, Michelstaedter states that in 'what follows', lies the possibility for 'liberation'. This latest remark overlooks the aporia in which the project is entangled, and this would have been enough to discard the preliminary attempt at a preface as naïve. In other words, while the argument of the paratext is coherent with the text in the definition of the general argument on rhetorical language, its thematizing of the strategies for overcoming inadequate affirmation is both undeveloped and 'optimistic', highlighting the draft nature of the piece.

This non-argued optimism is arguably the most substantial difference between the first preface and the text. That said, however, the complexities of the dialectic towards 'persuasion', as discussed above, point toward an interpretation of Michelstaedter's enterprise that does not rely on a simple opposition between adequacy and inadequacy of signification, but considers the dialectic of negations as the terrain on which a particular type of investment, infinite and in need of an impossible overcoming, can be conceived. In other words, the questions in this context are: can the 'liberation' of the first preface be read as a process, and not a final outcome? In this sense, can the first preface cast a new light on the second, dismissive paratext, or are they to be considered as diametrically opposed? And, given that both paratexts are ultimately crossed out from the final copy of the work, what is the ultimate 'project' of the text itself?

Before addressing these questions, a further point needs to be discussed. The first preface is the affirmation of the inadequacy of any affirmation, implying a problematic ground on which to develop a philosophical project. This is, in other words, the question on Michelstaedter's commitment. A few paths are open here to an interpreter. The first is the temptation to cut short and highlight this contradiction as the very reason for the dismissal. The second would be to think the mere presence of the contradiction, and moreover its self-conscious presence, as the sign of a «coazione a dire»[11] that leads to an utterance 'despite itself'. It is hard, however, to imagine how this could account for the rhetorical and stylistic complexities of *La Persuasione e la Rettorica*, which would be reduced to a mere (redundant) epiphenomenon. Our hypothesis of commitment would address this complexity, but needs to be demonstrated.

1.1.2   A Gnostic 'way to persuasion'?

The concern for the problem of unity and multiplicity comes to Michelstaedter most likely from his reading of the Presocratics, who constitute the most conspicuous set of sources in *La Persuasione e la Rettorica*[12]. That said, the story in the first preface has a curious Gnostic flavour: in its dualism, its inverse exegesis of biblical sources and, more indirectly, in the structural and thematic parallels with Gnostic interpretations of the Platonic demiurge. However, a few preliminary remarks are necessary in order to centextualize the discussion of these parallels. Michelstaedter's myth of the origin of language, this sort of declension in linguistic terms of the Gnostic prison, is not a direct allusion to a Gnostic text; similarities are to be found in a structural parallel, and in the reference to strikingly common sources. The possibility of demonstrating a direct intertextual link between Michelstaedter's oeuvre and the Gnostic corpus is in this sense highly improbable. Surely the letter to Gaetano Chiavacci dated 22nd of December 1907 opens a series of hypotheses: «Io voglio sapere qualcosa di più preciso su quella lettratura cabbalistica [he refers to his great grandfather Isacco Samuele Reggio (1784-1885)], specialmente sulle sue origini, poi voglio farmi consegnare dall'archivio i resoconti protocollati di tutte le sedute in cui quel mio bisnonno compì solenni atti di purificazione con mezzi cabbalistici (poi s'è possibile risalire più su)» (E: 268). To my knowledge, however, there is no fully developed study, not based on general speculations, that highlights the extent of Michelstaedter's knowledge of the area in question[13], or how far back in history he managed to reach in his readings[14], supposing that he followed through with the interest he manifested in the letter, and given that none of these works appear in any explicit form in his writings.

The second remark concerns the ironic nature of the paratext. Needless to say, the proposed exegesis, linked to the passage on harangues in the opening simile, should be intended, in its fictional status, as a figurative rendition of a philosophical argument that does not aim to enter the debate on religious exegesis, if not as a critique of religion from the outside, as a crystallized and self-reproducing form of 'rhetoric'. The importance of the choice of figurative language in the context of an attempt to come to terms with the aporia of signification will be addressed later in our research; what is important to stress here is that the ironic strategy is employed 'seriously', to exemplify an underlying philosophical problem and (theoretically and stylistically) conceive its overcoming.

In recent years the very category of Gnosticism has undergone a process of critical revision after the discoveries of Nag Hammadi, particularly in the work of Williams, who called its religious, social and historical unity into question, revealing it as a modern construct[15]. If Michelstaedter's myth, in its structure, is coherent with some aspects of the classic definition of Gnosticism given in the final document of the famous 'Colloquio di Messina' on the origin of Gnosticism[16] – where acosmism is translated in the paratext as an identification of language as evil – it comes to fit even more the much more careful definition provided by Williams under the label of 'biblical demiurgical tradition'[17]. Here, 'demiurgical' includes «those that ascribe the creation and management of the cosmos to some lower entity or entities, distinct from the highest God» («this would include most of ancient Platonism»)[18], and 'biblical' «denote[s] 'demiurgical' traditions that also incorporate or adopt traditions from Jewish or Christian scripture»[19]. The inverse exegesis of Michelstaedter's paratext is cleary drawing from Genesis and the Gospel of John; however the link with a Platonic demiurgical tradition is not immediately clear. The 'Creator' of the first preface is indeed the one God, a paradoxical figure who embodies at the same time 'persuasion' and the possibility of letting a fallacious word 'slip out', thus being the origin of imperfection, of 'rhetoric'. In this, nevertheless, as a 'creator of language' he is definitively imperfect, somehow distinct from his own perfection. This is not enough, yet, to sustain the parallel.

The *locus classicus* for all the demiurgical speculation of Platonic derivation is the *Timaeus*. In his contribution to the Sethian's reading of Plato, for example, Turner shows how the God of Genesis is interpreted, in the Sethian corpus, as a Demiurge, subordinate to a paradigm which is above him; and it is the reading of Plato's 'errant cause' that allows this development:

> but even in the Timaeus, the altogether reasonable Demiurge's positive intentions are hindered by another negative element that Plato introduces [...]: the works of 'Necessity' of the 'errant cause' as opposed to the 'divine cause'. It is this element of irrational Necessity that enters into the work of the younger Gods when the Demiurge commissions to fashion the mortal bodies of humans and to append certain necessary mortal additions to human soul[20].

In *La Persuasione e la Rettorica*, *Timaeus* is used as the main example for a critique of the later Plato, while at the same time offering the chance for a further explanation of the concept of φιλοψυχία. In the second appendix to the text, an extraordinary long quote from 68e, introduced as a 'dogmatic' development of a point in *Phaedo* (PR: 153), is interpreted as follows: «questo ἀναγκαῖον, questo αἴτον sono la χρεία, la deficienza di tutte le cose: il mancare dell'essere, il non-essere, *il male*» (PR: 153).

Interestingly, this passage makes the link between 'necessity', 'lacking nature of all things', 'non-being' and 'evil' explicit, in ways which support our argument. Furthermore, however, and this in the most crucial of parallels, it is a personification of 'evil', the god of φιλοψυχία, to whom Plato succumbs: «[i]l buon δημιουργός del Timeo, il τῷ ὄντι αἴτιον del Fedone, sono questo stesso male, questa stessa mancanza dell'essere, sono le incarnazioni del dio della che così ha vinto il divino discepolo di Socrate» (PR: 154).

The passage here strengthens the link between the first paratext and *La Persuasione e la Rettorica*, and supports the reading of the former under a Gnostic framework. Moreover, by identifying 'Necessity' with the god of φιλοψυχία, Michelstaedter underlines 'necessity' as the *locus* of a choice for the subject; 'love for life' is equated to 'cowardice' (PR: 17), thus opening the space for 'courage'. In this sense, the interpretation of the passage from *Timaeus* as a reification of 'necessity', leads to the dismissal of the 'divine disciple of Socrates' as succumbing to the rhetoric of φιλοψυχία. And yet, once again the same passage hints at the aporia of the 'courage', its 'impossibility', «il coraggio dell'impossibile» (PR: 43); if φιλοψυχία is 'necessity', the 'necessity of overcoming/resisting φιλοψυχία' is itself φιλοψυχία: god, the 'just' (PR: 40) god of 'persuasion' is thus infinitely alien.

1.1.3 Metaphysical nihilism, Verweltlichung, Entweltlichung and the risks of reification

By introducing Hans Jonas' terminology on Gnosticism, the argument is here focusing on the possibilities opened by the parallel between Gnostic speculation and negative thought in general, of the sort inaugurated by *Gnosis und Spätantiker Geist*[21]. In this sense, the parallel corroborates the stream of studies which, throughout the history of the interpretation of Michelstaedter, starting from the seminal contribution by Joachim Ranke[22], interpreted the philosopher as a precursor of existentialism.

More specifically, the importance of the comparison with the Gnostics allows us to articulate the question of a supposed metaphysic of foundation in Michelstaedter's philosophical project. This point can be clarified through Coulianu's argument on the difference between ancient and modern nihilism, seen as a different attitude towards transcendence[23]:

> If nihilism is the state that ensues from the 'unbuilding' of transcendence and the attitude that pursues transcendence in order to 'build it down', then we are entitled to notice that Gnosticism is the obverse of nihilism, for being the champion of transcendence; in this sense, Gnosticism would be 'the most powerful metaphysical nihilism in the history of western ideas[24].

In the first preface, in fact, on the one hand, transcendence is impossible, and «l'impossibilità della persuasione è causa che gli uomini parlano ancora, e senza fine parleranno»; on the other hand, in 'what follows', resides the possibility of a 'liberation' – was Michelstaedter a 'metaphysical nihilist'? The answer to this question is what polarizes the contemporary debate on the author.

Furthermore, the parallel with Gnosticism allows us to articulate the problem of signification in the horizon of 'liberation': the question of how the first paratext can be presenting a 'truth' about the human condition whilst 'outsourcing' the liberation from this condition, the achievement of a 'truth of signification', to a coming text.

Jonas discussed the same order of problems in his analysis of the Gnostic corpus, as a matter of objectification and permutation[25]. In the context of the opposition between *Verweltlichung* (being trapped in the world) and *Enweltlichung* (escape from or negation of the world)[26], the Gnostic myth, by revealing duality, at the same time objectifies *Entweltlichung* in the form of a story. This relationship between myth and reification becomes problematic: if, on the one hand, myth re-subjectifies the objective world, reified through rational objectivity[27]; on the other, the paradox of this 'objectification of the awareness' and of the movement towards *Entweltlichung* inside the signification of the myth reifies once again the human existential movement[28]. Once the myth becomes the *locus* of an instrumental knowledge, or leads to a structured sacramental practice that defines objective 'steps' towards *Entweltlichung*, it becomes part of the problem that it is set to overcome[29]. Working towards a historical interpretation of these different moments in the context of late antiquity, Jonas suggests the following movement: from myth, seen already as the «projection of an existential reality which seeks its own truth in a total view of things and may even at first satisfy its primary aspiration in such objective-symbolic representations»[30], to a re-interiorization into «subjective phases of self-performable experience whose culmination has the form of *ecstasis* or mystic union», where «Gnostic myth passes into mysticism» and «transcendence itself [could] be turned into immanence»[31]. In Michelstaedter's philosophical project, on the contrary, there is no space for a moment of objectification that is in any way external to the subjective existential movement towards 'persuasion', as either a consequence or a cause: signification, for Michelstaedter *must be* part of the emancipation, or it is its fatal halt, its rhetorical crystallization. In the context of hyperbolic negation, objectification is envisaged only if at the same time embodying its own self-negation. It is in this sense that it may be possible to think of *La Persuasione e la Rettorica* as mystical.

This is not the place for a discussion on the value of Jonas' contribution to the understanding of Gnosticism; rather the present discussion is an attempt to exploit some theoretical questions that arise from the engagement with Gnostic texts. In this sense, the problem of 'the word of revelation' and 'what to do with it' is crucial. The first paratext, in its explicit distancing of the moment of 'knowledge' from the moment of 'liberation', falls prey to the contradiction. But this could also be read in the opposite way: infinite negation implies that the adequate signification is something always yet to come, and 'liberation' is always necessarily something that 'follows': «my liberation is *necessarily* and *unavoidably what follows*», in the infinite movement of Socratic dialectic. This is precisely the reason why the first preface is to be rejected, and the reason why it is crucial to our ends.

1.1.4 The second preface

The second, restored preface gives an account of the use of positive examples with regard to 'persuasion', and does so with a strong self-reflexive aim, resulting in nothing less than an assessment of the value and the role of the text itself.

Io lo so che parlo perché parlo ma che non persuaderò nessuno; e questa è disonestà – ma la rettorica ἀναγχάζει με ταῦτα δρᾶν βίᾳ – o in altre parole «è pur necessario che se uno ha addentato una perfida sorba la risputi».

Eppure quanto io dico è stato detto tante volte e con tale forza che pare impossibile che il mondo abbia ancor continuato ogni volta dopo che erano suonate quelle parole.

Lo dissero ai greci Parmenide, Eraclito, Empedocle, ma Aristotele li trattò da naturalisti inesperti; lo disse Socrate, ma ci fabbricarono su 4 sistemi. Lo disse l'Ecclesiaste ma lo trattarono e lo spiegarono come libro sacro e non poteva quindi dir niente che fosse in contraddizione coll'ottimismo della Bibbia; lo disse Cristo, e ci fabbricarono su la Chiesa; lo dissero Eschilo e Sofocle e Simonide, e agli italiani lo proclamò Petrarca trionfalmente, lo ripeté con dolore Leopardi – ma gli uomini furono loro grati dei bei versi, e se ne fecero generi letterari. Se ai nostri tempi le creature di Ibsen lo fanno vivere su tutte le scene, gli uomini «si divertono» a sentir fra le altre anche quelle storie «eccezionali» e i critici parlano di «simbolismo»; e se Beethoven lo canta così da muovere il cuore d'ognuno, ognuno adopera poi la commozione per i suoi scopi – e in fondo ... è questione di contrappunto.

Se io ora lo ripeto per quanto so e posso, poiché lo faccio così che non può divertir nessuno, né con dignità filosofica né con concretezza artistica, ma da povero pedone che misura coi suoi passi il terreno, non pago l'entrata in nessuna delle categorie stabilite – né faccio precedente a nessuna nuova categoria e nel migliore dei casi avrò fatto ... una tesi di laurea. – (PR: 3-4).

There is a generalized interpretive habit of considering this preface a dismissal of the entire project of *La Persuasione e la Rettorica*, seen as something accomplished «per motivazioni tutte esteriori»[32], thus surrendering to the contradiction between theory and practice. In this sense, the eventual deletion of the paratext from the final copy (C) of the thesis, would *per se* be evidence of commitment, of investment in the process of signification. But on this there is more to be said.

After the word of 'what has been said many times, and with such strength', 'it seems impossible that the world had continued'. This *seeming* impossibility shows a clear intertextual link with the first preface, and witnesses the development of Michelstaedter's thought. In the first paratext, continuation, after the 'persuaded and persuading' word is simply impossible[33]. Two interpretive options open here. We could be inclined to hypothesize that the positive sources quoted in the second preface are not necessarily 'persuaded' voices, but voices which 'say persuasion', announce it, and in doing so orient themselves towards the hyperbolic way. Indeed, in the passage there is no explicit mention of these examples as 'persuaded'; the positive sources are introduced through the following verbs: to 'say', to 'proclaim', 'to repeat', 'to make live', 'to sing'. If we add to this the problem of the incommensurability between 'rhetoric' and 'persuasion', the doubt on the status of the sources can be fully stated: if the narrator is not 'persuaded', he wouldn't be able to utter what 'has been said many times', not even in a 'weaker' way. 'Rhetoric' and 'persuasion' are not two opposite poles of a continuum from zero to maximum 'force'. If this were true, the general opinion – which regards this group of positive examples as a rather transparent 'pantheon' of persuaded humans who have reached what the narrator is vainly trying to repeat[34] – would be radically put into question. The narrator, thus, may as well be positively engaged in that infinite and impossible hyperbolic movement that the sources are performing: saying, as he 'knows and can', the same.

The ways in which 'persuasion' is described and personified in the body of the text, however, only partially confirms this hypothesis. In fact, while it is true that the 'persuaded' is consistently presented in general terms as the 'who', or 'the one who' (for example, PR: 9; 10; 33; 34, and so on) – and the positive quotes are usually adopted to defend an argument *on* 'persuasion' – two of the positive examples of the preface are indeed treated in the body of the text as 'persuaded'. The first evidence is implicit:

> essere indipendenti dalla gravità vuol dire non aver peso. E Socrate non si concedette riposo finché non ebbe eliminato da sé ogni peso. – Ma consunta insieme la speranza della libertà e la schiavitù – lo spirito indipendente e la gravità – la necessità della terra e la volontà del sole – né volò al sole – né restò sulla terra; – né fu indipendente né schiavo; né felice né misero; – ma di lui con le mie parole non ho più che dire (PR: 66).

Surely, the rest of the positive examples of the paratext can be read, in their being 'speakable' (throughout the body of the text) not only through negations, as engaged in the process of «non concedersi riposo». But Socrates, having reached beyond this state, constitutes a potential contradiction in the paratext (is this enough to delete it?).

Christ is the second example: «perciò nella sua presenza, nei suoi atti, nelle sue parole si rivela, si <enuclea>, si fa vicina, concreta una vita che trascende la miopia degli uomini [...] [;] perciò ogni sua parola è luminosa, perché, con profondità di nessi l'una alle alter legandosi, crea la presenza di ciò che è lontano»; «perciò Cristo ha l'aureola, le pietre diventano pani, gli ammalati risanano, i vili si fanno martiri e gli uomini gridano al miracolo» (PR: 48). «Cristo ha salvato sé stesso poiché dalla sua vita mortale ha saputo creare il dio» (PR: 62). Here, however – and this is the significant difference from the first paratext – the possibility of a relationship between the 'persuaded' and the rest of humanity is also outlined[35]: «la via della persuasione non è corsa da <omnibus>, non ha segni, indicazioni che si possano comunicare, studiare, ripetere. Ma ognuno ha in sé il bisogno di trovarla e nel proprio dolore l'indice, ognuno deve nuovamente aprirsi da sé la via» (PR: 62). In this sense, if the relationship with the example of 'persuasion' leads to the orientation towards a personal, individual path, then the position of the narrator in the second preface can be explained in a way which diverges from the simple admission of impotence, as a particular declension of the *excusatio propter infirmitatem*: one which expresses commitment.

We can follow this alternative interpretation throughout the paratext.

Io lo so che parlo perché parlo ma che non persuaderò nessuno; e

questa è disonestà – ma la rettorica ἀναγχάζει με ταῦτα δρᾶν βίᾳ –
o in altre parole «è pur necessario che se uno ha addentato una perfida
sorba la risputi».

The fact that the narrator will not convince anyone can be read as a sign
that locates the project of the thesis before an acquired 'persuasion'; however,
the 'necessary spitting', the spitting of 'rhetoric' through the uttering of
'rhetoric' (the war with words against words) is entirely coherent with the
hyperbolic movement. What follows, in this sense, is not a liberation; it is a
liberating movement. Also the concluding passage of the paratext can be read
in this light:

> Se io ora lo ripeto per quanto so e posso, poiché lo faccio così che non
> può divertir nessuno, né con dignità filosofica né con concretezza
> artistica, ma da povero pedone che misura coi suoi passi il terreno,
> non pago l'entrata in nessuna delle categorie stabilite – né faccio
> precedente a nessuna nuova categoria e nel migliore dei casi avrò fatto
> … una tesi di laurea. –

The repetition of the word of/on 'persuasion' in an individual, singular
way, the avoidance of pre-existing categories and the explicit intention to
avoid the role of a 'precedent' originator of new categories, rhetorical
systems, seems once again coherent with the hyperbolic movement, boldly
trying to avoid the fate of its sources, which were historically misinterpreted.
Returning to our hypothesis, this passage works also as an implicit comment
on style, on the pragmatics of signification to be found in *La Persuasione e la
Rettorica*.

If this reading is plausible, it opens the option to interpret the concluding
remark ironically. In a preface written (also) for its readers (the academic
commission of the Istituto di Studi Superiori)[36], what is usually considered a
straight forward dismissal – a surrendering to 'rhetoric' which seems to clash
with the preceding narratorial remarks – becomes an antiphrastic comment:
'in the best of cases' (for you, professors who are reading me), 'I will have done
a degree thesis'. As we are about to see, this would be coherent with the
construction of the implied reader in the body of the text.

The second paratext introduced a complex and ambiguous relationship
with the examples on/of 'persuasion', an ambiguity replicated throughout
the text. Disentangling this problematic knot means to figure out the nature

of the «dire» and of the «ripetere», ultimately defining the narratorial position with regard to his own philosophical project. What can be said here, is that the 'exceptional importance' of the second paratext resides not in an explicit dismissal, but rather in the complex articulation of the tensions between the limits of 'rhetoric' and the necessity to 'spit it'. This is, in other words, the playing out of the problem of *Verweltlichung* and Michelstaedter's peculiar declension of *Entweltlichung*: a judgement on the coherence of Michelstaedter's enterprise can be imagined only inside this field of tensions.

1.2   Commitment in the body of the text

In his book on the semiotics of the narrative voice[37], Stefano Agosti reads the development of the novel in the twentieth century through a methodological framework centred on the voice of the narrator. The starting point is the idea of the narrative text up to the late nineteenth century as 'semantically closed'[38]; that is, meaning – understood here as a stable probation for the narrator (a truth, a metaphysics, a correct point of view, etc.) – is located somewhere *outside* the given text. Consequently, he traces how «solo nel Novecento si assiste, e da vari punti, alla rottura dello spazio epistemologico che garantiva l'articolazione del Discorso in quanto riproduzione del senso e manifestazione della verità, in quanto organizzazione logico-razionale (univoca) di contenuti sensibili e intellettuali semanticamente ipostatizzati»[39]. A privileged point of departure for tracing this change, according to Agosti, is the status of the narrator as both a repository of sense external to the text, and the *locus* of a privileged relationship with truth and its crisis at the turn of the century. As Lukács' *The Theory of the Novel*[40] and Goldmann's re-discussion of it argue[41], what enters into this crisis is a particular understanding of the hero, both in its 'positive' (the *locus* of sense[42]) and 'negative' (as the exemplification of the absence of values – the *locus* of a negative sense, yet in any case a 'sense', that is, the hero remains the centre for the organization of the truth of the text) manifestations. This crisis ultimately «involves the elimination of two essential elements of the specific content of the novel: the psychology of the problematic hero and the story of his demoniacal search»[43].

Agosti's attempt to find in the narrative voice a key point at which a particular understanding of the hero is put at stake – and thus the very stylistic tool (we will soon see at which level) for the emancipation of the novel from a stable foundation in a truth – is useful for the present enquiry on two different levels. Firstly, and most importantly, it gives methodological significance to the stylistic reading of a non-fictional text. In this sense, the question to ask would regard the status of an academic supposedly extra-diegetic narrator who, through the organization of the material and a series of examples and arguments, formulates a thesis and defends his point of view. This is, for example, the case in other essays by Michelstaedter, such as the short thesis on *Lessing e Baretti* of 1906 (SS: 3-57). Consequently, if the hypothesis is that *La Persuasione e la Rettorica* should be read as an attempt at stylistic/philosophical coherence (as an attempt at emancipation), then this attempt should have resonance in the text as an intra-diegetic, or homo-diegetic component. This second question is the focus of our discussion here, the point being whether the cognitive[44] and meta-discursive[45] features of the narrator remain present as a generic necessity for generalization and conclusion (after all, it is a degree thesis in philosophy); and if the striving for coherence implies the 'hyperbolic' approach, thus undermining the same generalizations and conclusions.

Alongside its strategic role in shaping our textual analysis, Agosti's framework allows us to tackle a second major question. As Taviani pointed out: «il linguaggio offre numerosi punti di contatto fra la rettorica michelstaedteriana e il tema della crisi delle parole che attraversa tutta la letteratura moderna: Hoffmansthal, Musil. [...] Svevo e Slataper, ma anche Tozzi e Pirandello, per la perdita di fiducia nel linguaggio e nel nesso che univa un tempo le parole e le cose»[46]. Further than this, the hyperbolic movement, at its limit, in its ultimate 'negation of the value of negation' has a very problematic relationship with a supposed 'absence of foundation', and seems to do nothing else but replace (linguistic) values with a meta-value, a meta-negation. What is interesting in this sense are the consequences for the idea of subject and subjectivity. Does the subject lose its ultimate foundation in the final moment? In *La Persuasione e la Rettorica*, the 'persuaded human', «colui che è per sé stesso non ha bisogno d'altra cosa che sia per lui nel futuro, ma possiede tutto in sé» (PR: 9): but is he a subject who has regained his unity, or one who finally overcomes the question of his foundations and, paradoxically achieves a unity of a different sort[47]? How is this performed in the text?

The enquiry in this sense is ultimately the way to test Michelstaedter's work in relation to its own philosophy and the context of its time[48].

1.3 Subject pronouns in *La Persuasione e la Rettorica*: fluctuations and their causes

The critical literature on Michelstaedter briefly acknowledges what Muzzioli calls the instability of the grammatical subject in *La Persuasione e la Rettorica*[49], but lacks a comprehensive discussion on the consequences of this instability for defining the nature of the relationship between the narrator and his object[50]. My argument is that this point of departure can be considered a privileged one in many ways: for addressing the levels of involvement of the narrator in the narrated matter (as a character), his possible intra-diegetic or homo-diegetic features, and for defining the narratorial perspective and point of view in relationship with his poetic. In this sense, the fluctuations of the subject pronoun act as a key for linking poetic and rhetoric.

The first evidence to support this argument comes from a crucial passage in *La Persuasione e la Rettorica*, where a dramatic turn in the tone of the narratorial voice takes place. This moment defines a sharp discriminant in the strategies of argumentation, and their development can be interpreted as an explicit commitment to a negative dialectic.

1.4 The discriminant: φιλοψυχία, 'veil of Maya', consciousness of the human nothingness

The discriminant which sanctions the shift in the strategies of argumentation in *La Persuasione e la Rettorica*, and in this way, the relationship between the narrator and its object, occurs in the pages where the narrator – at that point extra-diegetic and omniscient – introduces a series of examples to represent the experience of 'nothingness', the 'inadequacy' and lack of a stable ground that manifests itself to the (unwilling) subject. These are moments when the set of values, beliefs and certainties fails to provide a covering mask, and surrender to the appearance of the true human condition: the depictions of these experiences are the most dramatic to be found in *La Persuasione e la Rettorica*[51] and seem to invest the narrator himself, calling him to a choice of coherence.

Critics[52] have often acknowledged how the unwilling experience of the nothingness of human condition can easily be compared with and find its source in the Schopenhauerian definition of the 'veil of Maya'. We can draw a first parallel between the Schopenhauerian *Wille zum Leben* and

Michelstaedter's φιλοψυχία («amore alla vita, viltà» PR: 17); the definition of the latter as the basis of human self-perpetuation through the fulfillment of finite needs, and thus inadequate self-affirmation, echoes Schopenhauer's. Secondly, we can consider 'persuasion' as an overcoming of the *principium individuationis*, and thus understand 'rhetoric' as a development of the concept of the veil of Maya[53] as the horizon for human activity.

In the theoretical landscape outlined, the two thinkers share a further understanding of the human capability for developing consciousness of their situation: the possibility of seeing and seeing through the veil of Maya. This consciousness is the basis of a project of emancipation and overcoming. The fact that, as Muzzioli notes, the analytic definitions of this project and the consequences to which they lead are very different and may be the major point of distance between the two thinkers, does not diminish the value of the parallel[54].

Schopenhauer describes the lifting of the veil in moments where the normal interpretive framework (in terms of causes and effects) fails to give a believable interpretation of an experience:

> there lives only in the innermost depths of his consciousness the wholly obscure presentiment that all this is indeed not really so strange to him, but has a connexion with him from which the *principium individuationis* cannot protect him. From this presentiment arises the ineradicable dread, common to all human beings [...] which suddenly seizes them, when by any chance they become puzzled over the *principium individuationis*, in that the principle of sufficient reason in one of other of its forms seems to undergo an exception[55].

In an analogous way, in *La Persuasione e la Rettorica* this consciousness, along with the state of horror that the temporary lifting of the veil of Maya implies, is accepted as a part of the existential experience of all humans. More than that, Michelstaedter's texts describe this as a 'limit experience', a moment of revelation in which the subject is called for a reaction, an answer. As a consequence, the subject faces two options: 'covering', trying to thicken the veil of Maya in order to (vainly) prevent the penetration of these experiences; or, 'uncovering', facing the pain, putting oneself on the way to 'persuasion'. A description of the horror – often considered one of the best pages of Michelstaedter – is in many ways the crucial moment where the foundations of his whole philosophy are explicitated. The textile metaphor is kept: «i bambini

– quasi vite in provvisorio – hanno molto meno definita la trama, molto più varia e disordinata, qui densa e luminosa, lì sottile e oscuro-trasparente», and the obscurity below the veil of Maya can manifest itself, so that

> le cose si sformano in aspetti strani: occhi che guardano, orecchi che sentono, braccia che si tendono, un ghigno sarcastico e una minaccia in tutte le cose. Si sentono sorvegliati da esseri terribilmente potenti, che vogliono il loro male [...] Quando passano una camera oscura, sembra ai bambini che questi <Essi> gridino mille voci, che con mille mani li abbranchino, che in mille guizzi ghigni il sarcasmo nell'oscurità, si sentono risucchiati dall'oscurità, fuggono folli di terrore e gridano per stordirsi (PR: 22-23).

This also happens to adults, despite the 'thicker cover': «Ma quando per ragioni che non stanno in loro, il limbo della trama si solleva, anche gli uomini conoscono le spaventevoli soste. Li visitano i sogni nel sonno – quando rilassato, l'organismo vive l'oscuro dolore delle singole determinazioni impotenti ognuna per sé di fronte ad ogni contingenza, per cui, fatta più sottile la trama dell'illusione, più minacciosa appare l'oscurità» (ibid.). And so

> il riso sarcastico turba, guasta, corrompe le tranquille immagini famigliari ch'essi invano vorrebbero trattenere, e li grava con oscure immagini di biasimo e di minaccia» (ibid.), and while «cercano angosciati una tavola di salvezza, un punto saldo, tutto si scompone, tutto cede, fugge, s'allontana e tutto domina il ghigno sarcastico: <ùùùùùùùù ... niente, niente, niente, non sei niente, so che non sei niente, so che qui t'affidi ed io ti distruggerò sotto il piede il terreno>» (PR: 24).

This is the moment in which every human being «si sente impotente come un morto a curar la sua vita, e soffre in ogni attimo il dolore della morte» (ibid.).

The first point to be underlined here regards the voice which happens to sound to the ear of the person who experiences the lifting of the veil of Maya. In both examples this voice is defined as 'sarcastic'. For children, this sarcastic voice both laughs at them and takes them away with a 'thousand hands', threatening to disappear with them in the darkness. The children, who have a 'less tightly woven fabric', can reply to this undermining and terrorizing call only with the most elementary self-affirmation of a scream, which 'dazes' and attests to the first basic presence of the subject, and of the subject to itself. The dichotomy here is clear; the negative pole of the elementary affirmation of the scream is the sarcastic monster that takes one away, from what is safe (and illuminated) and in this sense, away from one's ('rhetorical') self.

More complex is the role of this voice in adults. Here, the 'sarcastic laughter' which appears in dreams acts as an undermining force that attacks and 'corrupts' the most reassuring idyllic images (for example the family) and prevents them being 'held' and 'kept'. This is the voice that shatters every certainty, revealing, through the weapon of sarcasm, its contingency and the 'nothing' which lies behind it.

The second important point regards the reaction of the subject to these moments of awareness. In a way that is similar to the child who tries to stop the sarcastic voice in the only way she/he can imagine (an inarticulate scream), the adult is engaged in a struggle against the experience of what is behind the veil. In order to stop the horror she/he attempts to reconstruct the certainty and value of his determinations, which in their recurrence are indeed the weapon to 'repress' the painful knowledge of the 'obscurity/darkness' that infects the pleasure found in the satisfaction of needs: «Al di sotto della superficialità del suo piacere egli sente fluire ciò che è al di fuori della sua potenza e che trascende la sua coscienza. La trama nota (finita) dell'individualità illusoria che il piacere illumina, non è fitta così che l'oscurità dell'ignoto (infinito) non trasparisca. E il suo piacere è contaminato da un sordo e continuo dolore la cui voce è indistinta, che la sete della vita, nel giro delle determinazioni, reprime» (PR: 21). This act of repression can however be more actively and systematically put into practice: «gli uomini hanno paura del dolore e per sfuggirlo gli applicano come empiastro la fede in un potere adeguato all'infinità della potenza ch'essi non conoscono» (PR: 21).

Here, for the first time in the text, the double movement which will characterize the construction of 'rhetoric' is outlined as the experience and subsequent repression of the 'deaf and continuous pain'. The net of finite determinations on which life is constructed, the world of phenomena, reveals itself as an attempt at 'repression'[56] in which human beings are more or less consciously involved. Thus far from being a simple, 'neutral' cover, it is an «empiastro», a 'protection' in order to 'heal'. That is 'what humans do', but at the same time, in order to represent this movement the narrator at least partially[57] puts into practice the opposite attempt, one oriented against 'repression' and towards description, or revelation. He is telling it. He faces the consciousness of the horror that comes from undermining the certainty of values[58], and his attempt to describe it is driven by the necessity of dis-covering rather than covering. How this dis-covering is linked with the voice of negativity, the 'sarcastic voice' we discussed above, and moreover how this process of facing the horror represented by/through the sarcastic voice is linked with a possible 'way to persuasion', needs to be discussed. But in order to better illuminate those links, we need to come back to our analysis of the grammatical subject that identifies the narrator in the text, and its fluctuation.

In the diegesis of *La Persuasione e la Rettorica*, the moment of the lifting of the veil of Maya indirectly assumes the value of a definitive question about the commitment of the narrator in relation to his matter. More than this, following the description of the experience of the human existential situation, arguably every voice embodied in the text will be located according to its position with regard to this experience. The point here is, assuming the experience of 'nothingness' as a discriminant, to explain what happens to the narrator before and after this moment, and his level of involvement in the diegesis.

1.5   The argumentation 'before': the hetero-diegetic narrator and 'we'

«*So che voglio e non ho cosa io voglia*» (PR: 7). In this way, *ex abrupto*, opens the first chapter of *La Persuasione e la Rettorica* (on 'La Persuasione'), with an 'I narrator' introducing himself[59] as a subject who is engaged in an experience which will reveal itself as the central moment in the argument of the narrator. This is, the (in this case self-conscious) experience of the will to possess, the will to satisfy a need for possession; the impossibility of which constitutes the theme of the first pages of Michelstaedter's thesis. Thus it is through a moment of self-reflection and self-analysis conducted by the narrator that the entire movement of the thesis finds its origin. But, is this enough to say that the narrator is intra-diegetic and thus part of the action?

This question can be further defined. After the opening sentence, the narrator offers a demonstration of the nature of desire (the will to possess) and its impossible fulfilment in the famous 'apologue of the weight'[60]: here, a weight hanging from a hook is described in its infinite will for the 'lower' and its infinite need to humor the force of gravity. The need/desire[61] of the weight can never be fulfilled, because at every point of its descent its necessity is always yet to be satisfied, it is always posited at a lower point toward which the weight will strive, so that «la sua vita è questa mancanza della sua vita» (PR: 8).

Campailla, in his article on the 'Postille Leopardiane di Michelstaedter' interprets this simile between the weight and the 'I' of the narrator through an analysis of the variants of the opening sentence, as found in manuscript A[62] of the work. He concludes that

> la lettura dell'autografo della *Persuasione* dimostra come il pensatore si sia tormentato su questa frase: in un primo tempo, egli aveva scritto più prosasticamente: <io so che voglio qualcosa e che non ho quello che voglio>, corretto poi in <io so che voglio e non ho cosa io voglia>, ed infine, eliminato il pronome di prima persona e conferito un tono di maggior universalità al concetto, nella forma lapidaria che appunto avvia la potente similitudine del peso, che <non può mai essere persuaso>[63].

Campailla hypothesizes a parallel between the 'I' of the narrator, the 'weight' and the 'universal', an equation to be discovered in the crossing out of the pronoun of the opening sentence and its contrastive and/or disjunctive role. In this sense, the stress seems to be put on the cognitive narrator who, putting himself in a 'third position', generalizes from an example something about human nature, and thus something about himself as well. This extra-diegetic component, however, does not wipe out the fact that the originating cause for this generalization is a personal statement regarding the narrating subject.

The apologue itself can tell us something more on this point. In fact, here we can find the first change in the grammatical subject; the narrator, who is also the author of an action (in charge of the experiment), shifts toward a *pluralis maiestatis*: «lo vogliamo soddisfare [il peso]: lo lasciamo andare, che sazi la sua fame del più basso, e scenda indipendente fino a che sia contento di scendere» (PR: 7). Within the apologue, the newly introduced 'we' is the subject who puts the experiment into action, allows it to happen; 'we' leave the weight free to fall, and thus 'we' are engaged in the enquiry and in the demonstration. The temporary equation between 'I' and 'we' is further established in the interpretive comment following the apologue: «tante cose ci attirano nel futuro, ma nel presente invano vogliamo possederle» (PR: 8). Furthermore, 'we' are generalized as 'all humans': «[n]é se l'uomo cerchi rifugio presso la persona ch'egli ama – egli potrà saziare la sua fame: non baci, non amplessi o quante altre dimostrazioni l'amore inventi li potranno compenetrare l'uno nell'altro»

(PR: 8-9); «[g]li uomini lamentano questa loro solitudine, ma se essa è loro lamentevole – è perché, *essendo con se stessi, si sentono soli*: si sentono *con nessuno* e mancano di tutto» (PR: 9). These considerations allow us to draw a temporary distinction. On the one hand, we have an extra-diegetic position, in which 'humans', 'we', and 'I' are the same simply because 'we' are all human beings (and this will sound less banal when the somehow extra-human figure of the 'persuaded' will be introduced). On the other hand, in the sub-plot of the exemplifying apologue, the 'we' narrator assumes an intra-diegetic role, as part of a series of actions (an experiment, in this case) which are conducted in order to make sense of the first statement of the 'I narrator' regarding himself. In synthesis, 'we' are the agent that permits the formulation of the self-consciousness of the cognitive narrator, of the extra-diegetic 'I' and/or impersonal voice.

A synthesis of our results can be schematized as follows:

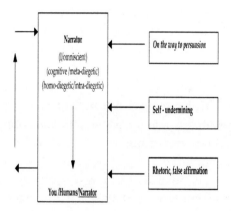

This last interpretation is less irrelevant than it might appear, because it introduces a hint of difference between the narrator and 'us', which will become a theoretical and stylistic strategy later in the text. A preliminary account of this peculiarity can be offered through the discussion of the position of the narrator and 'us' inside the theoretical framework of the text.

Humans lack 'everything' simply because they lack 'the possession of themselves'; however, so does the narrator (again intra-diegetic, when inside the sub-narration of an example): «[i]o salirò sulla montagna – l'altezza mi chiama, voglio averla – l'ascendo – la domino; ma la montagna come la posseggo? Ben son alto sul mare; e vedo il largo orizzonte che è della montagna; ma tutto ciò non è mio: non è mio in quanto vedo e per più veder non mai <ho

visto>» (PR: 8). According to what we anticipated in our introduction, this description can be subsumed under the category of 'rhetoric', or at least it is the preliminary cause for the development of inadequate 'rhetoric'. Furthermore, 'rhetoric' is not only a prerogative of the single (the 'I'), but is a process that can be shared by a 'we', who are the actual actors in the experiment. This means that 'we' humans can experience, in front of our eyes so to speak, facts which should give us consciousness of our own state. Until here, the equation between narrator, 'humans' and 'we', is working. However, in the first pages of *La Persuasione e la Rettorica*, this equation does not develop toward a place where the actual (self) knowledge of the narrator is deployed. This second level, the cognitive understanding of human condition, is the sole prerogative of the narrator, in generalizations such as «infatti è questo che l'uomo cerca» (PR: 93), «così dunque nella società organizzata ognuno violenta l'altro» (PR: 103): a statement in which the *pluralis maiestatis* is used in a cognitive position is nowhere to be found. Further in this analysis, it will be possible to understand how this difference, this peculiarity of the narrator, has its place in the theoretical discourse on 'persuasion': consciousness is the first step for a way towards the absolute (and 'we' seem not to be part of it).

'Rhetoric' allows enquiry (for 'us'), which allows consciousness (for the cognitive narrator). This consciousness can lead to a further step; the logical postulation of the possibility of another state, the state of pure (self) possession. The narrator underlines this point by introducing the first definition of 'persuaded human': «[c]olui che è per se stesso non ha bisogno di altra cosa che sia per lui nel futuro, ma possiede tutto in sé» (PR: 9). This 'colui', 'the one who', appears almost entirely as the logical opposite of 'humans': he is singularly capable of possessing everything in himself, unlike the 'human' who is defined precisely through this incapability, and he does not need anything in the future, as opposed to the human who is always 'yet to be', who is necessarily 'what follows'. Furthermore, as the text continues, this logical difference is semantically underlined through the constant use of the adversative conjunction 'but'[64]: «[m]a l'uomo vuole dalle altre cose nel tempo futuro quello che in sé gli manca: il possesso di sé stesso: ma quanto vuole e tutto occupato dal futuro sfugge a sé stesso in ogni presente» (PR: 9); «ma ognuno gira intorno al suo pernio, che non è suo, ed il pane che non ha non può dare agli altri» (ibid.).

At this point, a few pages inside the text, the narrator has already defined his aporia, and the direction of his struggle. He 'knows that he wants', he is conscious of the fact that he does not have, that he is searching 'in vain', and he knows 'what he wants': a (persuaded) state in which he 'does not ask for anything in the future'. This is the paradox. However, the narrator implicitly outlines the direction of his impossible search. As every human can do, as 'we' in fact do, he faces (acts in) an experiment: the apologue of the weight, in which the consciousness of the reasons for an existential state can arise. As a consequence of this experience, he derives the correct answers, while 'we' do not. 'We' are erased as positive actors, as readers 'we' can only 'learn' the result from the voice of the narrator, 'we' can share his point of view only passively, through his mediation; it is as if the narrator 'opened his eyes' after the experience and now tries to make us open ours (logically speaking: he becomes a further example). This difference is crucial, and it is one point of the discrimination between a human on the way to 'persuasion' and humans on the safe way of 'rhetoric'. But implicit consciousness is not yet an active emancipatory practice, and the narrator will introduce the theme of self-consciousness, leading to the crucial moment of the 'horror' of the obscurity and its consequent turn.

1.6 φιλοψυχία and the introduction of human self-consciousness

The structure of the relationship between the narrator, implied reader, and the object of the argument is generally stable in these opening pages of *La Persuasione e la Rettorica*, and invests the description of the experience beyond the veil. The 'I' and the 'we' continue to share their point of view, while the 'I' maintains exclusivity in the cognitive moment. In this way, we are taken through the first steps towards a phenomenology of «*questa continua deficienza – per la quale ogni cosa che vive muore ogni attimo continuando – ogni cosa che vive si persuade esser vita*» (PR: 11). The main theme here is the understanding of the consequences implied in the satisfaction of one's needs and determinate possession, and thus of the will to self-perpetuation. This determination is, in the narrator's words, «*mutarsi in relazione a una cosa*» (PR: 12): the construction of a relationship of reciprocal dependency between subjects, or subject and object[65] through (finite) possession; thus a 'will' that is in every moment a will for determination. In other words, this relationship is born as a consequence of the attribution of a value: «*ogni cosa in un punto non possiede ma è volontà di possesso determinato: cioè una determinata attribuzione di valore: una determinata coscienza*» (PR: 12).

The rhetorical way to defend and further explain this assertion is, again an example, a fictional experiment which offers support for a simile involving the object of the example and human beings in general; and again 'we' are involved as actors. If «per esempio il cloro è ingordo che è tutto morto», then «noi lo facciamo rinascere e lo mettiamo in vicinanza dell'idrogeno» (PR: 13). This time the experiment involves some knowledge of chemistry, and in particular the behaviour of two elements, hydrogen and chloride. The argument begins from a comparison between the human stomach and these two elements: «noi isoliamo una sola determinazione della volontà, per esempio in un corpo lo stomaco come vivesse per se stesso: lo stomaco è tutto fame, esso è l'attribuzione del valore al cibo, esso è la coscienza del mondo in quanto mangiabile» (PR: 13); «così quando due sostanze si congiungono chimicamente, ognuna saziando la determinazione dell'altra, cessano entrambe della loro natura, mutate nel vicendevole assorbimento» (PR: 13). In the case of hydrogen and chloride, the narrator assumes for the sake of simplicity that the valence of the second would be only for the first, and shows us how the life of one element exists only in the possibility of joining the other. In this joining it dies as 'singular', dies as itself:

> poiché la presenza dell'atomo di idrogeno avrà fatto palpebra all'occhio dell'atomo di cloro, che non vedeva l'idrogeno, e gli avrà chiuso l'orizzonte che era tutto idrogeno», leading to the fact that «il loro amore non è per la vita soddisfatta, per l'essere persuaso, bensì per il vicendevole bisogno che ignora la vita altrui. I loro due mondi erano diversi ma correlativi così che dall'amplesso mortale avesse d'attendere e poi soffrir la vita: l'acido cloridrico (PR: 13).

The reading of this experiment is a confirmation of our preceding argument, and yet it adds the personification of the description of the two chemical elements, making our first interpretation more poignant. Terms such as 'eyelid', 'eye', 'love'and 'mortal intercourse'[66], in a certain sense push the simile towards its referent, somehow before the intervention of the cognitive narrator[67]. The introduction of a metaphorical vocabulary related to 'sight', specifically the term 'eyelids', is of particular interest. Hydrogen becomes the eyelid of the atom of chloride, it closes the horizon of its sight and kills it in the mortal intercourse. The fulfilment of finite needs is the 'cover' that exhausts the subject in its will, avoiding the consciousness of a wider condition. The point here is that in the example, the attraction between the chemical elements, even if 'humanized', is correctly given as a mechanical process; the 'eyelid' is not an obstruction that the chloride has the power to remove or raise. On the contrary, the raising of an eyelid indicates a human activity implying consciousness and will. Thus if the eyelid is the fulfilment of a finite need, humans may have a way to understand the inadequate nature of this relationship, they can open their eyes, and as the metaphorical eyelid was hydrogen, the object of the desire, this raising is also an overcoming of the value of this relationship, its negation[68]. The power of this possibility, the particular escape route that the construction of the example implies, resounds throughout the generalizations, to complex organisms, and then to humans, where the concept of φιλοψυχία is introduced already carrying its sense of 'cowardice' and implying the possibility of an opposite choice, of 'bravery'[69].

This consideration takes us back to the narrator and the developing implied reader. As pointed out, both share the (mediated) experience of their condition and are engaged in experiments, but only the first moves from experiment to a generalized knowledge of contingency and the definition of something beyond it, the 'colui', the 'persuaded human'. If this is correct, then the narrator can be defined as someone who has raised his eyelids and is engaged in an overcoming: for our goals, the demonstration of this engagement and the attempt to put it into practice, is a further confirmation of our opening hypothesis.

1.7 The narrator 'after' the lifting of the veil: where are 'we'?

The opening pages of *La Persuasione e la Rettorica* seem to place the narrating voice in a position of coherence with the theorized 'way to persuasion'. That said, the cognitive prerogative of the narrator, with his constant generalizing and drawing conclusions about all humans, partakes at the same time of a movement of affirmation, of the establishment of a truth, which according to the categories of the text could easily be dismissed as 'rhetorical'. Value creation is in fact the very centre of the definition of inadequate affirmation. However, when the demand to come to terms with the consciousness of human contingency becomes dramatic, radical and unavoidable, and when the 'cover for the pain' is shown to be a failure, the strategies of the narrator change. The first sign of this difference is the disappearance of the pronoun 'we', and the introduction of a 'you'. This explicit address to an implied reader – the first of many fictional dialogues[70] – is introduced in *La Persuasione e la Rettorica*, as the incipit of the chapter on 'La Via alla Persuasione': «questo che fai, come che cosa lo fai? Con che mente lo fai? Tu ami questa cosa per la correlazione di ciò che ti lascia dopo bisognoso della stessa correlazione [...]? *O sai cosa fai?*» (PR: 31).

This substitution of pronoun has important consequences for our discussion. Following the introduction of an implicit dichotomy between the different reactions of humans and the narrator in the face of the horror of their contingency, the direct address to an implied reader, a 'you', locates that reader at a crossroads between two possibilities; the narrator is asking 'us': how do you react? Do you do like every other human or have you faced another possibility? Do you live and perpetuate contingency selling it to yourself as a (false) absolute, as an 'empiastro', or on the contrary, are you 'persuaded'?

The mode of narratorial questioning anticipates the answer of the implied reader: the narrator produces his interlocutor and engages in an undermining dialogue. «Tu dici che sei persuaso di quel che fai, avvenga che può? – sì? – Allora io ti dico: domani sarai morto certo: non importa?» (PR: 31). Here begins the process of undermining, and revealing the falsity of the values of the implied reader: «pensi alla fama? Pensi alla famiglia? Ma la tua memoria è morta con te, con te è morta la tua famiglia; – pensi ai tuoi ideali? Vuoi fare testamento? Vuoi una lapide? Ma domani sono morti, morti anch'essi; – tutti gli uomini muoiono con te» (PR: 31-2). The narrator asks the questions and draws the final conclusions:

> Allora ... allora ... il dio d'ora non è più quello di prima, non è più quella la patria, quello il bene, quello il male, quelli gli amici, quella la famiglia. – Vuoi mangiare? No, non puoi mangiare, il sapore del cibo non è più quello, [...] e poi l'odore, l'odore è nauseante: *pute di cadavere*; – vuoi una donna che ti conforti gli ultimi istanti? No, peggio: è *carne morta* [...]. Il dio che ti teneva in piedi, che ti faceva chiaro il giorno, e dolce il cibo, che ti dava la patria, il paradiso – quello ti tradisce e ti abbandona perché è rotto il filo della tua φιλοψυχία. (PR: 32).

In this moment, the implied reader shifts from co-author of the experiment to the narrator's cavy.

A few considerations can be drawn here. First of all, the utterance of the monologuing narrator is here double-edged, it is always a comment and an answer, it is dialogic in a Bakhtinian sense. Furthermore, the nature of the

hyperbolic movement, allows us a second remark. As much as the negative
dialectic is engaged in the dismissal of any external ideology – thus working as
a pedagogy, an education – it is also, and primarily, directed against one-self.
The motto: «non adattarti alla sufficienza di ciò che t'è dato» (PR: 62)[71],
implies a process of self-questioning, a personal overcoming of one's own stable
values. To face the horror without recourse to a cover has, as a consequence, the
necessity of constant replication of the process of dismissal that the painful
experience puts in place: «ognuno ha [...] nel proprio dolore l'indice» (ibid.).
The interlocutor of the dialogue, the 'you', needs thus to be interpreted also as
self-reflective, and the questions asked to the 'you' should be read also as self-
directed: is the text the result of a determination, of the satisfaction of the need
for its completion, or is it a tool for emancipation? Our argument on the
relationship between poetic and practice of signification is based on this self-
reflexivity. When Michelstaedter, in the crossed-out preface, writes «è pur
necessario che se uno ha addentato una perfida sorba la risputi» (PR: 3)[72], he
is giving preliminary evidence of this project.

Bakhtin's definition of *Icherzählung* in his interpretation of Dostoevskij's
Notes from the Underground, can help us to further clarify the above points.
In the *Notes*, the protagonist «tries to anticipate the possible definition or
evaluation others might make of him»[73]; and in doing so, he embodies the
possible reply of an imaginary interlocutor and defends his point of view
against it. The polemic is developed through a monologue that assumes the
forms of a micro-dialogue, in which: «all words in it are double-voiced, and in
each of them a conflict of voices takes place»[74]. If this can be said for the
passage discussed above from *La Persuasione e la Rettorica* and in different
ways throughout the text[75], it must be added that this implies an 'active'
involvement of the narrator in the diegesis. It is tempting to conclude that the
entire *La Persuasione e la Rettorica* is the story of the struggle of the narrator
against 'rhetoric', and thus a homo-diegetic narration; it is intra-diegetic only
to the extent that the narrator actively takes part in its development. But in
order to argue this point, another feature of the dialogical monologue against
the 'you' should be discussed.

Our recollection of the modes of *Icherzählung* and remarks on the self-
reflexivity of the dialogical process make it clear that the attack on the implicit
addressee is both a way to coherently formulate the most crucial question about
the will to 'persuasion', and locate the narrator himself and other voices
embodied in the text with regard to this will. We argued that the implied reader
is produced as a 'subject of rhetoric', and in this sense his φιλοψυχία is

composed of a set of inadequate values that the narrator is ready to acknowledge and dismantle. We also know that at the origin of the φιλοψυχία is an attempt to avoid pain, to find a 'cover from the eyes', an 'eyelid'. The narrator is engaged in the opposite movement. He assumes a tone of sarcasm beyond the veil, and reproduces its mechanisms. Given a series of certainties and values, his movement is one of sarcastic dismantling, of revealing how 'you are nothing, nothing'. In this sense, he is not closing his eyelids in front of the experience of pain, but is engaged in the negation of inadequate affirmations. This is a representation of the hyperbolic 'movement towards persuasion', and if this is true, the narrator can be read as intra- and homo-diegetic. In this sense *La Persuasione e la Rettorica* becomes the story of the struggle of a character – the narrator – on his 'way to persuasion': philosophical theory and the practice of signification reflect each other in this struggle.

While the scheme of the hetero-diegetic narrator and his argumentation before the painful experience of human condition did not have much to do with the description of the strategies towards 'persuasion' presented in the text, the following scheme – which synthesizes the interpretation in this section – does offer the possibility for a comparison with the hyperbolic way:

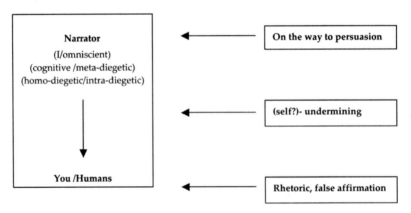

1.8 Back to the hyperbole, and some conclusions

Bakhtin, in his work on Dostoevskij, has no gentle words for the possibility of a dialogic style in philosophical writing, where «the genuine interaction of consciousnesses is impossible», with the exception of «someone who knows and possesses the truth [and] instructs someone who is ignorant of it and in error; that is, it is the interaction of a teacher and a pupil, which, it follows, can only be a pedagogical dialogue»: the pedagogic dialogue of the cognitive narrator. The narrator of *La Persuasione e la Rettorica*, as outlined above, partakes of this kind of genre. On the other hand, however, he is also engaged in a questioning and self-questioning dialogue. While this mode is surely oriented against the negation of objective values, at its limits it is negative consciousness turning against itself; the movement implies self-negation and negation of the presupposition of the negative mechanism itself: the value of pain. 'Persuasion' is in this sense the infinite point on this path, and for Michelstaedter writing philosophy means also writing *against* the systems of philosophy. This dialectic of negation implies a particular conception of pedagogy, alien to the one defined in the Bakhtinian analysis of the academic genre. The text itself offers a definiton of it, under the label of «educazione socratica»: «in questa vita ottusa e frammentaria, l'educazione socratica è *creatrice d'uomini.* [...] Essa risveglia nell'uomo il la richiesta del bene attuale e lo affrance dal pericolo di dar valore ai nomi così da essere per questi tratto a adattarsi all'irrazionalità di una qualsiasi vita sufficiente. [...] Questa educazione (ed è l'unica) dà all'uomo le gambe per camminare, e gli occhi per vedere: *non gli dà vie fatte, non gli fa veder date cose.*» (PR: 150).

This pedagogy, further defined in the interpretation of Socratic dialectic[76], has the features of an idealized perfection (a perfect and never resting mechanism of negation) and the strength of an ethical imperative. Here is one definition given by the narrator: «*[l]a sua vita non è un procedere, ma un permanere.* Ché *fermo* e *attuale* tenendo il postulato del valore della vita, le parole che gli uomini usano con presunzione di assoluto valore – in ciò ch'egli ne esige la sufficienza in rapporto ad ogni caso, quale avrebbero se questo valore contenessero – come a quel postulato inadeguate, vuote di senso le manifesta. Questa è la dialettica. –» (PR: 173)[77]. This endpoint in which the 'persuaded' 'consists', and does not 'proceed' in the future, is what the text is striving to achieve. As much as the narrator is not a 'persuaded', his attempt is to proceed on a path of negation until the (impossible) leap into the absolute 'permanere' becomes possible: a movement 'through activity to peace' (PR: 49). This 'activity' never stops, not even for a moment of self-satisfaction, and it is in this sense that Plato is considered a traitor of this 'way':

[i]l *Fedro* fa l'apologia della dialettica – e in ciò appunto non è più dialettico, ma apologetico. [...] Nel *Fedro* Platone realizza con efficacia insuperata il valore della *via socratica* di fronte all'altrui impotenza, e in quel punto *dandola come finita e considerandola, vi*

s'è già fermato. E poiché la via socratica perciò appunto e soltanto non è una via come un'altra, perché nega ogni fermata e si proclama sempre ancora non finita, il fermarvisi a compiacersene *è un abbandonarla per sempre* (PR: 172).

How can a philosophical text, and a degree thesis in particular, fulfil the requirements implied in this understanding of Socratic dialectic? The necessity for undermining, self-undermining and incompleteness, communicating the sense of its infinite reproduction, is in contrast with the necessity to provide results. This is the problem we will face in the rest of our enquiry. It is interesting to underline, as a preliminary remark, how also Bakhtin, in the context of his critique of philosophical writing, has a partially positive opinion of Socratic dialogue: «the idealism of Plato is not purely monologic. It becomes purely monologic only in a neo-Kantian interpretation. Nor is Platonic dialogue of the pedagogical type, although there is a strong element of monologism in it»[78]. Moreover, following Zappen, Bakhtin shares with Michelstaedter a predilection for the earlier Socratic dialogues: Bakhtin «distinguishes the Socratic notion of the dialogic nature of truth, and the dialogic nature of human thinking about truth, which he claims is characteristic of the earlier dialogues, from the 'official' monologism, which pretends to possess a ready made truth', and which he claims is characteristic of the later dialogues»[79]. The interpretation of the dialogues through an 'autobiography of the consciousness' – implicitly adopted by Michelstaedter – offers the chance to underline further parallels[80]. However, reading Michelstaedter through Bakhtin's understanding of Socrates seems rather counterintuitive. In fact, we would first have to discuss the 'translation' of Socrates in Michelstaedter' style, and then perform a comprehensive Bakhtinian reading of Plato[81], and finally, outline a comparison. Furthermore, it would be potentially misleading to define strict parallels between Bakhtin's 'democratic' ethic of dialogism[82] and Michelstaedter's ethic of undermining. The most useful adoption of Bakhtin is thus *strictu sensu* as a theoretical, methodological framework, which can guide us in the mapping of *heteroglossia* in *La Persuasione e la Rettorica*. This, with the attention to the role of the narrator[83], and dialogism as the underlying philosophy of language, make Bakhtin's framework the most useful point of departure. Our methodological strategy will be to read the text against itself. If it is true that the theoretical speculation in the text is also the outlining of a poetic, then our task will be to compare this poetic with the practice of textual signification. Only at the end of this process will it be finally possible to argue if the narrator-hero is carachteristic of a Nineteen-century literary approach (the stable centre of the organization of a sense, and an extra-textual truth, the truth of the belief in 'persuasion') or part of a new mode of understanding the subject. At stake will be the interpretation of *La Persuasione e la Rettorica* as a pedagogical, and in this sense apologetic, text (Plato's mistake), or one which goes 'against itself' and its genre: two crucially different ways of self-undermining.

Notes

1. FCM III 3 – 37.
2. Despite the many more and less recent editions of various sections of the corpus of Michelstaedter's legacy. See: PPA; PEE; Carlo Michelstaedter, *Sfugge la Vita. Taccuini e Appunti,* ed. Angela Michelis (Torino: Nino Aragno Editore, 2004).
3. See Campailla's introduction to his first edition of *La Persuasione e la Rettorica*: Michelstaedter, *La Persuasione e la Rettorica*: 28.
4. The preface is elsewhere described by Campailla as «per il passato sempre sacrificata e per la prima volta in questa edizione restituita all'unità del corpo cui appartiene» ibid.: 14.
5. Given the context of its publication: Asor Rosa, ''La Persuasione e la Rettorica' di Carlo Michelstaedter'.
6. The crossed-out variants are in square brackets; the unreadable, crossed-out variants are square brackets and underlined. My corrections are underlined: 'un' for 'una', and 'ed' for 'èd', and the addition of missing inverted commas.
7. This works coherently throughout *La Persuasione e la Rettorica* without the necessity of recurring to the classical references to the concepts.
8. His library at the moment of his death included the French edition of the Gospel of John and Luther's Bible in German.
9. See for example: Muzzioli, *Michelstaedter.*
10. Evidence of this are the notes on Parmenides in preparation for the drafting of the thesis Now published in PEE.
11. Asor Rosa, ''La Persuasione e la Rettorica' di Carlo Michelstaedter'.
12. On this: PEE; Benevento, ' 'La Persuasione e la Rettorica' di Michelstaedter e la 'Concretezza Artistica','; Piero Pieri, *La Differenza Ebraica. Ebraismo e Grecità in Michelstaedter* (Bologna: Cappelli, 1984): 67-83.
13. The article by Perna (Valerio Perna, 'Dal Libro alla Parola,' in *Il Maestro del Deserto Carlo Michelstaedter,* ed. Antonia Acciani (Bari: Progedit, 2005) tries to read Michelstaedter's adoption of fictional sub-genres in his work as a link with his Jewish background and Hasidic parables. However, Perna's results do not add anything which could not be explained through explicit interptextual references, such as Leopardi's *Operette Morali* or Plato's use of myth. A more general work on Michelstaedter's 'Jewishness' is the one by Pieri, *La Differenza Ebraica. Ebraismo e Grecità in Michelstaedter.*
14. Did he reach Middle Platonism – for example, Philo of Alexandria? This would add a very interesting dimension to our research, which in the context of this contribution limits itself to a structural comparison.

15. Michael Allen Williams, *Rethinking Gnosticism: an Argument for Dismantling a Dubious Category* (Princeton: Princeton University Press, 1996); Ioan P. Couliano, *The Tree of Gnosis: Gnostic Mythology from Early Christianity to Modern Nihilism* (San Francisco: Harpercollins, 1992).

16. Ugo Bianchi, ed., *Le Origini dello Gnosticismo: Colloquio di Messina, 13-18 Aprile 1966* (Leiden: E.J. Brill, 1967: XXVI-VIII.

17. Williams, *Rethinking Gnosticism: an Argument for Dismantling a Dubious Category*: 51.

18. Ibid.

19. Ibid.

20. John D. Turner, 'The Gnostic Sethians and Middle Platonism: Interpretations of the Timaeus and Parmenides,' *Vigiliae Christianae* 60 (2006): 19.

21. Hans Jonas, *Gnosis und Spätantiker Geist*, 2 vols. (Göttingen: Vandenhoeck & Ruprecht, 1992). While existentialism was originally to play the role of the 'key' for the 'lock' of the Gnostic corpus, 'by the early fifties the former lock had turned into a key and the former key into a lock to be opened'. Michael Waldstein, 'Hans Jonas' Construct 'Gnosticism': Analysis and Critique,' *Journal of Early Christian Studies* 8, no. 3 (2000): 344. The image of the key comes from Jonas himself: Hans Jonas, *The Gnostic Religion: the Message of the Alien God and the Beginnings of Christianity* (Boston: Beacon Press, 1963): 321-22 and, more in general, the entire chapter.

22. Ranke, 'Il Pensiero di Carlo Michelstaedter. Un Contributo allo Studio dell'Esistenzialismo Italiano'.

23. Here Coulianu is embodying a Nietzschean vocabulary of 'unbuilding', '*zugrunde richten*'. Nevertheless, this is most poignant inside our argument, if compared with Michelstaedter's definition of Socratic dialectic discussed above.

24. Couliano, *The Tree of Gnosis: Gnostic Mythology from Early Christianity to Modern Nihilism*: 250.

25. Jonas, *Gnosis und Spätantiker Geist:* Vol. 2, 1-23. See also: Waldstein, 'Hans Jonas' Construct 'Gnosticism': Analysis and Critique': 357.

26. Waldstein, 'Hans Jonas' Construct 'Gnosticism': Analysis and Critique': 362.

27. Ibid.: 363.

28. Ibid.

29. Ibid.: 364-5. Jonas discusses also alternative practices of *Entweltlichung* that emancipate themselves from the objectification of myth, such as modified states of consciousness in the form of mystic ecstasy, and ascetic practices. However, in Michelstaedter's case what we have is the text and a suicide. In refraining from a discussion of the latter, it is possible to frame the text inside Jonas' problem. It is interesting to note, however, a tendency towards interpreting the last weeks of Michelstaedter's life as a progressive asceticism, and thus his work as external to the problem of its signification (on this see for example: Campailla, *A Ferri Corti con la Vita*). While biographical speculation exceeds the goal of a close textual reading, such as the one proposed in this article, the biographer's worries and interpretive temptations are an indirect confirmation of the relevance of our framework.

30. Hans Jonas, 'Myth and Mysticism: a Study of Objectification and Interiorization in Religious Thought' *The Journal of Religion* 19, no. 1 (1969): 315.

31. Ibid.: 317. In this contribution, Jonas carefully acknowledges the fluidity of 'the borderline between mere sacrament [...] and some actual experiential verification of the real thing [...]', in the context of the practices of the cults. Nevertheless, also in this case, the two moments, the symbolic/objective and the experiential/subjective are kept separate. See: Jonas, 'Myth and Mysticism: a Study of Objectification and Interiorization in Religious

Thought': 318, and, more broadly, the entire framework of the article.

32. Asor Rosa, "La Persuasione e la Rettorica' di Carlo Michelstaedter,'.

33. The original idea however, remains in the text: '[c]hé s'egli vedesse [...] egli non si continuerebbe nel tempo poiché, come dice il popolo, <chi vede Iddio muore>' (PR: 17). This ambiguity strengthens the possibility for interpreting the sources of the paratext as 'non persuaded'.

34. See for example: Muzzioli, *Michelstaedter*; Benevento, ' 'La Persuasione e la Rettorica' di Michelstaedter e la 'Concretezza Artistica'".

35. We will discuss fully the case of Christ and its role in the articulation of a relationship with the 'persuaded' word in chapter 2, bringing to light the Kantian framework behind this articulation, and the theoretical and stylistic problems that this implies. In the present context, we can only focus on a more precise definition of the contradictions of the paratext and their possible overcoming.

36. As evidente of this, alternative sketches of a preface to be found in the autograph of *La Persuasione e la Rettorica* (FCM III 3 c) rework the theme of 'spitting out' rhetoric in a dialogue between Michelstaedter and a university professor: '[l']università è il tempio della rettorica e affermandomi di fronte alla rettorica [...] ho risputato i 4 anni che v'ho consumati'. The professor takes here personal offence, playing out once again Michelstaedter's project of 'war with words against words'.

37. Stefano Agosti, *Enunciazione e Racconto. Per una Semiologia della Voce Narrativa* (Bologna: Il Mulino, 1989).

38. Ibid.: 9.

39. Ibid.: 12. I wrote 'in a general sense', because this generalization does not prevent Agosti from acknowledging the predecessors of this process and briefly discussing the cases of Dostoevskij (through Bakhtin) and James (mainly through Todorov).

40. Georg Lukács, *The Theory of the Novel* (London: Merlin Press, 1971).

41. Lucien Goldmann, *Towards a Sociology of the Novel* (London: Tavistock Publications Ltd., 1975).

42. «[l'eroe è] il centro prospettico entro il quale convogliare e in base al quale ordinare il senso del reale» Agosti, *Enunciazione e Racconto. Per una Semiologia della Voce Narrativa*: 9-10.

43. Goldmann, *Towards a Sociology of the Novel*: 13. Obviously, our approach is far from Goldmann's attempt to find the factors that produce changes in the economic structure of society. This search is extraneous to Agosti's approach as well.

44. To remain within Agosti's framework, for a definition of cognitive narrator, as part of the hetero-diegetic (in this case derived from the reading of Manzoni's *Promessi Sposi*): «Se la voce verbale è quasi sempre al presente, il pronome di prima persona può, invece, non apparire. Al suo posto troviamo, o la costruzione impersonale; o la costruzione neutra, osservativa, della massima, della sentenza; o un soggetto generalizzante (<noi uomini siamo fatti così>) ecc. È la zona in cui la razionalità del discorso è supposta coincidere con quella dell'Auctor» Agosti, *Enunciazione e Racconto. Per una Semiologia della Voce Narrativa*: 125.

45. The meta-discursive narrator represents «quella fase del processo di *enbrayage* che si configura come la più prossima alla sorgente dell'enunciazione, di cui compone compiutamente, dal punto di vista linguistico, il simulacro: pronome di prima persona, deittici avverbiali e pronominali del 'qui-ora', voci verbali al presente (o al futuro). [...] Oggetto del suo discorso è il racconto stesso (i personaggi, le situazioni e i percorsi narrativi, gli eventi) e quanto ha a che fare con il racconto: il lettore per esempio, ma anche i testi su cui il racconto si fonda e il nesso attraverso il quale il racconto si fa: e cioè la

scrittura» (ibid.: 131). On this point and the preceding note, see also: Alessandro Costantini, 'Il Testo Letterario e l'Enunciazione (Appunti per una Teoria Semiotica),' *Strumenti Critici* 46 (1981).

46. Taviani, 'Attualità di Michelstaedter': 320.

47. Michelstaedter would say that the 'persuaded human' becomes God to himself; in this sense, alien to a problem of origin and foundation (PR: 62). See also our 'Introduction'.

48. It is clear how Bakhtin is important in this context, not least for the interpretation of the role of the narrator in the novel, as we will discuss through: Michail M. Bakhtin, *Problems of Dostoevsky's Poetics*, ed. Caryl Emerson (Manchester: Manchester University Press, 1984).

49. «La Persuasione inizia e termina come enunciazione di un <io>; ma nel suo corpo il più delle volte tratta impersonalmente (con la terza persona) di un'entità generale: l'<uomo> o gli <uomini>. Quando non si rivolge a un <tu> autoriflessivo, o a un <voi> che fa entrare nel testo l'uditorio immaginario, peraltro inserito con frequenti battute di obiezione e con interventi dialogici» (Muzzioli, *Michelstaedter*: 54).

50. To my recollection, articles entirely focused on the grammatical subject regard the 'poetic I' of Michelstaedter's poems: see for example Kanduth, 'Dal Tu all'Io nella Poesia di Carlo Michelstaedter'.

51. See on this point: Debenedetti, 'Michelstaedter'.

52. For the relationship between Michelstaedter and Schopenhauer, see for example: Angela Michelis, *Carlo Michelstaedter, il Coraggio dell'Impossibile* (Roma: Città Nuova, 1997); Raschini, *Carlo Michelstaedter*: 52 et passim; Taviani, *Michelstaedter*: 60-3; Cristina Benussi, *Negazione e Integrazione nella Dialettica di Carlo Michelstaedter* (Roma: Edizioni dell'Ateneo, 1980): 7 et passim; Brianese, *L'Arco e il Destino. Interpretazione di Michelstaedter*: 17-31.

53. The very first definition of veil of Maya to be found in *The World as Will and Representation* is a good example for showing the parallels with Michelstaedter: «[...] the ancient wisdom of the Indians declares that "it is Mâyâ, the veil of deception, which covers the eyes of mortals, and causes them to see a world of which one cannot say either that it is or that it is not; for it is like a dream, like the sunshine on the sand that the traveler from a distance takes to be water, or like the piece of rope on the ground which he regards as a snake"». Arthur Schopenhauer, *The World as Will and Representation,* trans. E. F. J. Payne, 2 vols. (New York: Dover Publication Inc., 1969): 8. It should be clear how the world of contingency built by Michelstaedter's god of φιλοψυχία, in which fulfilment of determinate needs defines a net of relationships that pushed the subject away from self-possession in the present, from unity, from objectivity, and condemns it inside an inadequate affirmation of itself in time and space, can be read through Schopenhauer. For references on this point, see preceding note.

54. Muzzioli noticed that «[Michelstaedter] non poteva accettare *in toto* gli aspetti contemplativi e platonizzanti [di Schopenhauer], e la stessa soluzione della *Noluntas* era troppo passiva. La distinzione del filosofo dal santo [...] certamente sembrò a Michelstaedter un comodo, opportunistico escamotage»; therefore «[...] quel sorprendente silenzio nell'elenco dei precursori della <persuasione>» (Muzzioli, *Michelstaedter*: 19-20). More specifically, what is absent in Michelstaedter is the interpretation of the Schopenhauerian differentiation between 'abstract' and 'intuitive' knowledge. If Michelstaedter accepts that the veil of Maya can be lifted through knowledge, he is highly conscious that this knowledge implies signification, and signification implies space, time, and the veil of Maya itself. I will argue in the second part of this chapter that this

consciousness is the main reason for the importance granted to language and style in the struggle for the avoidance of 'rhetoric'. Schopenhauer, in his explanation of human condition' finds himself, all together, in a safe place: «[w]e who are here looking for the theory of virtue, and who thus have to express in abstract terms the inner nature of the knowledge lying at its foundation, shall nevertheless be unable to furnish that knowledge itself in this expression, but only the concept of that knowledge» (Schopenhauer, *The World as Will and Representation*: 370). Given the impossibility of concurrently describing abstractly and putting into practice what is described, the philosopher calls himself out of the movement towards the penetration of the veil of Maya. The saint on the contrary requires a knowledge which is intuitive, and thus can only be comunicated through actions (Schopenhauer, *The World as Will and Representation*: section 66). But still it is expressed through language, through dogma, which has «mearly the value that the man who is virtuous from another kind of knowledge [...] has in them a scheme or formula» (Schopenhauer, The World as Will and Representation: 368). In *La Persuasione e la Rettorica*, the implications of signification and rhetoric (and thus space, time, veil of Maya) will be directly addressed, and a possible solution will be sought in the realm of aesthetics. In our chapter 4, we will fully address this point, and demonstrate the philosophical terrain on which the differences between the two philosophers are founded.

55. Schopenhauer, *The World as Will and Representation*: 353. The quote continues with a series of examples of this consciousness. We will see, further in this chapter, how this quote is revealing for the interpretation of Michelstaedter's category of 'persuasion'.

56. As is repeated at the start of the chapter on rhetoric: «Ma gli uomini si stancano su questa via, si sentono mancare nella solitudine: la voce del dolore è troppo forte [...] e chiedono una benda per gli occhi, *chiedono di essere per qualcuno*, per qualche cosa, ché di fronte alla richiesta del possesso si sentivano mancare» (PR: 53).

57. 'Partially' in the sense that signification is, according to the text, inextricably entangled in a 'rhetorical' net.

58. Intending values in Michelstaedter's sense, as 'possibilities for the satisfaction of determinate needs'.

59. The gender of the narrator in *La Persuasione e la Rettorica* is male. Furthermore, the general adoption of 'man' for 'human' and the identification of other voices (the dialogic interlocutors in the wide sense) as male render the orientation of the text fairly clear. It should be noticed, for example, that the group of 'persuaded humans' excludes female members. However, in other texts and particularly in the poems, female figures are linked in various ways with both a definition of and a struggle for 'persuasion'. The analysis of this implies a broad discussion of the differences of gender and the nature of the (female) figures with regard to the 'poetic I'. To my recollection there are no critical works that perform a gender analysis of Michelstaedter's oeuvre. I will from now on use the male when referring to specific singular voices found in the text, and will use the neutral word 'human' in the other cases, with the specific intention of leaving the question of gender open.

60. This apologue is so famous, that the sentence «chi pende dipende» (PR: 7) is, in the *vulgata*, almost automatically linked with the name of Michelstaedter. An interesting discussion of this apologue and its supposed intertextual link with Schopenhauer can be read in: Brianese, *L'Arco e il Destino. Interpretazione di Michelstaedter*: 21.

61. Indistinct in Michelstaedter.

62. As acknowledged, this is Michelstaedter's autograph draft, before the final copy.

63. Campailla, 'Postille Leopardiane di Michelstaedter': 247.

64. To the point that the entire structure of *La Persuasione e la Rettorica* seems to be built

around this use of the conjunction. 'But' is the link between the first part of the thesis devoted to the concept of 'persuasion' and the second part on 'rhetoric': «[m]a gli uomini si stancano su questa via, si sentono mancare nella solitudine» (PR: 53).

65. Or two inorganic beings, as chloride and hydrogen are in the figurative example we are about to discuss. We will see in chapter 4 how this figurative language partakes also of the philosophical conceptualization, and the theoretical consequences of this link.

66. This humanization is a tendency throughout the whole narration of the experiment. For example: «[p]er questo sentimento del tempo inutile il cloro nella lontananza dell'idrogeno *s'annoia*» (PR: 15).

67. This is one of the reasons why, in chapter 4, we will interpret the passage as an allegory. In the present context, what interests us is the use of the term 'eyelid' and the interpretation of this metaphor inside a theoretical framework.

68. The word of the 'persuaded' is revelatory, so that «allora i ciechi vedranno» (PR: 45).

69. From the 'single' fulfilment of a determinate need, the idea that «lo stomaco non ha fame per sé, *ma per il corpo*» (PR: 16) guides the narrator to a discussion on the body as a complex container for a series of activities that ultimately replicate a mechanism of self perpetuation. For humans, the «dio della φιλοψυχία » (PR: 17) organizes «il piacere» (ibid.) making sure that the use won't spill over into «abuso» (PR: 16). «Nella nebbia indifferente delle cose il dio *fa brillare* la cosa che all'organismo è utile; e l'organismo vi contende come in quella avesse a saziare tutta la sua fame, come quella gli dovesse dar tutta la vita: *l'assoluta persuasione*; ma il dio sapiente spegne la luce quando l'abuso toglierebbe l'uso; e l'animale sazio solo in riguardo a quella cosa, si volge dove gli appaia un'altra luce che il dio benevolo gli accenda; ed a questa contende con tutta la sua speranza; finché ancora la luce si spegne per riaccendersi in un altro punto ...» (PR: 16).

70. In this case, a dialogized monologue, in which the voice of the implied reader is imagined and anticipated by the narrator in his is allocutory monologue.

71. The following chapter will offer an interpretation of this passage, inside a discussion on the problem of exemplarity and categorial generalization.

72. The image is exploited also in PR: 173, where the negative act of 'spitting' the unwanted fruit is further clarified against the danger of considering the act as an end in itself. These themes will be crucial in our concluding chapter, where the definition of the text with regard to the project of 'persuasion' will be addressed.

73. Bakhtin, *Problems of Dostoevsky's Poetics*: 52.

74. Ibid.: 74.

75. For example, negative descriptions of 'persuasion' in the tone of those quoted in our introduction, can be read as a dialogical answer to an implied (rhetorical, in many senses) interlocutor: «egli non può prendere la persona di questi bisogni come sufficiente [...]: egli non può affermare se stesso nell'affermazione di quelli [...], egli non può muoversi a differenza delle cose che sono perché egli ne abbia bisogno: non c'è pane per lui, non c'è acqua, non c'è letto, non c'è famiglia, non c'è patria, non c'è dio – egli è solo nel deserto e deve crear tutto da sé» (PR: 34). It should be clear how all the negations of the series can be also interpreted as answers to an implied rhetorical voice; moreover, in reading the list of proposed (and negated) values, this voice seems very close to the 'you' we discussed just above.

76. For an interpretation of Michelstaedter's pedagogy in terms of correct or incorrect dialectic, see: Raschini, *Michelstaedter*: 143-50.

77. On this topic, with particular regard to the different interpretations of Plato given by Michelstaedter and Nietzsche, see the important: Cacciari, 'La Lotta 'su' Platone'.

78. Bakhtin, *Problems of Dostoevsky's Poetics*: 100. A further analysis of Platonic dialogue as

apomnemoneumata, and the role of the hero/Socrates, see Michail M. Bakhtin, *The Dialogic Imagination. Four Essays*, trans. Caryl Emerson and Michael Holquist (Austin: Univerity of Texas Press, 1981): 24-6.

79. James P. Zappen, *The Rebirth of Dialogue: Bakhtin, Socrates, and the Rhetorical Tradition* (Albany: State University of New York Press, 2004): 164. Zappen sees *Protagoras* and *Gorgias* as the two dialogues in which Bakhtinian dialogism is mostly expressed, because «the Socrates that Bakhtin finds in this early dialogues is a Socrates who tests and contests and creates idea in dialogue or discussion (*dialegesthai*) – not dialectic (*dialektikē*) – with others. This Socrates is not the speaker/writer/rhetor [...] but the listener/reader/responder» (Zappen, *The Rebirth of Dialogue: Bakhtin, Socrates, and the Rhetorical Tradition*: 13). The affinities with our quote from Michelstaedter are clear. We could also read the differences in Plato's dialogism in terms of his 'second navigation', sharply satirized in one of the most famous apologues of *La Persuasione e la Rettorica*: 'Un esempio storico' (PR: 66-73). See: Giovanni Reale, *Storia della Filosofia Antica*, 3 vols., vol. 1 (Milano: Vita e Pensiero, 1976); Francesco Sarri, *Socrate e la Nascita del Concetto Occidentale di Anima* (Milano: Vita e Pensiero, 1997).

80. Michail M. Bakhtin, 'Forms of Time and Chronotope in the Novel,' in *The Dialogic Imagination. Four Essays* (Austin: University of Texas Press, 1981): 130-1.

81. Which would, in general, address the definition of the border between early, dialogic dialogues, and later dialectic. On this point, see at least: Terry Penner, 'Socrates and the Early Dialogues' in *The Cambridge Companion to Plato*, ed. Richard Kraut (Cambridge: Cambridge University Press, 1992); this is also one of the tasks of Zappen, *The Rebirth of Dialogue: Bakhtin, Socrates, and the Rhetorical Tradition*.

82. On Bakhtin's ethic, see, for example: Galin Tihanov, *The Master and the Slave: Lukàcs, Bakhtin, and the Ideas of Their Time* (Oxford: Clarendon, 2000); G.M. Morson and C. Emerson, 'Extracts from a Heteroglossary' in *Dialogue and Critical Discourse: Language, Culture, Critical Theory*, ed. M. Macovski (New York: Oxford University Press, 1997).

83. For the Bakhtinian analysis of the voice of the narrator and its role as 'word between words' in Dostoevskij's dialogic novel, see: Bakhtin, *Problems of Dostoevsky's Poetics*: 250-1 et passim.

CHAPTER TWO

The Narrator and the Embodiment of Exemplary Quotes

Ich trink Wein aus zwei Gläsern.

Paul Celan

At the infinite point of the hyperbolic movement, the leap to 'persuasion', as the exemplary construction of Beethoven's biography shows, implies an ultimate radical negation: the negation of the value of negation itself. If the hyperbole must become a line, the utterance of the 'persuaded human' assumes a radically different linguistic status; if the Socratic dialectic takes to the limits of 'persuasion', the word of the 'persuaded' is – to remain within a Bakhtinian vocabulary – nothing less than perfectly monologic.

The goal of our enquiry is to offer a comprehensive interpretation of this leap. In this chapter, however, the important point is that this transformation – an overcoming of contingency that results in an absolute self-possession and self-expression – implies a disavowal of the tools adopted for its achievement. The question on the self-undermining and centrality of the narrator should be read under this light. On the one hand, the leap resembles a romantic *topos*, as defined in Paul De Man's study on *The Rhetoric of Romanticism*: «the paradox of a wisdom that lies somehow beyond cognition and self-knowledge, yet that can only be reached by ways of the process it is said to overcome»[1]. On the other, the final negation of the value of the hyperbolic way to 'persuasion', logically calls into question all the assumptions on which the path is founded and through which it develops: the status of the subject/narrator as a centre for acquiring a rational knowledge of its condition, and the *locus* of a coherent will which would lead towards the 'justice' of 'persuasion'.

If this is true, then a certain degree of self-undermining should be expected, and so the questioning of the status and value of a particular dialectical practice of signification. On a theoretical level, this movement could once again be interpreted as a romantic project of «innocence recovered at the far side and by way of experience, of paradise consciously regained after the fall into consciousness»[2]. On a stylistic level, however, we could question the strategies of (self) undermining with regard to the *locus* of linguistic foundation in the text[3]; and position *La Persuasione e la Rettorica* inside the recent debate on Michelstaedter, that opens to stylistic readings[4] and suggests a contextualization of the author inside the problematics of the Italian Novecento.

Much of what is at stake in this agenda has to do with the interpretation of the fate of the narrator: explicitly, as the centre of the organization of the different voices in the text and at the same time shaped through this relationship; and implicitly, as one of the characters in the complex net of affirmation and dismissal which constitutes the production of meanings in the text[5]. In this second chapter, we will address the explicit level, starting from an analysis of the practice of quotation in *La Persuasione e la Rettorica*. More than being the first and most immediately identifiable of the intertextual voices in the text, quotations exemplify in many ways the order of problems we face in further analysis of the narratorial dialectic.

Exemplary quotes are borrowed from exemplary figures: authors of exemplary sentences who have a particular relationship with the concept of 'persuasion', a relationship which, as discussed, oscillates between the status of 'prophet of persuasion' and 'persuaded human' with crucial consequences for the coherence of the argument. In order illuminate these consequences, we will firstly present a reading of Michelstaedter's idea of exemplarity, and interpret this idea in light of the general categories of his philosophy. Secondly, we will analyze the textual context of the narratorial utterance in which the external voices are embodied together with the technical strategies adopted for this embodiment, and we will defend a definition of the quotes and the quoted sources as exemplary, both in terms of the conclusions reached in the philosophical argument and the particular attitude towards 'persuasion' that they display. Finally, we will return to our general framework and ask ourselves what is the consequence of this 'positive' external utterance in the economy and agenda of *La Persuasione e la Rettorica*.

2.1 Theorization of exemplarity in the text

In *La Persuasione e la Rettorica*, there is a moment in which the narrator defines the 'way to persuasion' as a solitary path, the individual/subjective movement of a person engaged in the overcoming of his own peculiar contingency. Its opposite, 'rhetorical' movement, seeks 'persuasion' in the imitation of an example, of an authoritative figure of 'persuasion': an act that is unavoidably destined to result in an empty repetition, a rhetorical systematization and generalization inadequately derived from the individuality and irreproducibility of the example itself. If we consider the large number of exemplary quotations embodied in the first part of the text, we can read these passages (PR: 61-2) as a sign of indirect self-reflection on the practice of borrowing: the distinction between the correct and 'rhetorical' use of examples becomes in this sense the theoretical knot through which it is possible to read the text against itself.

2.1.1 The theory

The interpretive component at the very core of a rhetorical practice of exemplarity is the major problem faced by the narrator in his discussion of exemplarity inside a theory of 'persuasion' (and consequent poetic, poetic of exemplarity)[6]. The text is written from the position of a narrator who orients himself towards 'persuasion'; nevertheless, the adoption of positive examples risks taking part in a rhetorical systematization performed in support of the narratorial argument, threatening to entangle the subject in the «accontentarsi di quanto già dato» (PR: 62).

The theoretical question on exemplarity is addressed in *La Persuasione e la Rettorica* by insisting on the perlocutionary[7] nature of the example, or better, insisting on the adoption and quotation of the example exclusively in and for its perlocutionary sense: the positive example is something that 'moves towards action', and the 'exemplary person' a voice which is able to induce a movement to 'open the eyes' of the reader. Ethically, it points towards the path of 'persuasion' – one without foundations or a determined endpoint – without reducing this path to a system. More than the simple induction of a moral lesson or a general rule derived from the particular case[8], the focus on the perlocutionary tries to leave the interpretation of the matter for the manner, as a signpost for the reader of the necessity of not adapting to the sufficiency of what is given (PR: 62). Even the exemplary quote becomes insufficient, and calls for the personal engagement of the subject in an individual ethical struggle towards 'justice'. The following passage illustrates this point:

I primi Cristiani facevano il segno del pesce e si credevano salvi; avessero fatto più pesci e sarebbero stati salvi davvero, ché in ciò avrebbero riconosciuto che Cristo ha salvato se stesso poiché della sua vita mortale ha saputo creare il dio: l'individuo; ma che nessuno è salvato da lui che non segua la sua vita: ma seguire non è imitare, mettersi col proprio qualunque valore nei modi e nelle parole della via della persuasione, colla speranza d'avere in quello la verità. *Si duo idem faciunt non est idem.* [...] La via della persuasione non è corsa da <omnibus>, non ha segni, indicazioni che si possano comunicare, studiare, ripetere. Ma ognuno ha in se il bisogno di trovarla e nel proprio dolore l'indice, ognuno deve nuovamente aprirsi da sé la via, poiché ognuno è solo e non può sperar aiuto che da sé: la via della persuasione non ha che questa indicazione: non adattarti alla sufficienza di ciò che ti è dato (PR: 61-2).

This argument on exemplarity is clearly conducted in an attempt to avoid the formalization of an example into a doctrine, a safe and passive practice, or a rhetorical system. Moving from the *si duo idem faciunt non est idem*[9], the exemplary figure has the role of inducing in the subject a striving for 'knowing thyself' on a way which does not have any 'signposts', and is to be individually created. The encounter with the exemplar is thus a moment of revelation correlative to the experience of the horror[10], with the indirect function of revealing the true value of the latter. However, we are about to see how complicated and potentially incoherent this indirect 'foundational' function really is.

2.1.2 *Theoretical problems: the authority of the interpreter*

In the quote above, a definition of a correct use of exemplarity is given through an example and partially as a consequence of it. If we can read the example of Christ and the first Christians in order to understand a theory of exemplarity, we can at the same time discuss the practice of quoting the positive example in relation to the 'rule' that the example is there to affirm. In this sense, the interpretation of the figure of Christ brings out some problematic issues.

The first problem concerns the authority with which the narrator invests himself in order to be in charge of the interpretation of Christ[11]. The example of Christ is there to define the rule of 'following' versus 'imitating', and thus asserts the perlocutionary status of an example versus the deterministic induction of a moral and rhetorical rule. However, it is clear that at the basis of this interpretation is a determinism: the example of Christ is contradictorily adopted in order to *define the rule of the perlocutionary*; that is, it offers as a rule the imperative of avoiding the definition of a rule. This point arises with the definition of Christ as a 'persuaded'[12]. The acronym ΙΧΘΣ of 'Jesus Christ of-God Son the Saviour', which for the narrator is the mistake at the foundation of the rhetoric of religion, is corrected into the plural ΙΧΘΥΕΣ, 'Jesus Christ of-God Son of-Himself Saviour': Christ saved himself, because he managed to create god from his mortal life, to create the 'individual'. This example, which gains further importance from its position before the theoretical paragraphs on exemplarity, seems to split the general perlocutionary intent of the example into two distinct moments of interpretation. The first is an act by the interpreter of the example (the narrator) which acknowledges Christ as the one who saved himself, and thus as 'persuaded'; the second, consequent on the first, is the effective perlocutionary push towards 'persuasion'. The acronym does not state 'Jesus Christ the one who makes you save yourself', but 'the saved', and *therefore* an example to follow. We have already seen, in our discussion of the delated paratexts, how inside the framework of *La Persuasione e la Rettorica*, this judgement on the 'persuaded' nature of a subject is quite difficult to defend.

In the case of Christ a logical question arises: how can we humans of 'rhetoric' interpret and judge something non-rhetorical? How can we recognize something outside our (rhetorical) language? The two poles are incommensurable. In relation to the acronym of the fish, in the moment in which we consider ΙΧΘΣ as ΙΧΘΥΕΣ, our interpretation does not evade fixing Christ as a definite value, a 'rhetorical' definition of 'persuasion', thus positing the example as the foundation for a rhetorical system, a 'religion'. In other words, the degree of formalization that is a consequence of the definition given by the narrator becomes the basis for a pedagogy of 'persuasion'[13]; and the narrator adopts an authoritative stance as the *correct* interpreter of the example. Assuming the role of teacher, he becomes an authority on the transmission of a rhetorical system on the matter of 'persuasion'. In this sense, if the plurality of ΙΧΘΥΕΣ works as a word underlying the subjective nature of the path to 'persuasion', it fails when the acronym is revealed. We could argue that Christ is considered 'persuaded' because he has perlocutionary value, it spurs to engage with his individual emancipatory path. In other words, Christ's word could be intended as the origin and the cause of the narrator's attempt: a moving revelation. If this is true, nevertheless the narrator finds himself in the problematic role of the interpreter, invested with an authority that risks crystallizing the example inside a fixed rhetorical system.

This self-affirmative movement of the narrator, both because of his self-investment as a hermeneutical authority, and the activity of defining rules which are foundational for the philosophical argument, is exploited in other larger exemplary narratives which punctuate the entire text: apologues, parables, dialogues, myths, to quote a few. In chapter 4 we will focus on these sub-genres and their dialogical relationship with the academic frame. In the case of quotes however, this point is interwoven with a further problem. In the practice of exemplary quotation, as the sentence is exemplary, so is the source (the 'name' of the original author) and his status. The interpretation of the position of this author in relation to 'persuasion' is something we need to analyze further.

2.1.3 'Imitating' and 'following'

In the above passage on exemplarity, two different ways of relating with an example – 'imitating' and 'following' – are presented as antithetic practices in relation to 'persuasion': «ma seguire non è imitare, mettersi col proprio qualunque valore nei modi e nelle parole della via della persuasione colla speranza d'avere in quello la verità» (PR: 62). These provide a framework for further analysis of the practice of quotation.

The incommensurability between the realm of 'rhetoric' and that of 'persuasion' becomes here the basis for a dismissal of 'imitation' as a practice which is blind to this incommensurable nature, and rhetorically affirms the absolute value of a relative understanding. On the contrary, 'following' is a strategy developed in full knowledge of the contingent nature of the practice of the example and its intrinsic inadequacy in defining a general rule.

It is interesting to underline how this insistence on the incommensurability of the two is treated. It reminds us of the discussion on the relation between example and rule which we find in readings of Lyotard, such as that by Gelley: «though the rule or law as such cannot be formulated, its point (or *pointing*) emerges from what Lyotard has termed "a symbolization ... through permutations of instances". The example does not stand alone, but inaugurates a dynamic that displaces the instance. Each variant or alternative [...] shifts the direction of the argument»[14]. In other words, «Lyotard's aim is to guard us against [an] automatic bridge or linkage [...] between, say, a thesis or principle and the call for its application or actualization, the injunction»[15]. In *La Persuasione e la Rettorica*, the concept of 'following' seems to be conceived in order to preserve the impossibility of defining the rule, and the insistence on the perlocutionary function of the example (its openness) stresses the irreducibility of the 'rule of persuasion' to the statement of its example. However, as we pointed out, the authority with which the narrator invests himself while defining Christ as a 'persuaded', and the 'transparency' in the interpretation of the example which derives from this investment build an automatic bridge between rule and example, which is, in Michelstaedter's terms, the inadequate affirmation of a value. Thus, as Gelley points out, the movement from story to interpretation to the final injunction[16] is inverted by the guiding presence of the authority: «if the interpretation is already determined by an "authoritative" instance, it is at the other end, the level of injunction, that we should look for a source of the interpretation, of whatever "meaning" is to be imputed to the story»[17]. Again we find Michelstaedter's 'false affirmation'[18].

On the other hand, if *La Persuasione e la Rettorica* is to be considered entirely as a text engaged in a narratorial-driven pedagogy, the judgement on the relationship between rule and example, the ambiguity in the relation between theory and practice of exemplarity and the determinism which seems to hide under this practice (with the consequent affirmation of the ideology of the narrator and its role as a centre, a foundation of the text) should have a relatively smaller role than what a further interpretation of the categories of 'following' and 'imitating' reveals. In fact, investing the concept of 'imitation' with all the negative attributes of 'rhetoric', and assuming 'following' as a path coherent with 'persuasion' implies a radical negation of the pedagogical project and an attempt to link the attitude towards 'persuasion' with the Kantian understanding of the relationship between genius and aesthetic examples[19].

A reading of the relevant passages of the *Critique of Judgement* reveals a similarity in vocabulary:

> genius is the exemplary originality of the natural gifts of a subject in the free employment of his cognitive faculties. In this way the product of a genius […] is an example, not to be imitated (for then that which in it is genius and constitutes the spirit of the work would be lost), but to be followed, by another genius; whom it awakens to a feeling of his own originality and whom it stirs so to exercise his art in freedom from the constraint of rules[20].

In this quote, we can almost immediately read the main features of Michelstaedter's understanding of exemplarity: the example of the genius is not there to be imitated (*Nachmachen*), but to be followed (*Nachahmen*[21]), the function of the example is perlocutionary (it awakens the genius to a feeling of his own originality and so forth), and the 'following' is free from the constraints of rules. As David Lloyd synthesizes, «the genius stands outside the repetition of an exemplary pedagogy, since his skills can be neither communicated nor learnt and since the originality of the genius is not progressive but returns always to the same ground in nature»[22]. It is difficult here not to see the parallel with the statement on 'persuasion' given by the narrator of *La Persuasione e la Rettorica*: «la via della persuasione non è corsa da <omnibus>, non ha segni, indicazioni che si possano comunicare, studiare, ripetere» (PR: 62)[23]. The adoption of Kantian concepts as the only correct approach to the problem of exemplarity, leads logically to the rejection of any possible pedagogy. If in Kant «his example [of the genius] produces for other good heads a school, i.e. a methodical system of teaching according to rules, so far as these can be derived from the peculiarities of the products of his spirit», and «for such persons beautiful art is so far imitation, to which nature through the medium of a genius supplied the rule»[24], in Michelstaedter this perspective coincides with 'rhetoric', with the «mettersi col proprio qualunque valore nei modi e nelle parole della via della persuasione, colla speranza d'avere in quello la verità» (PR: 62), and thus the inadequate foundation of an ideological system. The progressive faculty of 'taste', and its relationship with pedagogy, seems to not have a place in Michelstaedter[25].

A few points which arise from this comparison need to be addressed. First of all, we should point out how Kant's discussion deals with the realm of aesthetics and aesthetic judgement. It may sound quite odd, in a highly self-referential academic work such as *La Persuasione e la Rettorica*, to find such a drastic attack against 'teaching through rules', and in favour of artistic production: after all, the thesis is engaged in the definition of 'concepts', for example the 'rules of persuasion' and the 'rule of rhetoric'. It is in this sense, that the judgement by Thomas Harrison, that «to continue to live Michelstaedter [...] would have had to shift more of his energy into the production of art»[26] gains its full importance[27]. And it is in this sense that our approach to *La Persuasione e la Rettorica* is conceived: the idea of reading the text 'stylistically', and the focus on the ultimate self-undermining aim that the text should perform, are ways to explore the degree of rejection of a pedagogical model of argumentation. The point is to see whether the 'ruins' which remain after the 'war with words against words' can be understood as a coherence between theory and practice, from an aesthetic point of view, or more specifically, under the umbrella of the Kantian genius.

Now that we have made the terms of Michelstaedter's concept of exemplarity clear, the relationship between the asserted necessity of (self) undermining and the necessity of rejecting a pedagogy can be defined. In order to do this, it is worth focusing again on the final clause of the quote on exemplarity: «la via della persuasione non ha che questa indicazione: non adattarti alla sufficienza di ciò che ti è dato» (PR: 62). This statement is coherent with the hyperbolic movement towards 'persuasion': it was this dialectic of 'not content oneself' that gave us the chance to hypothesize the dialogic nature of Michelstaedter's work. Moreover, just above this clause, the origin of this 'indication' is given: «ognuno ha in sé il bisogno di trovarla [the way to persuasion] e nel proprio dolore l'indice» (PR: 62). The 'pain' refers here to the consequence of the experience of the horror beyond the veil of Maya – the moment of consciousness which imposes the ethical choice between 'persuasion' and 'rhetoric' – and once the choice towards 'persuasion' is made, the dialectical rule to be followed is the infinite, hyperbolic, 'never content'. However, once again, this 'indication' and the further indication of its origins in the experience of pain, are nothing more than the statement of a rule; maybe 'the rule to end all the rules': a pedagogical foundation at the origin of the project of 'persuasion'. The rejection of 'imitation' shifts the teaching inside a sort of 'pedagogy of the way to persuasion', a teaching on how to become geniuses: by following the rule of pain, and by avoiding being content, *ad infinitum*, we become geniuses/persuaded[28].

This attempt carries some important consequences for our argument. Firstly, it rescues the philosophical/academic project by asserting that it acts as the *locus* of consciousness: both the rule and the practice of the project of (self) undermining. Secondly, the project of 'persuasion' is rescued inside the perspective of the writing of the text; the text becomes a moment on the path which should allow the final overcoming of the reasons of the text itself. It is worth reminding ourselves how this movement towards an 'infinite consciousness' which will regain 'immediacy' is in fact coherent with the romantic *topos* defined by De Man; and how our project of mapping and questioning the hyperbolic movement in the writing of *La Persuasione e la Rettorica* gains further weight from this argument.

The introduction of a 'pedagogy of genius' is paradoxical in the measure in which it is destined to overcome itself, and implies the measurability of the movement to 'not be content' through the mathematical function of the hyperbole[29]. Moreover, this introduction replicates features belonging to a pedagogy of aesthetic judgement, namely[30]: the re-introduction of 'time' (pedagogy is a process and so is the movement along the hyperbole); the relationship between teacher and pupil, in which the teacher holds the power, for example as interpreter of the examples; and a statement of the inadequacy of the exemplary role of the teacher and the example because of their incommensurability with a rule. These points map the ambiguity played out between the rejection and affirmation of the pedagogical status. We will now point out both a series of strategies which are coherent with the concept of 'following' an example, that is a highly original and individual exploitation of the source by the narrator. We will also highlight how quotations work to establish and defend the narratorial point of view as a system that can explain the movement of 'persuasion'.

2.2   Phenomenology of the exemplary quotes

Our interest in the practice of quotation in *La Persuasione e la Rettorica* resides in the nature of the quotations as clearly identifiable external voices which potentially disrupt the flow of the narratorial utterance on thematic and formal levels[31]. In coherence with the method outlined in the preceding chapter, this 'other' utterance needs to be analysed in two different steps: firstly, interpreting this presence in its relationship with the narratorial voice, in order to define its degree of dialogism and reciprocal orientation; secondly, comparing the results with the theoretical discussion on exemplarity in the text.

2.2.1   Multilingualism, Greek and aphorisms

The multilingual aspects of *La Persuasione e la Rettorica* have been underlined and related to Michelstaedter's background to the degree that they have assumed the status of truisms: 'Michelstaedter spoke in the language of his sources'[32]. What concerns us, however, are the ways in which, and the possible rhetorical reasons why, a language other than Italian is deployed.

Michelstaedter's use of foreign languages encompasses German, ancient Greek and the dialect of the Veneto region, the latter limited to the quotation of the lyrics of a folkloric song[33]. The predilection for a foreign term or sentence is generally preferred when the possibilities offered by the chosen language allow the explanation of a passage in a synthetic and/or aphoristic way, particularly in cases where the foreign language allows meaningful wordplays, double senses and rhymes. The case of German is emblematic here. It first appears inside a discussion on the relativity of values and the consequences for contingency in terms of the attribution of truth to a certain point of view: «*alle haben recht – niemand ist gerecht*» (PR: 39). The narrator plays here with the word '*gerecht*' meaning both 'right' in an ethical sense – to be a 'right person', to be 'upright' – and in the sense of being 'right about something', saying something 'correct' or 'true'. This intention is made explicit through the following translation and explanatory paraphrase: «tutti hanno ragione – nessuno ha *la ragione*. Poiché non v'è effetto senza causa, ogni cosa nel mondo ha ragione d'avvenire; a ogni causa è giusto il suo effetto, a ogni bisogno la sua giusta affermazione – ma nessuno *è giusto*» (ibid.). By means of rephrasing, the initial defining sentence is rendered intelligible and coherent with the argument. However, the disruption of the foreign language, the italics[34] and the positioning at the beginning of the paragraph[35] – leading to the broader translation, paraphrase and following argument around the same topic – put the German sentence in the foreground and invest it with the status of an aphorism[36]. The second German occurrence works similarly, but the disruption of the narratorial flow is further emphasized by the adoption of a poetic/proverbial mode in metrics and rhymes: «*Beredt wird einer nicht / durch fremder Reden Macht, / ist nicht sein eigen Geist / zur Redlichkeit gebracht*» (PR: 48). Again, the word play is made explicit in the given footnote («[i]ntraducibile: *redlich* = onesto, e <dicibile>», ibid.)[37], and the whole utterance is once again an aphoristic comment, but this time closing the paragraph[38].

The example of the use of German brings to light a pattern for interpreting the use of ancient Greek; the latter commonly adopted throughout Michelstaedter's academic career and artistic production[39]. In this context, it is extremely difficult to talk of the 'originality' of the Greek in the text in a strict sense, without pointing to a possible intertextual source, which is most likely one of the thinkers assumed as a positive support for the argument through 'identifiable' marks of quotation and reference. This is the case for the term φιλοψυχία, which is of Platonic derivation[40], but in the text assumes the status of a philosophical category representing an entire speculation on existence, in ways impossible to render immediately in translation; hence a translation is given in a footnote using two terms that make its double meaning explicit: «amore alla vita – viltà» (PR: 17). More correctly, we should imagine the adoption of Greek terms and quotes as a continuum[41], with the fully referred examples to be found in the 'Appendici Critiche' at one end, and at the other, the implicit borrowings and elaborations of single terms and original sentences, which partake of the field of the narratorial utterance, alongside and in dialogue with explicitly recognizable external quotes.

An example of this latter pole can be found already on the very first page of *La Persuasione e la Rettorica*, inside the description of the 'apologue of the weight'. Here the narrator offers in brackets a Greek translation of part of his preceding Italian sentence: «e nessuno dei punti futuri sarà tale da accontentarlo, che necessario sarà alla sua vita, fintanto che lo aspetti (ὄφρα ἂν μένῃ αὐτόν) più basso» (PR: 7). Campailla[42] clearly and correctly points out how the narrator recurs to the Greek in order to play with the possible contraposition between the transitive form of μένειν which leads to 'waiting for someone or something', and the intransitive form: 'to stay, to consist'. This possibility in the Greek verb gives to the 'apologue of the weight' a different thickness, impossible to render in Italian. The Italian sentence will thus require a series of explanatory comments at the end of the apologue to articulate the fundamental dichotomy between relative and absolute possession. In doing so, the narrator introduces an inductive generalization, assuming an extra-diegetic position, as discussed above in chapter 1. The adoption of Greek, on the contrary, already implies the possibility of a dualistic opposition between transitive and intransitive forms and thus embodies in one word, practically all that is at stake in the philosophy of the text: the possibility of absolute versus relative, of a non-relational, or mono-directional life and language versus a violent relational and social existence: 'persuasion' versus 'rhetoric'. In this example Greek acts as an alternative to the extra-diegetic attitude. The development of the Greek term throughout the text offers further evidence of the investment that is at stake here. As Campailla again briefly points out[43], the narrator will exploit the ambiguity of meaning all the way through the first part of the text. Firstly, the transitive/intransitive dichotomy is made explicit: «colui che è per se stesso (μένει) non ha bisogno d'altra cosa che sia per lui (μέοι αὐτόν) nel futuro, ma possiede tutto in sé» (PR: 9); furthermore, it becomes part of the original aphoristic sentence: «Ἕως ἂν παρῇ μοι ἐλπίς τις – μένει μοί τι» (PR: 13). The following translation/paraphrase of this aphorism in Italian loses the poignancy of the Greek, not being adequate to translate the intransitive alternative to which the verb reminds: «fin quando io voglia ancora in qualche modo, attribuisco valore a qualche cosa – c'è qualcosa per me» (ibid.). Finally, the term becomes so charged that it can stand alone, in the context of an iconographic synthesis of the narratorial argument, in the paragraph which concludes the demonstration of the «cerchio senza uscita dell'individualità illusoria» (PR: 19). «[M]ένει γὰρ αὐτῷ ἅπερ ἂν αὐτὸν μένῃ. La realtà è per lui le cose che attendono il suo futuro» (ibid.), writes the narrator, reproducing the same pattern of aphorism/translation seen above. He then introduces his 'circle', the schematic definition of the results of his argument: «Μένει τι - μένει μέ τι – πάρεστι ἐλπίς - ἀρκῶ»[44] (ibid.). The further explanation in Italian once again fails to reproduce the level of synthesis of the 'circle', which retains both the full complexity of the argument and the dichotomy between the choice of human illusory affirmation in the fulfilment of finite needs; and, on the opposite, intransitive side, the pure self-possession of the persuaded, his staying, his consisting.

The adoption of Greek terms charged with a particular philosophical meaning is not particularly original in a philosophical context, however the example above allows us to highlight two important features for understanding of the embodiment of quotes. Firstly, the importance acquired by the Greek term is not acknowledged by the narrator through a rational discussion of the reasons motivating his choice of the term and its value in the context of his theory. Even more than in the case of φιλοψυχία, which is translated and appears inside the discussion on self-perpetuation – explicitly becoming the synthetic appellative of the 'benevolent and prudent god' (PR: 17) – the ambiguity is left to the reader. Further exploitation of this ambiguity becomes a sort of subtext, in which the Greek underpins the parallel Italian discourse with a poignant immediacy, reaching its endpoint in the image of the circle and in production of aphorisms. Thus we arrive at our second point: it is clear, both in what we said about the use of German and in the present case, how a complex philosophical demonstration seems to lead to a climactic conclusion, a final emblematic synthesis encapsulated in a single aphoristic formula. At this point, the sub-genre 'aphorism' (which enters into a complex 'mirroring' dialogue with the narratorial logical/academic argument) is the place in which multilingualism is fully developed in the direction of synthesis, density, complexity and, as we will argue, exemplarity. It is in this precise context that the majority of the 'positive' quotes embodied in support of the demonstration are found. This implies that the external voice, when explicitly acknowledged as such, enters the text in a sub-generic role that is elsewhere fulfilled by an original sentence.

2.2.2 Quoting in support of an argument

In his book dedicated to Michelstaedter, Muzzioli affirms that ancient Greek – the language both of the most important sources for the author's philosophy and of the major examples of the humans on the way to 'persuasion' – becomes, in *La Persuasione e la Rettorica*, a privileged mode of expression that emancipates itself from the rhetoric of the degree thesis and resembles the 'unity' in which 'persuaded souls' can communicate the word of/about 'persuasion'[45]. The investment in Greek aphorisms, original and quoted, and the adoption of this sub-genre for Italian synthetic sentences, as if to replicate or echo the imported voices, could be intended in this sense. Brianese, in his essay on the theoretical relationships between ancient philosophy and Michelstaedter, seems to orient his interpretation in this direction: pointing out that *La Persuasione e la Rettorica*, despite being conceived as an enquiry on the concepts of rhetoric and persuasion in Plato and Aristotle, is mainly concerned with the philosophy of the Presocratics, in particular Heraclitus and Parmenides[46] (leaving the discussion of Platonic and Aristotelian texts to the 'Appendici Critiche'[47]). He further states that «si ha spesso l'impressione che a Michelstaedter il linguaggio dei greci sia come connaturato, quasi la forma più adatta d'espressione di un pensiero sempre sul punto di travolgere ogni barriera linguistica e metalinguistica. Si ha la sensazione insomma che il Goriziano parli greco anche quando parla la propria lingua, e che anche per questo riesca a dare armonica collocazione alle parole dei Padri del pensiero occidentale»[48]. This 'harmonic placement' of positive sources needs to be further discussed. It is clear that this harmonization is not mono-directional, that is, it is not only a movement *from* the narrator *towards* the sources, as a sort of attempt at replicating a Presocratic style; but – given the re-encoded, cut and pasted nature of quotes in general – a sort of dialogical encounter, the phenomenology of which needs to be mapped. Brianese's reading of Michelstaedter's use of the 'filter' of Schopenhauerian metaphysics of will as a foundation for the context of the borrowing, while its mediation is a 'betrayal' of the Presocratics is coherent with our argument[49]. These two positions are the preliminary theses which we are about to verify and complicate in our interpretation of the praxis of quoting.

The first feature that is relevant for our reading is the absence of secondary sources in the work, with the exception of a comment on Mullach, the editor of the *Fragmenta Philosophorum Graecorum* on which Michelstaedter was working at the time of the thesis, and a brief remark on Gomperz, author of a history of ancient philosophy, *Griechische Denker*[50]. The comments on these sources are by no means intended as a synthesis, systematiszation or 'shortcut' for an interpretation of the Greek references[51]. The narrator engages in an unmediated dialogue with his sources, and thus the discourse on 'persuasion' is developed. The direct bridge and complete withdrawal from validation of the argument through the use of authoritative secondary sources is coherent with the need to avoid 'rhetoric'; for 'rhetoric' manifests itself in the creation of a closed system of values, and if the academy is one of the *loci* where systems are built and crystallized, then the development of the argument in *La Persuasione e la Rettorica* cannot (directly/rhetorically) bank on previous knowledge: it must avoid rules derived from secondary sources. The adoption and exclusive discussion of primary sources can thus be considered as not just an attempt at a coherence between theory and practice, but, once again, a positioning of the text on the hyperbolic 'way to persuasion'.

However, it is not only the status of primary sources that is striking, but the peculiar group of authors from whom the quotes are borrowed. If we refer to the counting of the quotes by Aurelio Benevento[52], we will see how:

nel quadro complessivo [...], ai primi posti troviamo i presocratici, Parmenide, Eraclito e poi Empedocle, che sono per Michelstaedter i veri fondatori del pensiero filosofico, seguiti da Platone, la voce di Socrate e il vero maestro di pensiero – citato dai dialoghi 'socratici', Gorgia, Fedro, Apologia e anche Repubblica, ma ignorato negli ultimi dialoghi [...] – e dai poeti tragici, Sofocle anzitutto e poi Eschilo – mentre è ignorato il moderno razionalista Euripide – e da un poeta lirico nutrito di pensiero filosofico, come Simonide. Sul versante del pensiero religioso occupa significativamente il primo posto l'Ecclesiaste, seguito dal Giovanni dell'Apocalisse, oltre che da Isaia e dagli evangelisti Luca e Matteo, mentre altrettanto significative sono le citazioni da Lucrezio e dal Petrarca dei Trionfi[53].

A simple listing of the sources allows us to place the text in the debate of its time: from the preference for Ecclesiastes to the complex and conflicting relationship with Nietzsche; from the preference for the Presocratics and indifference towards Empedocles to the crucial adoption of Socrates, before Plato's 'betrayal'[54], as a positive example, in clear contrast with the Nietzsche of the *Birth of Tragedy*[55]. Keeping in mind the genre of the work (an academic thesis on 'the concepts of "persuasion" and "rhetoric" in Plato and Aristotle'), the choice of 'authorities' sounds quite original[56]. In fact, if we assume that quotation of an example is, in Aristotelian terms, part of a rhetoric, and if the realm of rhetoric implies an attention to audience, then the very fact of employing a group of sources such as those in *La Persuasione e la Rettorica* to discuss and defend a reading of Plato and Aristotle[57] puts the very core of the 'argument of authority'[58] at stake. It is highly unlikely that the immediate readers, the panel of professors in Florence, would have recognized those proposed 'authorities' as such. The 'attention' for the reader, in this sense, seems to go in the direction of shock and displacement: shock for the absence of secondary sources and extensive quotes from Plato and Aristotle; displacement for the overwhelming presence of the Presocratics, Ecclesiastes, and the New Testament. The dialectic which presupposes the assertion of exemplary quotes as authorities on the matter of 'persuasion' is open to further interpretation. The movement of defining, recognizing and judging an example as authoritative, and the consequent construction of a panel of exemplary sources, a 'canon of/on persuasion' which is 'other than' and against the rhetoric of secondary sources (and any other possible group of authorities, namely Plato and Aristotle themselves), is a movement of substitution; its analysis can offer an object for the comparison of the theory of exemplarity with its stylistic practice.

A second feature of the practice of quoting is an apparent 'freedom' in the choice of the borrowings. The quotes are not systematically clustered around an explicit discussion of the philosophical position of the source, but reinforce narratorial statements, along with other authors who share, indistinctly, the same place and position. In this practice, the lack of an explicit logical defence for the choice of a particular author can be considered as an attempt to avoid the rhetoric of the positive yet inadequate explanation of 'persuaded example' through a system. In Bakhtinian terms it could be read as an identical orientation of the borrowing and borrowed voices in relation to the debated topic, where the adoption of an authority to replicate and echo the argument of the narrator is seen as evidence of the academic/monologic nature of the text. Alternatively, an interpretation of this practice under of the concepts of 'following' and 'imitating' (correct and incorrect relationships with an example, respectively) is the ultimate test of the internal coherence of the narratorial project.

Diepeveen, in his book on modern American poetry[59], offers a framework to link the practice of quotation with the appearance of dialogism in the text; he links a Bakhtinian reading with the specific intertextuality of quotes, working towards a dialogic reading of the genre. A recontextualization of some of his statements inside the object of our research can help us to synthesize our findings. Firstly, Diepeveen insists on the 'accuracy' of the practice of quotation versus allusion, where the freedom allowed the borrowing voice implies possibilities which tend to merge the external into a monologic utterance of the borrower: 'while *quotation* originally meant "to mark the number of", to simply refer to something, *allusion* has its Latin source in "to play with" – its form of reference suggests much more an interaction between borrower and source'[60]. This first distinction leads to the listing of a series of technical features of quotation which work as graphic signposts for the disruption caused by the quote in the flow of the text: italics (in the case of a foreign language), quotation marks – which according to Diepeveen «always signal appropriation of another voice of speech with which the author does not completely want to identify», for example in the use of cliché under inverted commas[61] – and, inside the academic genre, the colon, the indication of the reference, and so forth. However, if these features supposedly mark the presence of an external voice, they are not enough for us to speak of dialogism[62]. Indeed Bakhtin dismisses the academic genre as monologic; the mere presence of a dialogue between voices does not automatically imply the dialogic orientation of the text. This distinction underlies our construction of a continuum of quotation with the pole of 'hidden allusion' at one end and 'fully referred quotes' at the other. This explicit status is indicative of a particular relationship. While academic writing as a genre, and a degree thesis specifically, implies a formal rule for quotation – a system of referencing, as in the 'Appendici Critiche'[63]– *La Persuasione e la Rettorica* immediately deflates this expectation.

The first quote in the body of the text comes from Petrarch's *Triumphus Aeternitatis*, and it is not referenced: «<Non avrà loco fu sarà né era / ma è solo, in presente e ora e oggi / e sola eternità raccolta e 'ntera>» (PR: 9). The lines are reproduced as a poem, interrupting the flow of the voice of the narrator (first of all visually, through the quotation marks and the 'shorter' lines of hendecasyllables) and through the divergent texture of the imported voice (a more ancient Italian, in metrics, recognizable as something 'other'). On another level, the placement of the quote builds a strong relationship of coherence with the narratorial utterance; it reinforces and paraphrases the preceding sentence: «Colui che per sé stesso [...] non ha bisogno d'altra cosa che sia per lui nel futuro [...], ma possiede tutto in sé» (ibid.). In one of the rare footnotes in the body of the text, we find a further comment and a quote with its author identified: «e Parmenide: οὔ ποτ' ἔην οὐδ' ἔσται, ἐπεὶ νῦν ἔστιν ὁμοῦ πᾶν, / ἐν ξυνεχές·» [Neither was it once, nor will it be, since it is in the present, all together, one, indivisible[64]](ibid.). The introductory formula 'and Parmenides' and the positioning in a footnote give the sense that the comment of the Presocratic is a further synthetic, aphoristic explanation of what was discussed above: a further paraphrase. Some points can be stressed here. Firstly, something is missing in the academic reference. In the case of Petrarch, we do not find the name of the source (probably readerly knowledge of the classics is assumed) while in Parmenides we miss the quotation marks, the precise reference of the fragment and the translation from ancient Greek.

A further example will demonstrate the full range of play between marks, reference and translation. At the end of the first chapter[65] – after the 'apologue of the weight', the explanation by the narrator, the quotes from Petrarch and Parmenides and a further argument by the narrator – the final statements of the opening pages (PR: 7-10) are 'outsourced' to three references. Firstly, a sentence by the narrator, underlined by the use of italic, is paraphrased/commented through a quote from Saint Luke (his name is given as a reference in brackets, and lacks any further indications) without quotation marks or translation, and becomes, in the new context, an explanatory aphorism: «*chi non ha la persuasione non può comunicarla* (μήτι δύναται τυφλὸν ὁδηγεῖν) (S. Luca)» [Surely a blind man cannot lead the blind[66]](PR: 10). Following this, a sentence from Plato's *Gorgias*, identified only through the title of the Platonic dialogue, is embodied as a translation of a sentence by the narrator. Or, better said, the narrator's utterance is a sentence from *Gorgias* translated in Italian and subsequently repeated in Greek; the 'echo' engaged by the two utterances, becomes even stronger, as does the embodiment: «persuaso è chi *ha in sé la sua vita*: l'anima ignuda nelle isole dei beati (ἡ γυμνὴ ψυχὴ ἐν τοῖς τῶν μακάρων νήσοις) (Gorgia)» (ibid.). The last quote of the group, which is also a synthetic comment that closes the first chapter, comes from Saint Matthew: «Ma gli uomini cercano τὴν ψυχὴν e perdono τὴν ψυχὴν. – (S. Matteo)[67]». Recalling Diepeveen's argument that full academic reference indicates a 'maximum' distance between the borrowed and the borrowing voice, in *La Persuasione e la Rettorica* this distance is diminished[68] by a relative freedom in the formal choice of embodiment, without completely merging it into the narratorial utterance. It is as if the attempt to preserve a unity between the narrator and his source does not reach the point of fully wiping out the difference. With the addition of the 'name', the force of the 'argument of authority' is preserved, and the power of an 'exemplary quote' and 'exemplary source' is added. We can add further weight to this first evidence of a reduction of distance and diminishment of barriers through a comparison with the context of the narratorial utterance. We have seen how, from the very first pages of the text, Greek is established as the second language of the narrator, and exploited for the sake of forging synthetic, powerful and emblematic sentences. The presence of Greek quotes without (literal) translation is thus more than a graphic disruption, it exhibits a continuity with the narratorial practice. The quote from Saint Matthew, with its partial translation, works under this same principle.

A final point is related to the positioning of the quotes in the text. The narrator's argument tends to work towards the building of final aphoristic sentences, which synthesize his conclusions through a powerful statement, or sit at the start of a paragraph, as a comment on its opening. All the examples cited here are positioned in the same fashion, playing the role of the final aphorism with the addition of the authoritative exemplarity of the named source. This is maybe the most consistent feature of quotation, and at the same time the sign of a 'formal' unity of point of view.

This unity has its consequence for the content. The quotes often work as a condensation, paraphrase and interpretation of the argument, and the latter evolves as an explanation and/or a preparation of the condition for the embodiment of the quote. In this sense, explanatory quotes and sources can be considered as the object of a problem of interpretation, which implies a potential fall into 'rhetoric', as asserted in the theory on exemplarity discussed above. Does the embodiment of exemplary sources partake of the same ambiguities and contradictions which characterize the theoretical argument on 'following' and 'imitating' an example? Is the narrator 'following' or 'imitating'?

2.3   Ambiguity in the theory and practice of exemplarity

In this chapter, we discussed the reasons why Michelstaedter's theorization of exemplarity is ambiguous with regard to the necessities of 'following' an example and the ways in which the same theory of 'following' is argued in the text: the 'following' which leads to the freedom of the Kantian genius and in our reading invests the exemplary borrowing with a perlocutionary function is supposed to avoid the 'rhetoric' of the example, as systematized in formal analyses such as Suleyman's[69]. The 'interpretation' of the exemplary, if oriented towards the achievement of 'persuasion', is external to the problematic of interpretation and injunction; seen as 'rhetorical' generalizations, and inadequate affirmations of ethical values. However, the very presentation of the argument on exemplarity in the text shows features which, instead of projecting the narrator on the path of 'following', partake of a pedagogy delivered through examples which we called a 'pedagogy of persuasion', a teaching which sets itself in a potentially contradictory position with the path to 'persuasion'. In line with Gelley[70], we have pointed out how the links between 'story', 'interpretation' and 'injunction' are not mono-directional (as in Suleyman, originating from the narration towards a moral lesson), but move (also) in the opposite direction: from an intended and pre-conceived moral lesson towards the choice of an 'appropriate' example and the authoritarian narrowing down of its possible meanings. Indeed, the issue of authority involved in the pedagogy through exemplarity, is crucial in the broader problematic of authority that are fundamental to *La Persuasione e la Rettorica*. The choice of quoting the Presocratics, and more generally the entire 'pantheon' of exemplary authors as authorities on the matter of 'persuasion', is not necessarily a direct act of investing in a shared acknowledgement of their value – namely their value to support a discussion on Plato and Aristotle – but rather, a poignant attempt to establish a series of texts (and authors) as a proper (new) authority for the argument of the narrator. If one of the aims of *La Persuasione e la Rettorica* is to dismantle the positions of Plato and Aristotle on the two concepts, then the overwhelming presence of the Presocratics as a positive authority implies the definition of an original 'truth', historically located before the Platonic and Aristotelian 'corruption'. It is irrelevant if this is a 'truth of persuasion' or a 'truth about persuasion'; the point is that it is established and affirmed in a strong relationship with the logical defence of an argument by the narrator: it is affirmed through and because of the narratorial argument.

The first component in this movement of substitution of authorities is the definition of the philosophical concepts of 'persuasion' and 'rhetoric' by the narrator; the second, a reading of the philosophies of Plato and Aristotle as a fall into 'rhetoric', a moment of corruption in the history of philosophy. This comparison and dismissal are carried out both in the famous fictional apologue entitled 'Un Esempio Storico' (PR: 66-72), and in the defence deployed in the 'Appendici Critiche'. The third component is the exemplary sources: the Presocratics and all those who 'repeated' (PR: 3) their voice in the history of philosophy and art. Thus, the dismissal of Plato and Aristotle implies the establishment of a (new) authority, which allows the quotes to work at the rhetorical level of a 'demonstration through authority'. The importance and the role of the three components in their movement of substitution/ establishment lays bare the pedagogic nature of the narratorial voice.

In order to further demonstrate this point, we ought to introduce some considerations on the relative freedom and originality which characterizes the process of borrowing in the text. We have defined this 'freedom' as a *direct* relationship with the borrowed utterance; one that excludes any general discussion of the philosophical positions of the source, omits secondary sources, or any general systematization of the borrowed material, if not presented as the original argument of the narrator. Moreover, the practice of quotation seems to merge the borrowed utterance with the narratorial voice;

what Muzzioli calls the 'community of word' between the 'persuaded'[71], which we called, maybe more sceptically, 'paraphrase'.

On the one hand, these considerations seem coherent with the principle of 'following', which, in a Kantian sense, is evidence of the freedom of the genius in a state which cannot develop[72] (as Lloyd points out), and are thus coherent with the state of 'persuasion'. The examples are taken as a mere 'occasion' for the creation of a subjective, individual result, and their presence is an acknowledgement of this 'occasion'. On the other hand however, as the narrator does not fully escape the role of interpreter of the quotes, we could also argue the opposite.

The positioning of the quotes at the end of a demonstration, and their general aphoristic status help us to illuminate this point. Introductory sentences to the quotes, such as «onde dice il filosofo: [...]» (PR: 26); «questo ha detto l'oracolo di Delfo quando ha detto: [...]» (PR: 46); «Perciò Cristo ha l'aureola: [...]» (PR: 48); «per loro [gli uomini dell''educazione civile contemporanea'] disse Cristo: [...]» (PR: 95); «Elettra parla a loro quando dice a Crisotemide: [...]» (PR: 119), are all ways to reinforce the argument of authority at the end of the narratorial argumentation. However, a widespread insistence on the use of 'therefore', through synonyms or alternative formulation, builds an equation between the narratorial and the borrowed utterance which makes it possible for the argument of authority to work in two directions. It is true that the narrator 'is right' because he is coherent with an authority, but also, and more poignantly, the authority is affirmed as such because it is coherent with the argument of the narrator. This is crucial, because *La Persuasione e la Rettorica* deploys a series of 'persuaded authorities' which are not immediately recognizable as examples on the matter; their introduction is defended through the narratorial argument. The colon is exploited as the 'equal' of an equation which denotes a transparency of interpretation that is completely extraneous to the perlocutionary aim of the example to be 'followed'. Because it is based on the apodictic activity of the narrator, who defines the rules by which the example is 'exemplary of persuasion', the academic demonstration which precedes (and rarely follows or surrounds) the quotes is there to fulfil this pedagogical role.

The establishment of the Presocratics as original authorities on 'persuasion', and the substitution of any other possible authority on the matter, works through a crucial mediation: the narratorial argument is affirmed, and then contrasted with a reading of Plato and Aristotle in which their idea of 'persuasion' is dismantled. Because the Presocratics are 'saying the same thing as the narrator', the Platonic and Aristotelian points of view can be called a 'betrayal'[73]. What on one level was a logical argument, now becomes historical, and the Presocratics are given the status of original authorities on the topic.

This process has been possible only through an affirmation of indisputable value in the logical argument; the narrator invests himself with the authority of interpreting and defining the rule beyond the chosen example[74]. It is in this sense that a reading such as the one by Brianese[75], who sees *La Persuasione e la Rettorica* as producing its Greek sources as Schopenhauerian, gains its full value. This 'production' is embodied in the voice of the narrator, who, starting from his Schopenhauerian framework, interprets the authoritative sources and normalizes them in coherence with his ideology. The logical/academic genre of which the narrator partakes is improperly used to narrow down the possibilities embodied in the aphoristic quotes, endangering in this way the project of exemplarity and its relationship with 'persuasion'. The avoidance of an explicit discussion of the 'positive sources' comes in this sense indirectly back into the text as a system which is both a historical systematization and an affirmation of the validity of the argument of the narrator: we ought to call it, in contradiction with the agenda of an hyperbolic 'way to persuasion', its very foundation.

2.4   Conclusions

In both the theorization of exemplarity and its practice in the text it is possible to discover an ambiguity and incongruence which leads us to underline the affirmation of the point of view of the narrator and his rhetorical, logical/philosophical way of argumentation. On a theoretical level, within the concept of 'following exemplarity', which should free one from the rhetorical definition of rules, an exception is given in the form of the 'only' (PR: 62) rule of «non adattarti alla sufficienza di ciò che t'è dato» (ibid.). This statement was enough for us to imply a 'pedagogy of persuasion' in contrast with the following of its path. On the level of practice, the privilege accorded to the utterance of the narrator in relation to the production of the quotes as exemplary of 'persuasion' shows how this pedagogy, despite its artifice (consistently peculiar embodiment of the sources, high level of integration with the narratorial utterance, and so forth), remains the aim of the text.

At the core of this ambiguity of the text, on a theoretical level we discovered the Schopenhauerian definition of the origin of the discriminant between 'persuasion' and 'rhetoric' in the experience beyond the veil of Maya. It is this point that the 'rule', the 'only' rule which should lead to the absence of rules appears in the text; it is the engine that moves the hyperbolic way to persuasion, yet becomes sufficient for the narrator, who seems, in its affirmation, to comfortably 'adapt to the sufficiency' of this statement.

If considered in the economy of our general question on the status of the narrator in *La Persuasione e la Rettorica*, the present analysis shows how the foundation of Michelstaedter's philosophy is affirmed through the practice of exemplarity, but at the price of incoherence with the dialogical movement towards 'persuasion'; the narrator is affirmed in his role as the centre of the text, as the carrier of a definable (monologic/metaphisical) sense which founds the argument, produces it and ultimately 'returns to itself' as the 'truth of the text'. Hence, the narrator is affirmed in his heterodiegetic, authoritative, pedagogical component, that seems far from our hypothesis of a comparison with the narratorial strategies of the Italian Novecento.

This position of the narrator is precisely what constitutes the first level of undermining of his authority. This is not a paradox, if we consider that our interpretation of exemplarity started from a theory derived from the text itself. In other words, while the narrator provides a definition of 'following' as the rule for dealing with positive sources, his practice of quotation fails to fulfil this requirement; there is, in this sense, a contradiction between theory and practice that leads to the dismissal of the authoritative role of the generalising narrator. This is rather clear if we consider that *La Persuasione e la Rettorica* is conceived as an attack against systematization. Nevertheless, the importance of this point should not be underestimated. The undermining is an indication that the text fails to achieve a stable and authoritative conclusion. It does not fabricate a coherence, but rather exposes the narrator to the necessity of avoiding the fall into the construction of a philosophical system. If the 'way to persuasion' is a perpetual negation of one's own achievements, then the contradiction between theory and practice highlights the fact that the narrator cannot rest in a positive, conclusive affirmation. In a general sense, the text is called to define an argument, and by doing so, necessarily invests in a 'rhetorical' language. The contradiction that follows shows the inadequacy of the effort, negating it and moving the project on the hyperbolic way. On the other hand, by performing its inadequacy, the narrator ironically[76] evokes what he can only achieve in a negative sense: he engages in the 'war with words against words' as the only tool to address something which is necessarily 'other' than his contingent language.

A second level of undermining of the narratorial hermeneutical attempt with regard to exemplary quotation derives from what we could call the intrinsic failure of repetition. The embodiment of the positive quotes maintains a distance between narrator and source – a distance which allows the argument of authority – while at the same expressing an identical point of view. We called this process a defence, a confirmation, an echoing, a transparent interpretation: all definitions which have at their core the concept of 'repetition'. In the crossed-out preface to *La Persuasione e la Rettorica*, the narrator locates himself with regard to the ones who 'said persuasion', as someone who repeats the same words, as he knows and can: «se io ora lo ripeto per quanto so e posso» (PR: 4). This repetition cannot be, in any case, a hermeneutical transparency, a perfect equation, simply because it is necessarily engaging in a time-bound dialectic: it is 'interpretation'. In chapter 4, we will discuss this point to the end, following Paul De Man's analysis of the figure of allegory. In the present context, it is enough for us to highlight how a second level of undermining appears in the text not as a contraposition between theory and practice, but rather as the result of a dialectic between sections of the text, between practice and practice, form and form.

The full extent of this point can only be understood in the light of the complex juxtaposition of sub-genres, argumentative strategies and rhetorical figures that constitute the stylistic complexity of the text. In order to address this complexity, we will now move to an analysis of the treatment of the 'negative quotes', and their emblematic role in the organization of the voices in the text. This analysis will complete our framework, on which basis the fourth chapter will provide a general interpretation of the status of the text as read 'against itself'.

Notes

1. Paul De Man, *The Rhetoric of Romanticism* (New York: Columbia University Press, 1984).
2. Ibid.: 267. The quote continues: «the idea, in other words, of a teleological and apocalyptic history of consciousness is, of course, one of the most seductive, powerful, and deluded topoi of the idealist and romantic period» (ibid.) If this 'delusion' fits with De Man's reading of Kleist's *Über das Marionettentheater*, for sure it reminds of Michelstaedter's contradictions, both in his textual production and existential experience, as we outlined in our 'Introduction'. On this 'delusion' in regard to the project of 'persuasion', see for example Bini, 'Carlo Michelstaedter: the Tragedy of Thought'.
3. Furthermore, if the stylistic analysis reveals the absence of an affirmed centre of truth, and thus defines the self-referentiality of the text inside a negative logic of self-undermining, we

should again move back to the theoretical level and ask ourselves about the philosophical value of the 'hyperbolic' metaphor for 'persuasion', and its degree of certainty for our interpretation of the author. This is the kind of methodology which we outlined in the first chapters of our work.

4. Taviani, 'Attualità di Michelstaedter'; Muzzioli, 'Il Vociano Michelstaedter'.

5. This is coherent with Agosti's narratological approach for the analysis of the novel in the twentieth century, as discussed in our first chapter. See: Agosti, *Enunciazione e Racconto. Per una Semiologia della Voce Narrativa*.

6. In fact, while the two functions of an exemplary narrative, the narration itself and the injunction – as defined in Suleiman's seminal work: Susan Rubin Suleiman, *Authoritarian Fiction: The Ideological Novel as Literary Genre* (New York: Columbia University Press, 1983)– can be avoided in a simple example of a category, what is shared by both example and 'moral' exemplarity is the moment of interpretation, the hermeneutic link between the example and what the example stands for. If, as Suleiman states: «every story of an exemplary nature [...] is sooner or later designated, by the parabolic text itself, as needing interpretation, that is, as containing a meaning other (or more) than the immediate meaning of the events it recounts» (Suleiman, *Authoritarian Fiction: The Ideological Novel as Literary Genre*: 30), this is true also for the 'simple' example as the definition of a category. (On this point, see: John D. Lyons, *The Rhetoric of Example in Early Modern France and Italy* (Princeton: Princeton University Press, 1989): 10 et passim). This is the first concern of the narrator: interpreting an example without 'freezing' it into the rhetoric of a system; an example which avoids the degree of formalization that seems to be the necessary environment for its appearance.

7. Austin defines a perlocutionary act as follows: «the perlocutionary act may be either the achievement of a perlocutionary object (convince, persuade) or the production of a perlocutionary sequel»: see J. L. Austin, *How to do Things with Words* (Oxford: Clarendon Press, 1975): 118. In our context the term will be used to define the consequences of the 'persuasive word': moving the interlocutor on her/his own individual path to 'persuasion'.

8. With all the problems implied. For a historical excursus of this powerful rhetorical strategy, which strongly relies on the feature of 'induction', see: Wanda Ostrowska Kaufmann, *The Anthropology of Wisdom Literature* (Westport: Bergin & Garvey, 1996).

9. The Latin maxim *duo cum faciunt idem non est idem*, generally ascribed to Terence, appears in Arthur Schopenhauer, *Parerga and Paralipomena. Short Philosophical Essays*, trans. E. F. J. Payne, II vols. (Oxford: Clarendon Press, 1974): 463, as Campailla acknowledges in his note (PR: 317). See also the note in the English translation: Carlo Michelstaedter, *Persuasion and Rhetoric*, trans. Russel Scott Valentino, Cinzia Sartini Blum, and David J. Depew (New Haven, London: Yale University Press, 2004): 57. However, the exact variant adopted by Michelstaedter appears in Gottlob Frege's 1892 article on *Sinn* and *Bedeutung*; the quote can be now found in: Gottlob Frege, *The Frege Reader*, ed. Michael Beaney (Oxford; Malden, MA: Blackwell Publishers, 1997): 155. Given Michelstaedter's interest in mathematics, this could be a point of departure for further analysis, which unfortunately exceeds our goals.

10. See our chapter 1.

11. For a discussion on authority as a function for the efficacy of the rhetoric of exemplarity, see De Man's reading of Kleist's *Ueber das Marionettentheatre*, in: De Man, *The Rhetoric of Romanticism*: 263-90.

12. We could discuss, inside a Kantian framework, the figure of Christ as exemplary in the sense of «the necessity of the agreement [...] in a judgement that can be considered as an

example for a general rule that cannot be stated» Immanuel Kant, *Critique of Judgement,* trans. J. H. Bernard (Mineola, New York: Dover Publications, 2005): section 18. This is coherent with the idea of the incommunicability of 'persuasion' in terms of the definition of a rule; moreover, the «positing of such a generality [of the rule] as the condition for predication and communicability» (Alexander Gelley, 'Introduction,' in *Unruly Examples. On the Rhetoric of Exemplarity*, ed. Alexander Gelley (Stanford: Stanford University Press, 1995): 9) is coherent with the ways in which 'persuasion' is introduced in the argument of the text. In any case, the problems arising in the excerpt remain.

13. Following De Man: «teaching becomes possible only when a degree of formalization is put in the subject matter» De Man, *The Rhetoric of Romanticism*: 270.

14. Gelley, 'Introduction': 13.

15. Alexander Gelley, 'The Pragmatics of Exemplary Narrative,' in *Unruly Examples. On the Rhetoric of Exemplarity,* ed. Alexander Gelley (Stanford: Stanford University Press, 1995): 156.

16. Suleiman's model: *Suleiman, Authoritarian Fiction: The Ideological Novel as Literary Genre.*

17. Gelley, 'The Pragmatics of Exemplary Narrative': 145.

18. It is for this reason that a reading such as Brianese's, who sees Michelstaedter 'producing' the Presocratics as Schopenhauerians is possible: from the Schopenhauerian framework of the narrator we move to the understanding of the Presocratic examples. See: Brianese, 'Michelstaedter e i Greci. Appunti per un Confronto'.

19. Michelstaedter's critique of Kant as a «proletario della filosofia» comes in a sharp passage against philosophy as a 'rhetoric' of «risolvere problemi» (O: 666). Furthermore, in the notes on Empedocles, Michelstaedter produces a critique of *a priori* categories: «io arrivo alla realtà in sé attraverso la realtà dei sensi quando applico a questa i valori del mio *IO assoluto*. Ma siccome io *filosofo*, bisogna ch'io dica che questa applicazione non è arbitraria, ma che ho *applicato categorie assolute esistenti a priori in ogni anima*» (PEE: 64-5). This dismissal is evidence of Michelstaedter's familiarity with the work of the German, and similarities between the concept of 'following' an example and the behaviour of the Kantian genius imply a theorization which cannot be invested by the above critique; on the contrary, it can be conceived as a solution to the problem. We will see in our chapter 4 how Michelstaedter's investment in genius and artistic language partakes of a romantic development and critique of Kantian categories.

20. Kant, *Critique of Judgement*:121.

21. See: David Lloyd, 'Kant's Examples,' in *Unruly Examples. On The Rhetoric of Exemplarity,* ed. Alexander Gelley (Stanford: Stanford University Press, 1995): 266.

22. Ibid.

23. The continuation of Lloyd's quote is of some further interest: «Paradoxically for the aesthetics, the repetition proper to genius is one that cannot *develop* and for precisely that reason leaves the freedom of the subject intact» (ibid.). Our former discussion on the state of 'persuasion' as the moment of pure self-possession, emancipated from time and space on the line of absolute Justice (see our first chapter), shows how much the concept of 'persuasion' shares with a Kantian definition of genius. These points will gain their crucial importance in the final part of our enquiry, where we will try to link the poetic of *La Persuasione e la Rettorica* with the rest of Michelstaedter's artistic production, and in particular with the Leopardian and romantic influences in Michelstaedter's philosophical framework.

24. Kant, *Critique of Judgement*: 121. However, Michelstaedter's speculation seems to ambiguously live between two poles: 'it is an art if it only shows this by examples; it is a

science if it derives the possibility of such judgements from the nature of these faculties, as cognitive faculties in general' Kant, *Critique of Judgement:* 96. The goal of our research is also to come to terms with this ambiguity.

25. See again: Lloyd, 'Kant's Examples':266.

26. Thomas Harrison, 'The Michelstaedter Enigma,' *Differentia: Review of Italian Thought,* no. 8-9 Spring/Autumn (1999): electronic copy, page numbers not given.

27. In this sense, the reflection on aesthetics has a rather explicit importance in the development of the argument on the language of the 'persuaded'; much more than is argued for example by Stella: «il problema estetico ne risulta avviluppato e assorbito tanto da non affiorare se non per implicazione e incidentalmente nelle espresse domande di conoscenza e nei momenti di precisazione del processo logico» Vittorio Stella, 'La Riflessione sull'Arte in Michelstaedter' in *Dialoghi Intorno a Michelstaedter,* ed. Sergio Campailla (Gorizia: Biblioteca Satale Isontina, 1987): 137 ; this 'definition of the logical process' shifts the definition of the 'persuaded' to the realm of aesthetic.

28. The text addresses the problem of education in its critique of Plato's *Republic,* dismissing it as «ammaestramento che ha un determinato scopo sufficiente nella vita» (PR: 148). This is considered a betrayal of Socratic education: «[a]himè, non più l'educazione che sommuove dall'intimo l'individuo, e imponendogli l'identità con sé stesso (persuasione) lo porta alla giustizia e alla pace [...]» (ibid.).

29. Which is a measure of inadequacy.

30. The article by Lloyd we quoted above is devoted to a discussion of these points.

31. The concept of 'disruption', and the focus on the formal marks that testify the disruption embodied by the quoted voice (for example quotation marks, italic, etc) is borrowed from the analysis of modern American poetry conducted by Leonard Diepeveen, *Changing Voices. The Modern Quoting Poem* (Ann Arbour: University of Michigan Press, 1993).

32. For links with the biographical background, see for example Asor Rosa, "La Persuasione e la Rettorica' di Carlo Michelstaedter'; Campailla, *A Ferri Corti con la Vita* for the interpretation of ancient Greek as a sort of atemporal language of the 'persuaded human', see Muzzioli, *Michelstaedter:* 15. We will briefly discuss this latest point in the next sub-chapter.

33. PR: 35. It is known that Michelstaedter had a rough knowledge of French (see our introduction).

34. In the manuscript, italics are rendered through underlining, sometimes in pen, sometimes in pencil, this supporting the hypothesis of a stress, a further emphasis, added in the context of a later correction. For an interpretation of this feature in the manuscripts, and the connection between underlining in pencil and a preaching, oral, tone, interpreted as «intenzione dialogica della scrittura michelstaedteriana, il continuo riferimento ad un interlocutore» see Franchi's editorial note in Carlo Michelstaedter, *Il Prediletto Punto d'Appoggio della Dialettica Socratica e Altri Scritti,* ed. Gianandrea Franchi (Milano: Mimesis, 2000).

35. The end of the preceding paragraph is a quote in ancient Greek from Simonides. Its position as a concluding aphorism shows the parallel between narratorial original aphoristic sentences (often in a foreign language), and the strategies of embodiment of intertextual sources, to which this first part of our chapter is devoted. In this case, the 'double disruption' (Greek quote and German original) can be seen to support our argument, and underline an attempt by the narrator to adopt the style of his quotes, orienting each utterance in the same direction of the embodied voices not only at the level of ideology, but also, inextricably, at the level of form.

36. See for example the definition given by Bice Mortara Garavelli: «una sentenza dotata di capacità definitoria è l'aforisma [...], che concentra in una sola proposizione o in una composizione brevissima giudizi e riflessioni morali, resoconti di esperienze, asserzioni riguardanti un sapere specifico (filosofico, politico, medico ecc.)» Bice Mortara Garavelli, *Manuale di Retorica* (Milano: Bompiani, 2002): 248. The relationship between aphorism as a sub-genre and the problem of writing 'against' rhetoric will be addressed later in this chapter, and more comprehensively in our last chapter.

37. The manuscript A of *La Persuasione e la Rettorica* shows the genesis of this short poem through a series of attempts and variants, attesting to the originality of the utterance and reinforcing its emblematic importance (it is a note between page 66 and 67 of the manuscript A: FCM: III 3 c). There is a particular effort to put the sentence in the shape of an epigrammatic poem.

38. The few more German quotes come from the Austro Hungarian code (PR: 99, 101) and in this sense they are not original inventions of the narrator. The context in which they appear (PR: 101) is the discussion of the rhetoric of the State and its organization and therefore they partake of the pole of 'rhetoric'.

39. There are no specific enquiries into the original Greek adopted by the author, in terms of philological sources, developments, and so forth. This topic will not be addressed here, both for lack of specialized competence in the area, and relative importance for our goals. We will consider original ancient Greek sentences more as a sub-genre, which has strong parallels with the embodied intertextual quotes, and reveals a common orientation of narratorial and imported voices.

40. In the *Apology of Socrates* (37, C) and in *Gorgias* (512 e), the meaning of the term is coherent with Michelstaedter's use, but in *La Persuasione e la Rettorica* the term is highly charged and assumes an original value in the speculation.

41. We speak of a continuum, given the various loose and approximate ways in which the quotes, as we acknowledged, are referred in the text, particularly in the first part. We will come back to this point in the next section.

42. Campailla, Sergio, note in PR: 309.

43. Ibid.

44. Translated by Campailla in his 'Notes' as: «qualcosa è – qualcosa è per me – mi è possibile la speranza – sono sufficiente» (PR: 311): 'something is – something is for me – for me hope is possibile – I am sufficient'.

45. Muzzioli, *Michelstaedter*: 14-5. In chapter one we discussed the ambiguity of the positive examples as 'examples of persuasion'.

46. Brianese, 'Michelstaedter e i Greci. Appunti per un Confronto': 23-48: 28 et passim. For a discussion of the unifying reasons for the definition of a singular foundational element in the Presocratics, I find of the highest interest the contribution of Havelock: Eric A. Havelock, 'The Linguistic Task of the Presocratics' in *Language and Thought in Early Greek Philosophy,* ed. Kevin Robb (La Salle: Hegeler Institute, 1983).

47. With modalities of embodiment of the quotations which are drastically different from the first part, and which we will have the chance to analyze.

48. Brianese, 'Michelstaedter e i Greci. Appunti per un Confronto': 25.

49. However, our goal is far from Brianese's theoretical/philosophical interpretation of the supposed fidelity to the positive sources, and instead focuses on the structures of this production and embodiment, and the degree of difference/dialogue established between this construction and the ideology of the narrator.

50. Theodor Gomperz, *Greek Thinkers: A History of Ancient Philosophy* (London: Murray,

1901-12). The presence of this text is evidence of the fact that Michelstaedter had knowledge of secondary sources, and furthermore, that they play a part in the development of his speculation. On the one hand, this is confirmation that the avoidance of a discussion of and through secondary material is a conscious decision; on the other, it opens the possibility of a study of the hidden and implicit presence of these sources in the text. Unfortunately, the latter exceeds the object of our study.

51. In fact, it is a comment regarding an intervention by Mullach on the original Greek text, challenged by Michelstaedter in order to doctor his quote (PR: 13). Mullach is by no means explicitly acknowledged as a secondary source on which the position of the narrator of *La Persuasione e la Rettorica* is moulded.

52. In his list, Benevento does not explicitly specify the categories under which a sentence is defined as a quotation. For example, he seems to acknowledge a series of quotes, regardless to the presence of a reference to the text and graphic marks (quotation marks, inverted commas, and so on). This is the case with the sentence «*si duo idem faciunt non est idem*» (PR: 62), discussed above. I think that an enquiry into the intertextuality of Michelstaedter's work in order to define the opaque border between intentional and unintentional quotation – see at least: William Iwin, 'What is an Allusion?,' *The Journal of Aesthetics and Art Criticism* 59, no. 3 (2001); Ziva Ben-Porat, 'The Poetics of Literary Allusion,' *PTL: A Journal for Descriptive Poetics and Theory of Literature* 1 (1976) - and between that and intentional and unintentional allusions and paraphrase risks complicating the matter to the point of losing the sight of the most important feature of the text. As we will discuss later, Michelstaedter's practice of embodying quotes in the voice of the narrator, minimizes the discontinuity between the two texts but does not reach the point of erasing the minimal acknowledgement of the source, the borrowed authority, the example. This is the very cause of a problem of exemplarity which concerns us in our reading of the interaction of the ideologies of the text, and I assume that where the source is omitted, as in the case of Schopenhauer, this exemplary nature of the quote is lacking. This happens for example in the case of a hidden allusion to Aristotle's *Physics* (207 a): PR: 11. Furthermore, Benevento does not distinguish between quotes embodied in support of the argument and negative examples, which are attacked and undermined; a crucial distinction in our treatment of the matter. While the habitual embodiment of the 'Preface' as part of the object of analysis is again foreign to our approach, the exclusion of the 'Appendici Critiche' (probably caused by the fact that Benevento is reading the text in the Adelphi 1983 edition by Campailla, without the appendices) is coherent with our analysis in this chapter. In fact, the treatment of quotes in the 'Appendici' is clearly closer to the rhetoric of the academy; an extensive re-encoding of Plato and Aristotle counterpoints the logical dismantling of the shifts in their philosophy, with the goal giving 'acceptable' support to the first part of the thesis. In chapter 4, I will discuss this strategy, so close to the rhetoric against which *La Persuasione e la Rettorica* is devoted. Despite these differences, I am convinced that Benevento's work needs to be acknowledged as one of the few cases in which a close reading of the text through the framework of rhetorical analysis is deployed with the goal of a philosophical understanding of the author.

53. Benevento, ' 'La Persuasione e la Rettorica' di Michelstaedter e la 'Concretezza Artistica'': 120.

54. As discussed in our chapter 1.

55. This 'fight on Plato' has been comprehensively treated by Cacciari in his excellent article: Cacciari, 'La Lotta 'su' Platone'.

56. See also, for example, the entire quotation of a short song in the dialect of Veneto (PR: 35).

57. «The proof from a number of particular cases that such is the rule, is called in Dialectic induction, in Rhetoric example» (Aristotele ret. 1.2.1356b., Lyons, *The Rhetoric of Example in Early Modern France and Italy*: 6).

58. As in Perelman Olbrechts-Tyteca: «L'argomento del prestigio più nettamente caratteristico è l'argomento d'autorità, che si serve degli atti o dei giudizi di una persona o di un gruppo di persone come mezzo di prova in favore di una tesi» Chaïm Perelman and Lucie Olbrechts-Tyteca, *Trattato dell'Argomentazione. La Nuova Retorica* (Torino: Einaudi, 1966): 323. See also their pages on the model and anti-model: Perelman and Olbrechts-Tyteca, *Trattato dell'Argomentazione. La Nuova Retorica*: 383-92.

59. Diepeveen, *Changing Voices. The Modern Quoting Poem*.

60. Ibid.: 9.

61. Ibid.:13. While I agree in principle, I would speak rather about 'narrating voice' than 'author', even if the context is, as in Diepeveen, a poem.

62. Nor for Diepeveen: his text is devoted to defending the coincidence of quotation and dialogue in his corpus, in ways which are too far from the context of our analysis to be discussed here.

63. We have already acknowledged the difference in the quotation practice of the 'Appendici', giving the reasons for the necessity of addressing this topic in chapter 4. See also the accurate referencing in the academic works collected in the volume of *Scritti Scolastici* (SS).

64. My source for texts and translations from Parmenides is: Parmenides of Elea, *Fragments*, ed. David Gallop, trans. David Gallop (Toronto, Buffalo, London: University of Toronto Press, 1984). Michelstaedter quotes vv.5-6 of 'Fragment 8' (Parmenides of Elea, *Fragments*: 64-5).

65. Of the Campailla edition we are quoting.

66. Saint Luke, VI, 39.

67. 'For whosoever will save his life will lose it', Saint Matthew, XVI, 25 (*The Bible. Authorized King James Version*. Edited by Robert Carrol and Stephen Prickett. Oxford, New York: Oxford University Press, 1997).

68. The only fully referred quote in the body of the text is from Aeschilus (PR: 23).

69. Suleiman, *Authoritarian Fiction: The Ideological Novel as Literary Genre*.

70. Gelley, 'Introduction'.

71. See above in the present chapter.

72. See: Lloyd, 'Kant's Examples': 266.

73. «Nel *Fedro* Platone realizza con efficacia insuperata il valore della *via socratica* di fronte all'altrui impotenza, e in quel punto *dandola come finita e considerandola, vi s'è già fermato*» (PR: 172).

74. Moving the project away from the Kantian 'reflective judgement'.

75. Brianese, 'Michelstaedter e i Greci. Appunti per un Confronto'.

76. This is the 'second', general irony, not directly adopted for the dismissal of ideologies or points of view, which we discussed in our introduction.

CHAPTER THREE

Examples of Rhetoric: Negative Quotes and Undermining Strategies

Fadensonnen / über der grauschwarzen Ödnis.

Paul Celan

«$\mathbf{M}$a dimmi, non potresti tu di Eraclito convertirti in Democrito? La qual cosa va pure accadendo a me cha la stimava impossibilissima?»[1]. This exhortation by Giacomo Leopardi in a letter to Pietro Giordani is emblematic of the shift in the object of analysis in this third chapter. Here we conduct an enquiry into the parodic and sarcastic strategies adopted by the narrator of *La Persuasione e la Rettorica* in order to undermine a philosophical/ ideological position and reveal it as an example of 'rhetoric': hence, we are introducing the concept (and practice) of laughter. We are not however about to draw a comprehensive parallel between the laughter of *La Persuasione e la Rettorica* and that of the poet from Recanati; instead, we will be concerned with interpreting the exploitation of satire and a particular type of parody – which we will define in Bakhtinian terms as 'stylized parody' – in the light of the importance that 'sarcastic laughter' gains in the text. 'Sarcastic' is in fact the voice from beyond the veil of Maya which utters the horror of the consciousness of the 'nothingness' of human beings and human values[2]. Given that sarcasm and parody are, generally speaking, two ways of dismissing an argument, we will map their different prerogatives and read them through the dialectic of dismissal, undermining and self-undermining implied in the hyperbolic movement.

The object of analysis which offers us the opportunity to approach such themes is once again quotation. Yet in this chapter, the focus will be on intertextual voices embodied as negative, 'rhetorical' examples. In *La Persuasione e la Rettorica*, apart from the 'Appendici Critiche', there are very few cases in which an external voice is directly quoted as an example of 'rhetoric' and presented in order to be dismantled by narratorial reasoning. However, the rare occurrences are important for understanding the ways in which the dialectic developed by the narrator in his stylistic practice refers to the theoretical and poetic statements in the text. Again, we are entering into a discussion of the ways in which, and the reasons why, the text does or does not deliver that which it professes. Moreover, 'negative quotes' offer us a small enough object to highlight stylistic practices which are recurrent and crucial for the interpretation of the strategies of dismissal and the mechanisms for juxtaposition of sub-genres, and which are are widely adopted in other contexts in the text.

In the case of the embodiment of negative quotes – examples of 'rhetoric' – what enters directly into play is the philosophical role given to the dialectic of undermining and its stylistic consequences. In order to approach this problem, we will focus on what is arguably one of the most complex occurrences.

3.1   The «grosso signore» and Hegel

On a few occasions in the first part of the text, 'negative quotes', as examples of 'rhetoric', appear in a context which renders their embodiment by the narrator, complex and revelatory of a stylistic struggle to embrace a dialectic that would avoid falling into a logical determinism; that is, the monologism of a simple affirmation of a philosophical truth 'against' a negative example. The adoption of a series of different strategies – sarcasm, satire, parody – performs an immediate distancing from the reproduction of the same (academic, philosophical) rhetoric he is attacking, both theoretically and stylistically. In this sense, the analysis offers the chance to understand the philosophical concept of 'persuasion' through the stylistic practice of the narrator, further comparing the style with the poetic expressed in the text. The complexity and incongruence of the example we are considering, not least its 'ambiguities', will embrace also the interpretation of other, more 'linear' treatments of negative examples.

3.1.1   The «grosso signore»

The borrowed voice with which we are concerned is the one of Hegel's *Philosophie der Geschichte*. It occurs at the beginning of the chapter on 'La

Rettorica nella Vita', where the narrator introduces a fictional dialogue to represent the role of the human in modern society, with its false certitudes, search for safety, and development of rhetorical values. The dialogue is a fictional recollection of a discussion that the narrator had with a «grosso signore» after an «abbondante pranzo» (PR: 89). Here, in a climactic and paroxistic development, the sarcastic/questioning role of the narrator presents his interlocutor with the ridiculous nature his positions[3]. The prototype of the 'average man' of the time is dismantled: his advertised temperance, his balance between enjoyment of life and avoidance of excesses, and, the need to fulfil the duties of a social role in order to «portare il contributo alla grande opera di civiltà in pro dell'umanità» (PR: 91), are shown in their negative light as fragile covers that guarantee the safety of self-perpetuation and render humans blind to the pain of their condition. The dialogue lays bare the mechanism behind 'fear of death', 'self-perpetuation', 'rhetoric' and 'blindness towards death'. The search for small and temporary pleasures, «ma non da eccentrico! Ma nella via e nel modo come il nostro provvido tempo facili e leciti che li offre» (PR: 90); joy for the benefits guaranteed by fitting into a social role, «[l]o stipendio ... corre ed è sicuro», «c'è la pensione: – lo Stato non abbandona i suoi fedeli» (PR: 91), and the safety of this kind of existence, «appartengo ad una cassa per ammalati [...]. Il nostro ospedale ha tutti i comodi moderni [...].» (ibid.), all lead to the ultimate, ridiculous blindness: «ma infine morire – moriamo tutti!», protests the narrator, and the ready answer is «fa niente, sono assicurato pel caso di morte. [...] Come vede [...] sono in una botte di ferro, come si suol dire» (PR: ibid.).

It is interesting to point out how the major philosophical themes of Michelstaedter's thought are synthesized here in a form derived mainly[4] from Leopardi's *Operette Morali*. Bellucci identifies a parallel between this passage and the *Dialogo di Tristano e di un Amico*[5], and supports it through Michelstaedter's epigraph from the *Palinodia*: «di molti / tristi e miseri tutti, un popol fanno / lieto e felice» (PR: 89)[6]. She further stresses the common polemic «contro lo scientismo, il tecnicismo, il macchinismo, il grasso ottimismo borghese»[7], showing the extent to which this intertextual reference – seemingly carrying a degree of intentionality both at the level of the chosen sub-genre and its development under the umbrella of the quote from the *Palinodia* – is of great importance for opening the possibility of an interpretation of the core of Michelstaedter's philosophy through a Leopardian lens, with particular regard to the definition and consciousness of the 'nothingness' which represents the existential condition, the ways to affirm it, and the consequences for the thinker/artist/poet facing it. In this sense, a reading of Michelstaedter's interpretation of Leopardi, drawing on a wide range of critical studies, beginning with the seminal works of Campailla[8], allows not only to outline stylistic parallels, borrowings of images, lexicon, genre, structure, and allusions and so forth, but takes us to the most important problems in our enquiry: the interpretation of Michelstaedter's nihilism, the relationship between it and 'persuasion', the role of language (and art in particular) in the uttering of this nihilism and – again – the consequences for the project of 'persuasion'[9]. Daniela Bini, in her study on 'Leopardi e Michelstaedter tra Autenticità e Inautenticità'[10] shows the possibilities offered by this point of view, and offers evidence for interpreting Michelstaedter through this intertextual comparison[11]. Given the pertinence and strength of this theme for our goals, this will be a concluding point in our final chapter, where we will try to define Michelstaedter's works by locating them in a net of possible contextualizing references[12].

A further theme which brings together this passage of *La Persuasione e la Rettorica* with the Leopardian speculation is the critique of the construction of philosophical systems of thought. On the level of genre, the option for the philosophical dialogue or the 'operetta morale' can be discussed in both authors as an attempt to avoid the rhetoric of philosophy or, in Michelstaedter's case, of the academy. Moreover, on the level of content, the intolerance of systems, so present in Leopardi[13], directly follows this Leopardian dialogue in *La Persuasione e la Rettorica*, thus emphasizing the meaningfulness of the link. While dialogue could be interpreted generally as a more open genre, in fact, the position of the «grosso signore» is explained in the text as an example of the opposite, as the high peak of systematization, the individual 'dreamed' by Hegel as the 'apex' of his philosophical system.

3.1.2 Hegel

The final utterance of the man in the 'botte di ferro' and the narrator's comment on his own stupor are followed by a series of Hegelian quotes. These borrowings function in the text as an explanation of the preceding dialogue:

> Quest'uomo del suo tempo [...] è dunque l'individuo sognato da Hegel al sommo della chiesa gotica che gli antichi ignoravano – all'ultimo momento della libera evoluzione del sistema della libertà; – egli è l'obiettivazione della libertà fine a sé stessa e di sé stessa gode; è la persona ch'egli veste nell'esercizio della sua carica, quella è la

seconda natura – la libertà morale, medio concreto che unifica l'idea e le passioni umane – fine essenziale dell'esistenza soggettiva, unione della volontà soggettiva e della *volontà razionale*: questa è dunque l'idea divina, ciò che Iddio ha inteso fare col mondo per ritrovare sé stesso. – (PR: 92).

Generally speaking, this paragraph is composed as a series of sentences from Hegel, and explains the man of the dialogue as a Hegelian product. It is a 'transparent' equation where the man in the 'botte di ferro' = Hegelian philosophy = rhetorical system blind to human existential status. This equation extends the dismissal of the character in the dialogue to the philosophical source which is considered to be his origin (his cause). The satire[14] of the man in the 'botte di ferro' reveals itself more or less directly as a satire of Hegel. Hegel (an implicit and clearly drastic interpretation of Hegel) is put on stage in order to ridicule the 'social consequences' of his philosophical rhetoric, and subsequently pilloried and spaced out. From this point on, the relationship of the narrator with this source is characterized by a series of affirmed distances and rejections of the embodied voice. On a thematic level, the deafness of the «grosso signore», his unbelievable and unshakeable optimism in the face of narrator's questioning, and the ultimately impossible mediation between the points of view of the two interlocutors (their reciprocal deafness), account for this first movement of spacing-out.

In the text that follows the dialogue, this distance and the parodic/dismissive treatment of Hegel are carried out as a comment and an explanation 'with' and 'through' an Hegelian vocabulary. In the reduction, translation and paraphrase of quotes from the *Philosophie der Geschichte*, we can see how the critique, which in the satire of the «grosso signore» was circumscribed through the mimesis of the dialogue to the level of the 'existential consequences' of a philosophy, moves to the level of the philosophical style and vocabulary through which the philosophical thoughts are expressed. On a formal level this shifting implies the choice of parodic sub-genre: if the dialogue of the man in the «botte di ferro» is a satire on the consequences of Hegelianism as an apology of an 'ideology of insurance', the subsequent discussion of Hegel dismisses his rhetoric and philosophical ideology with and through his vocabulary. It is a parody which completes the equation: man in the «botte» = Hegel, man's words = Hegel's rhetoric. This is the second movement of spacing-out. The series of translations/paraphrases from the *Philosophie der Geschichte,* exploited by the narrator in order to build and demonstrate[15] his equation, all in all fit with a broad definition of parody: «a repetition with critical distance, which marks difference rather than similarity»[16]. This is a broad definition[17] because it embraces a series of different poles of the discourse on parody: mainly the question of the solidarity/distance from the parodied object and the question of the seriousness or comic nature of certain parodies (we could also say: the various degree of dismissal in which the parody is engaged, and the tools to obtain it)[18].

It can also fit narrower requirements. It is clear that the narratorial feeling towards Hegel is not at all sympathetic, indeed the intent is to dismiss the philosopher after having ridiculed him, thus the question of solidarity/distance that parody seems to imply can assist us in identifying the rhetorical strategies that the narrator is exploiting in order to fulfil his intent, and fits with a more structured definition of the genre[19]. To say that parody implies both a certain 'vicinity' and 'distance' from the parodied source, is to acknowledge the ambiguity of the process of embodying a foreign style in order to parody it. The etymology of the term gives a full account of this ambiguity, the prefix 'para' describing 'both nearness and opposition'[20], a feature originating with Aristophanes' *Frogs*[21]. One of the clearest manifestations of this ambiguity, and the one that most concerns us, is the the necessity for the parodying text to 'perform' or 're-encode' the parodied one in terms of point of view, discourse, genre or vocabulary, in order to perform, paradoxically enough, the very parodic distance itself[22]. Bakhtin's comment on this topic, with reference to the opening sonnets of *Don Quixote* is famous: «In a parodied sonnet, the sonnet form is not a genre at all; that is, it is not the form of a whole, but is rather *the object of representation*: the sonnet here is the *hero of the parody*. [...] But, in any case, what results is not a sonnet but rather the image of a sonnet»[23].

In the case of the Hegel example, the adoption of a parodic mode, following the satire against the social exemplification of Hegelianism, allows the narrator to shift the target of dismissal to the level of style and thus to a particular rhetoric. In a vocabulary closer to the text: the narrator reveals the 'rhetorical' nature of the philosophy of the German: «Quest'uomo del suo tempo – colla sua προθυμία e la sua <botte di ferro> è dunque l'individuo sognato da Hegel al sommo della chiesa gotica che gli antichi ignoravano» (PR: 92). In this sentence we already find two re-encodings of Hegel – the allusions to 'the men of his time' and 'the gothic church ignored by the ancient' – fully acknowledged as such in a series of footnotes: a rare yet crucial appearance which will play a further role in the process of undermining and dismissing.

The exploitation of these Hegelian borrowings in the constitution of the parody can be understood in Bakhtinian terms as 'parodic stylization'[24]; these together resolve in a stylization of the German philosopher, in the sense of a conventional rendering of the embodied voice and its objectives[25]. This reduction to conventionality – or the reduction of Hegel to what Hegel has to be in order to fulfil his function in the economy of the text, a very common feature in the practice of quotation[26] – is conducted through a juxtaposition of translations and paraphrases which become a series of maxims, slogans, marked words and sentences in order to evoke a well known rhetoric. Juxtaposition is crucial to the intent of ridicule; it is in fact organized starting from «l'uomo del suo tempo», to the depiction of this man as «l'obiettivazione della libertà che è fine a se stessa e di se stessa gode», and finally as «ciò che Iddio ha inteso di fare col mondo per ritrovare se stesso» (PR: 92). The substitution of 'the State'[27] with the man in the «botte di ferro», with the latter climactically ascending to become 'god's will' renders the passage comic; the former satirical depiction of the man and his present re-definition in Hegelian terms (words) turn the paragraph into a satirized parody, a conventional rendering that has the goal of stressing the opposition between the hosting and the hosted voice[28].

3.2   Parody and 'persuasion'

Following this analysis, it is possible to define a general tendency in the text to treat negative quotes in accordance with a positive versus negative dichotomy, not dialectic and without mediation, coherently with the hyperbolic movement. We have discussed the contradictory nature of this agenda in the case of exemplary quotes and the few 'flags' in the text[29] which, while seeming to undermine the project, stand as moments of self-reflection in the general economy of the text and its objectives. It is now possible to approach a specific interpretation of how the type of sarcastic/parodic undermining in which the narrator is engaged fulfils the requirements implied by the ethic of 'looking beyond the veil of Maya'.

At first glance, the parody of Hegel seems to be a repetition of the sarcastic voice discussed in our first chapter: the voice that resounds in the obscurity, when humans experience the painful nightmare that gives them sudden consciousness of the groundlessness of their values, and beliefs. The «riso», il «ghigno sarcastico» (PR: 22, 23), which says «niente, niente, niente, non sei niente, so che non sei niente» (PR: 23), are clearly reproduced in our example, when the interlocutor of the dialogue, the «grosso signore», is ridiculed by a voice who (in the general tone of the mimesis, in its role in producing the climactic paroxism and, explicitly, in the concluding sentence) lays bare the cover against fear of death that gives birth to this 'rhetoric'. To this extent the narrator locates himself with regard to the 'way to persuasion'. But can we extend this interpretation to the treatment of Hegelian quotes? In order to answer this question, we need to address one final point in the reading of the narratorial parody; here, the narrator addresses the most important ambiguity of the genre and, in some rhetorical ways tries to 'turn' parody against itself: this is the final moment of spacing-out and rejection of Hegel.

If the dialogue with the «grosso signore» carries the weight of the critique of the 'social consequences' of Hegelianism, and the parodic quotation of the German shifts the focus to his language – his peculiar 'rhetoric' – then 'stylized parody' may be the most aggressively oppositive way to adopt the parodic genre. We could argue that in the possible practices of parody, Michelstaedter's use occupies a very traditional place (traditional mostly in its burlesque dismissal of its object) in comparison with broader and more comprehensive definitions such as the one adopted by Hutcheon. However, despite this drastic dismissal by the narrator, which seems to converge with the necessity of reproducing the irreducible dichotomy between 'rhetoric' and the 'way to persuasion', a certain degree of ambiguity remains. This is precisely the ambiguity implied by parody as a genre. The parodied text can be treated only after having become part of the parodying one, and thus, using the example of the sonnet we quoted from Bakhtin, the parody of a sonnet is (a figure of) a sonnet. The narrator of *La Persuasione e la Rettorica* seems in this particular case clearly aware of this point, and in the footnotes he sets up the final attempt of spacing his source out of the re-encoding text, rendering it in this way a sort of 'absolute negative' which exceeds the possibilities of parody.

In the first of the footnotes on Hegel (PR: 92) (where the reference for the translations/paraphrases we discussed is given), the narrator's ultimate dismissal of Hegelian style comes from an admission of impotence: «non traduco le citazioni da Hegel perché dispero di poter riprodurre in italiano il loro ineffabile callopismatismo –»; consequently, the following references are presented in their original language. This statement, while obviously a flag to underline the parodic treatment in the Italian re-encoding of Hegel in the main text, is also a comment on the insufficiency of that same parodic treatment. If the quotes are untranslatable because any translation would fail to reproduce their 'ineffable kallopismatism', then Hegel is in a sense 'beyond parody'. While in the body of the text the parody works precisely through and because of the translations, the inherent loss of Hegelian style in the process of embodiment/translation renders the parody inadequate and underscores a distancing of the narrator from the source.

3.3   Reciprocal orientation of genres

In stressing the role of the narratorial utterance in defining the insufficiency of the re-encoding parody for the 'reproduction' of Hegel – which on the one hand shifts the parodic role to the quotes in the footnote, and, on the other, sanctions the otherness of Hegelian rhetoric with regard to the positive project of the text – we are introducing a discussion on the reciprocal orientation of two different sub-genres. Firstly, we have what we could call the 'academic narrator', expressing himself at the margin of the text (in a footnote) with all the characteristics of the academic genre outlined in our first chapter: omniscience, cognition, meta-diegesis. In coherence with this status, he affirms his ideology on different levels. In the footnote itself, he addresses both the dismissal of Hegel's 'optimistic rhetoric' and the parodic translation, with the consequence of pushing the parodic effect to the limit; he thus underlines the opposition between the encoded and the encoding text, stressing the rejection of the model through the impossibility of its reproduction. Moreover, the role of the generalizing narrator is extended both before and after the introduction of the parodic sub-genre. As for the role of the narrator after the parody, we will see how the dismissal of Hegel is followed by a further affirmation of the narrator's philosophical framework[30], offering to the dialectic movement towards 'persuasion' nothing more than a substitution, from the error of Hegel to the correction of *La Persuasione e la Rettorica*.

If what we wrote above was to be the end of the interpretation, a general understanding of the narratorial argumentation in the text would not move too far from the Bakhtinian critique of the academic genre as 'monologic'. That is, the different and divergent embodied and discussed ideologies unavoidably converge in a development, elaboration and affirmation of a single point of view, namely the result of the enquiry. The presentation of the debate is a step towards the definition and discussion of a problem, yet concurring to define a single, 'correct' solution. However, in the case we are studying, there is more than a simple substitution of the incorrect with the correct, and further complication resides again in the peculiarities of parody. Firstly, we must acknowledge that parody, despite being labelled as inadequate by the 'academic narrator' from a meta-linguistic position, is not deleted from the text and still plays a role. Therefore, it allows a reading of the passage from the point of view of parody itself. In doing so, we immediately face the fact that parody carries within itself not only a self-reflexive, but a meta-linguistic nature. If for the formalists, and to a great extent Bakhtin[31], the meta-linguistic power of parody is the engine for ideological and formal change, and the development of genres, we should discuss the extent to which, in our case, a parody so critically directed against the 'optimism' of philosophical writing invests and potentially undermines the 'optimistic', cognitive and meta-linguistic position of the text's 'academic narrator'. We have two genres facing each other, both with a generalizing status.

3.3.1 Which parody works for 'persuasion'?

Elsewhere in the text, Socratic dialectic defines the 'way to persuasion': «e poiché la via socratica perciò appunto e soltanto non è una via come un'altra, perché nega ogni fermata e si proclama sempre ancora non finita, il fermarvisi e il compiacersene è *un'abbandonarla per sempre*» (PR: 172). Given the undermining possibilities of parody, its power to 'negate', we shall therefore begin our interpretation of the adoption of this sub-genre in the text by questioning if and how the parody of Hegel matches the requirements of 'negation of every stop' and 'proclamation of itself as always unfinished'. The problem is to understand if and how the sub-genre 'stylized parody' is coherent with the narratorial agenda of infinite dismissal. The first part of this problem, the hetero-directed aim of parody, is clearly solvable simply because 'parodic stylization' can, by definition, be a useful strategy for undermining an 'other' voice[32]. The second part can be addressed through an analysis of the so called meta-fictional feature of parody, its property of 'reflect[ing] in both "meta-fictional" and comic fashion on other authors as well as on the composition and audience of the parodied work itself'[33]. To say that these self-reflective and self-questioning possibilies embodied by parody are at the centre of both the theoretical debate and literary/artistic production of postmodernism is almost a truism. We can start here by quoting two sources which are in various ways closer to the present analysis. The first appears in Bakhtin's discussion on the Sentimental novel:

what predominates in the novel are various forms and degrees of parodic stylisation of incorporated languages, a stylisation that, in the most radical, most Rabelaisian representatives of this novel-type [...] verges on a rejection of any straightforward and unmediated seriousness (true seriousness is the destruction of all false seriousness, not only in its pathos-charged expression but in its Sentimental one as well); that is, it limits itself to a principled criticism of the word as such[34].

The specific reference to the sub-genre 'parodic stylization' is the most important clue for our interpretative goals. The second quote, from Foucault's *Nietzsche, Genealogy, History*[35], posits a link between the concepts of parody, carnival, and Nietzsche's 'philosophy of the sunrise', indirectly offering a theoretical clarification of the narrator's use of parody in *La Persuasione e la Rettorica*.

the historical sense gives rise to three uses that oppose and correspond to the three Platonic modalities of history. The first is parodic, directed against reality, and opposes the theme of history as reminiscence or recognition; the second is dissociative, directed against identity, and opposes history given as a continuity or representative of a tradition; the third is sacrifical, directed against truth, and opposes history as knowledge[36].

With particular regard to the first point, the 'new historian' «will not be too serious to enjoy it; on the contrary, he will push the masquerade to its limit and prepare the great carnival of time where masks are constantly reappearing»[37], and «the parody [...] serves to emphasize that "monumental history" is itself a parody. Genealogy is history in the form of a concerted carnival»[38]. Two features of this definition of parody are relevant to our context (one in which one of the main philosophical goals is the revelation of the rhetorical nature of values, in this case: history): undermining and self-reflection (meta-fiction). Parody in this sense is a crucial tool in what Vattimo, in his discussion of *Human, all too Human*, defined as historical philosophy: «La filosofia <storica> che lavora con il metodo della <chimica> è quel sapere che <rischiara gradatamente e progressivamente> la storia del mondo come rappresentazione e ci solleva, <per qualche momento, al di sopra dell'intero processo>»[39].

This being 'above the process' fits with Michelstaedter's agenda of 'persuasion' in a number of ways. Firstly, it resembles an investment in the 'consciousness' of human condition; and secondly, the 'gradual and progressive' showing the world as 'representation' works in *La Persuasione e la Rettorica* as the dialectical movement which should lead to a process of emancipation. This latest consideration however, brings a crucial theme into the discussion, one concerned with the status of meta-language that the parody may or may not acquire, and the philosophical consequence of this possibility. Foucault's reading of Nietzsche posits parody as self-referred, as a parody of itself, itself involved in the 'concerted carnival', while Michelstaedter's parodic stylisation seems to reach this status only *ad infinitum*, working in the text as a useful meta-language for evaluation and dismissal, on the threshold of the leap into self-possession.

If this were the only way to interpret the investment in this sub-genre however, the presence of parody, framed by the discourse of what we called an 'academic narrator', would undermine the never-ending movement of laying bare the rhetorical nature of values and systems by 'stopping'; that is, by reaffirming a narratorial point of view as a foundation, and valid standpoint for the dismissive/parodic project itself. However, the meta-linguistic feature of parody not only avoids this 'failure' but helps us to highlight the basic form of a mechanism which is pervasive in the text, and which ultimately reduces the 'academic narrator' to the status of one (inadequate) voice among others. This is the second level of undermining: a second, linguistic, relativization.

3.3.2   *Dialectic movement and meta-language*
In the context shown above, it is possible to demonstrate how self-reflexivity is introduced by parody not at the level of the sub-genre, 'in a vacuum' so to speak, but in the more poignant and effective context of the text in general, and in its relationship with the narratorial utterance. We can interpret this through an analysis of parody as a meta-language, a second degree generic tool for laying bare the mechanisms of an external ideology; a narrow definition, which seems to fit our purposes. However, Roland Barthes, in *S/Z*, stresses some negative consequences:

> [f]or multivalence (contradicted by irony) is a transgression of ownership. The wall of voices must be passed through to reach the writing: this latter eschews any designation of ownership and thus can never be ironic; or, at least, its irony is never certain. [...] Employed on behalf of a subject that puts its imaginary elements at the distance it

pretends to take with regard to the language of others, thereby making itself even more securely a subject of the discourse, parody, or irony at work, is always classic language. [...] This is the problem facing modern writing: how to breach the wall of utterance, the wall of origin, the wall of ownership?[40]

Michele Hannoosh, in her study on the reflexive function of parody, tries to overcome Barthes' critique of the genre as «the voice which gives [...] unity»[41] by stressing its self-reflexive nature[42]. This would directly «challenge the notion of fixed works altogether, and thus leave itself open to the same playful critical treatment»[43]. This 'openness' is defined as a 'rebound': «[i]n rebounding upon itself, leaving room for other versions or even suggesting the forms these might take, parody ensures that the tradition it revises will continue even beyond itself»[44]. In continuity with Bakhtinian readings[45], this approach, in its stesss on the diachronic movement of intertextuality, offers an answer to Barthes. However, it fails to address the major point of the passage in *S/Z*. If parody is open because it allows further parody[46], it does not mean that the meta-linguistic right of the genre to comment upon other texts from a privileged standpoint is necessarily put into discussion, nor does it mean that each single parodic text necessarily ceases to perform as (in Barthesian terms) 'classical writing'. If it is true that some parodies are highly self-reflexive, the fact that parody indirectly implies the logical possibility of a self-critique is not enough to allow a generalization of the self-reflexive feature[47]. The same point could be made of any argumentative utterance, which critiques and therefore can be critiqued, and of language in general[48].

In Michelstaedter, parodic stylisation does not necessarily open to a 'critique of parody' or a 'parody of parody'. In the case of Hegel, Barthes' doubts are absolutely poignant. In the project of the text, parody and other dismissive strategies are temporary tools, which in reaching 'persuasion', have to be dismissed through a language which is not a privileged standpoint of (further inadequate) judgement. Here Michelstaedter will find himself at the limits of the problem of 'with words, make war against words', at the limits of a language which is by definition 'rhetorical' and now is supposed to mutate into its opposite. Negation through parody, irony, satire and other tools shows its inadequacy and need to be overcome.

But the very first problem is to demonstrate that the movement of parody is hyperbolic, if it is a movement at all. In fact, the case we are examining works as a mechanism of substitution; Hegelian ideology and rhetoric is targeted, embodied and removed through the meta-linguistic tool of parody. Parody is positively affirmed as the (temporary, if we consider the infinite point of its overcoming) standpoint for negation. However, the frame in which the parody takes place implies a further movement of substitution. The 'generalizing narrator', in his introduction to and guidance of the interpretation of the parody, deploys a further meta-language which acts upon the parody and the parodied text. In doing so, he turns the negation of Hegel into an affirmation of the narratorial point of view, as we quoted: «infatti è questo che l'uomo cerca, è così che crede giungere alla gioia – né può uscire di sé per vedere di più – soltanto egli paga l'ignoranza con l'oscuro tormento» (PR: 93). In this statement, the narrator summons the foundational cause for the hyperbolic movement: the 'obscure torment', as the inadequacy of 'rhetoric', calls for a more correct reaction and relationship with 'pain', without performing it, it substitutes 'cover' for 'cover', system for system. This position of affirmation, seems to fit with what Nietzsche calls 'romantic pessimism'[49], linking Michelstaedter once more with the Schopenhauer that he wants to avoid:

> può essere però anche la volontà tirannica di che soffre atrocemente, lotta, è torturato a voler imprimere il sigillo di una legge, di un obbligo vincolante a quanto ha di più personale, individuale e intimo, alla vera idiosincrasia del suo dolore, e per così dire vendicarsi di tutte le cose marchiandole a fuoco con la sua immagine, l'immagine della sua tortura. Quest'ultimo è il pessimismo romantico nella sua forma più espressiva, si tratti della filosofia schopenhaueriana della volontà o della musica wagneriana: il pessimismo romantico, l'ultimo grande evento nelle sorti della nostra cultura[50].

However, once again, the value of this interpretation is threatened by the bi-directional nature of the meta-linguistic process of negation. Not only is the narrator claiming its right to interpret parody; but the parody is there to put the pretences of the language and modes of the generalizing narrator into question, leading to the development of a dialectic between genres. It is worth offering some remarks on this point.

3.3.3 A dialogue between meta-languages
Following these temporary conclusions, we could comment that a contradiction, similar to the one we outlined in the case of exemplary quotes, takes place in the text. In both cases, the contrast is between 'persuasion' as

'seduction', the skill of 'moving towards action', and an 'academic rhetoric', didactic, monologic, and based on a foundation in 'truth'. The a-rhetorical status of the first is not fulfilled by the pedagogy of the second type, which is affirmed in the text, and compromises the dialogic possibilities of the parodic genre. However, before surrendering to the power of the 'academic narrator', the meta-linguistic status of the parody, which on one level puts at stake the dialectic movement of the text, can be considered also as the place from which to start to locate the very possibility of dialogism in *La Persuasione e la Rettorica*.

In our understanding of the passage, we have stressed how parody ultimately works as an extension of the 'academic narrator', a further tool of his affirmation which could be substituted by other strategies of dismissal: satire, academic discussion of quotes, and so forth. Moreover, we demonstrate how the narratorial frame shrinks the possibilities of the sub-genre by indicating preferential interpretation and asserting that the sub-genre itself was inadequate to reflect the 'optimism' of Hegel's style. Thus in this way the source is spaced out. We acknowledged the fact that this judgement fulfils the need to deal with the ambiguity of rejection-acceptance of the parodied text by the main text, defining the relationship between the narrator's and Hegel position as mutually exclusive. At the same time, we pointed out that the parody is not crossed out from the text; it is there, and keeps working according to its prerogatives. I would say that, as much as the meta-language of the narrator is engaged in relativizing the power of parody, parody works towards the relativization, opening the possibilities of undermining, laying bare the rhetorical mechanisms of the 'generalizing narrator'.

In order to defend this hypothesis, it is necessary to reiterate some previous points. Firstly, the parody of Hegel is a parody of philosophical systematization that targets both the blindness of the optimistic solutions (through the link with the dialogue with the «grosso signore») and the style (the philosophical rhetoric). Secondly, if our critique of the 'generalizing narrator' as positively affirming the foundation of his philosophy is true, and if it is true that he is a 'romantic pessimist', the implication is that the parody of Hegel, indirectly refers to the 'optimistic', or 'imperfectly pessimistic' voice of the narrator himself. Again, parody works on a stylistic level, laying bare the rhetorical mechanisms of the narrator. Therefore, the paroxism to which Hegel is pushed resounds throughout the text and invests the 'pathos charged', often declamatory, tone of the argumentation: its certainty. Parody is the rhetorical device which shows, in the text, the rhetorical nature of that which Thomas

Harrison defined as «one of the most rhetorically thick pieces of writing in the Italian early 20th century»[51]. In this sense, its self-reflexivity does not work at the level of the sub-genre, but at the level of the whole text, crucially opening the possibilities of dialogism.

The meta-language of parody and the meta-language of the 'academic narrator' thus enter into a dialogue in which they orient themselves 'against' each other, resulting in a reciprocal relativization. While the parody is 'inadequate' and needs the intervention of the narrator both before and after it to guide its interpretation, to correct the rendering of the translation, the narrator is revealed by the parody as an inadequate 'rhetorician'. Hence, the hyperbolic negative dialectic of the 'way to persuasion' finds its way to be performed in the practice, while being undermined in its academic theoretical affirmation. As a consequence, *La Persuasione e la Rettorica* loses its stable centre.

3.4   A second level of undermining

The conclusions we draw from our reading of the satire of the «grosso signore» and the parody of Hegel offer evidence for further generalization and reveals the importance of our framework for discussing general dynamics of the dialectic between forms which takes place in the text. The choice of focusing on negative quotations and their context of appearance, as explained at the beginning of this chapter, was suggested by the complexity offered by the Hegelian example: its strategic value in the development of the philosophical argument, the elaborate structure of the parody and the multiple links with other voices and sub-genres – for example the narratorial comment in the footnote, the sarcastic dialogue and general narratorial explanatory and generalising frame in the body of the text. Moreover, reading the Hegelian quotes through the theory of parody has helped us to highlight points which are crucial for our interpretation of the complex stylistic shifts which take place throughout *La Persuasione e la Rettorica*. Firstly, the ambiguity that derives from the embodiment not only of an external point of view, but of a language and vocabulary which is itself the object of undermining; secondly, the presence in the text of sub-genres which claim a meta-linguistic status and a positive value for alternative definitions of a philosophical argument. The latter potentially work as alternative generalizations, and by doing so put the value of the 'generalizing narrator' into question.

That said, it is possible to confirm the importance of these remarks by widening the results of our analysis in order to encompass other forms of satiric-ironic dismissal that take place in the text; this is a first step towards outlining what we called a second level of relativization that works as a dialectic between forms, between different sub-genres. On the point of satiric-ironic dismissal, a few more examples from different contexts in the text can test the value of our findings. The first comes from the 'Appendici Critiche', and is the dialogue between the 'I' of a «signore conosciuto e stimato» (PR: 160) and his own foot (PR: 160-3). This is conceived as a critique of the organicist view of society, and reworks the theme of the part versus the whole through the example of the stomach and its relationship with the entire organism (PR: 16). The development of this theme leads to a sarcastic dialogue in which the protagonist implicitly tries to defend the conception of Plato's *Republic* – the very conception attacked previously – against the argument counterposed by his foot and, inexorably, loses and dies. The context of the appendices, where 'negative quotes' are embodied in the text in a more orthodox way – fully referred and part of a comprehensive interpretation of the source – nevertheless allows a reading that stresses similar dynamics to those discussed above, particularly with regard to the sub-generic dialectic. The dialogue, in an attempt to avoid the rhetoric of the academic demonstration, calls Plato's system into question as much as it stresses a necessary stylistic difference from the hermeneutical system provided by the preceding academic argument, structured as a step by step critique of the philosophy of the Greek. Both sub-genres are conceived around the same topic and with the same goal. But while the rational academic sub-genre falls into a 'rhetoric' of false affirmation and systematization, thus needing the correction of the dialogue, the dialogue finds its interpretation through the framing narratorial voice. This is the dialectic which needs now to be discussed in its philosophical implications.

The same results can be obtained for the pages on «il conto [che] non torna» (PR: 37-9), even if further complications – worth highlighting at this point – are introduced. This passage is an ironic example used to explain the relative nature of rights and duties, and is synthesized with the framing motto: «*alle haben recht, niemand ist gerecht*» (PR: 39). The addressee of the remark is the implied reader and interlocutor of the text, addressed with a «voi». After a brief dialogue in which the interlocutor of this utterance defends his reasons for not following the path towards 'persuasion' («assai abbiamo da portare ognuno la nostra croce perché tu ci venga a imporre l'insopportabile, e a togliere quei sollievi ai quali abbiamo diritto»; «faccio i miei *doveri* d'uomo, di figlio, di cittadino, di cristiano». PR: 37), the narrator invites 'us' to try an experiment, to find the mathematical solution to the rights and duties of a member of a family, using as variables the points of view of the relatives. The introduction of these different variables makes the equation unmanageable and impossible. Hence the rejection of the language of mathematics as the solution of the problem of 'rhetoric' is attached to a critique that dismantles the preceding excuses of the narrator's interlocutor. Once again, as in the dialogue with the foot and others discussed in this chapter, a climactic movement leads to the final dismissal: from «[c]ominciate *quasi* a dubitare della matematica», to the final «poveri matematici, quanta fatica vana quando i dati non vi son dati, ma ve li dovete cercare, – e quando i dati sono dati, quanto lavoro inutile! Che avesse ragione il caro capo e refrattario alle matematiche di Sesto Empirico?» (PR: 38). While this passage lays bare, in coherence with the general discussion on science to be found in the text, the inadequacy of the presupposed objectivity of mathematical language, and 'our' inadequacy as faithful followers of inadequate affirmations, it also provides the terrain for a degree of self-referential critique. Shortly after, in fact, we find the passages in which the hyperbolic 'way to persuasion' (PR: 40) – in a rhetorical sense – is 'literally' translated into the mathematical function of 'hyperbole', and exploited to define the philosophical point. Despite the positioning of this mathematical argument in a footnote, with an ironic *incipit* that echoes the preceding polemic («a soddisfazione dei matematici» PR: 41), the investment in the possibilities of this demonstration is clear, and the references to the formula throughout the text are a confirmation of it[52]. This intratextual link gives extra importance to the experiment on 'rights and duties' and constitutes a dialectic in which the 'positive' affirmation of the hyperbolic way to 'persuasion' is itself in danger of being dismissed and relativized as 'rhetorical'. Or is it that mathematical language cannot offer a solution to 'rhetoric', but can precisely define a path towards this solution[53]? Once again, the juxtaposition of sub-genres confirms our results in a broader context.

This last point confirms the role of irony and sarcasm in the second level of undermining in the text[54]. However, the passage also widens the applicability of our results, encompassing not only ironic/sarcastic dismissal, but different strategies of signification employed in the argumentation, and the dialectical consequences of this juxtaposition. This is the hypothesis which will guide our next chapter: the repetition, with the goal of clarification and reinforcement, of philosophical points through different sub-genres results in a dialectic which relativizes the different utterances in their attempt at adequate signification, with the consequence of undermining, on a stylistic level, any stable foundation in a 'positive' language.

However, the following chapter will further complicate this hypothesis. Together with the juxtaposition of genres, the dialectic works also as the link between conceptualization – mostly a prerogative of the generalizing narrator – and a variety figurative representations. In approaching this further reading, we will also analyze ways in which, on a theoretical level, the problem of defining an 'adequate utterance' which avoids rhetoric is tackled, and if and how the dynamics which we highlighted can be read with regard to this problem.

Notes

1. Letter to Pietro Giordani, 18 giugno 1821. In: Giacomo Leopardi, *Tutte le Poesie e Tutte le Prose*, ed. Lucio Felici and Emanuele Trevi (Rome: Newton & Compton, 1997): 1216.
2. The presence of a relationship between consciousness of 'nothingness' and laughter is in fact the basis for an unavoidable comparison with Leopardi. On this point, see for example: Daniela Bini, 'Giacomo Leopardi's Ultrafilosofia' *Italica* 74, no. 1 (1997); Daniela Bini, 'Leopardi e Michelstaedter tra Autenticità e Inautenticità' in *Italiana*, ed. Albert N. Mancini, Paolo Giordano, and Pier Raimondo Baldini (New York: American Association of Teachers of Italian, 1986). We will come back to this topic in our fifth chapter. The letter to Giordani continues the delineation of the origin and the field of Leopardi's laughter: «[v]ero è che la Disperazione si finge sorridente. Ma il riso attorno agli uomini ed alle mie stesse miserie [...], quantunque non derivi dalla speranza, non viene però dal dolore, ma piuttosto dalla noncuranza» (Leopardi, *Tutte le Poesie e Tutte le Prose*: 1216). Lonardi is one of the many critics to map the presence and development of the concepts of the laughter of desperation and the laughter of carelessness, and their relationship with the opposite concept of pity (until the famous «Non so se il riso o la pietà prevale», of *Ginestra* 201): see Gilberto Lonardi, '«Alter Ridebat... Flebat Alter»: A Proposito di Democrito/Eraclito in Leopardi,' in *Il Riso Leopardiano. Comico, Satira, Parodia. Atti del IX Convegno Internazionale di Studi Leopardiani* (Firenze: Leo S. Olschki Editore, 1995). His reading could be the starting point for a comparison with Michelstaedter, but such an enterprise is premature in this context. In chapter 5 of the present volume we will offer some remarks based on the hypothesis of Michelstaedter's ontological nihilism.
3. We can read this as Socratic irony. Without the need to engage in the debate around this point in Plato, we can resort to Vasiliou's definition of what he calls 'conditional irony': 'the irony lies in the fact that if the antecedent were true, then Socrates would really believe the consequent; however, it is clear to the reader, though not always to the interlocutor, that Socrates believes that the antecedent is false, which therefore suggests that he believes the negation of the consequent'. Iakovos Vasiliou, 'Conditional Irony in the Socratic Dialogues' *The Classical Quarterly*, New Series 49, no. 2 (1999): 462.
4. Fabiola Pagnanelli correctly points out the fundamental similarity in the «dislivello ontologico o pragmatico degli interlocutori» as «una delle caratteristiche principali dell'ironia 'macrostrutturale' tipica dei dialoghi leopardiani» Fabiola Paganelli, 'Il Sorriso

Tragico di Carlo Michelstaedter' in *'Quel Libro Senza Uguali'. Le Operette Morali e il Novecento Italiano,* ed. Novella Bellucci and Andrea Cortellessa (Roma: Bulzoni, 2000): 61. In this, she follows F. Secchieri, *Con Leggerezza Apparente. Etica e Ironia nelle 'Operette Morali'* (Modena: Mucchi, 1992). The main difference resides in the faith in the stylistic possibilities of the maieutic role, adopted here with the sarcastic intent of pushing the position of the interlocutor to paroxism without resolution. Fabiola Pagnanelli, for example, considers Michelstaedter's occasional investment in the possibilities of maieutic as the main difference between the style of dialogue in the two thinkers. She stresses this category to the point of focusing her comparison exclusively on dialogues where maieutic is absent, thus avoiding the important *Dialogo della Salute* (DS). See: Paganelli, 'Il Sorriso Tragico di Carlo Michelstaedter': 60. In our context, the mockery is a crude stylization for sarcastic goals, and a tongue-in-check exploitation of Socratic irony. At the same time, however, it exemplifies the movement of relentless questioning which leads to a dismissal of inadequate values. It is a sort of mock(ing) maieutic, which cannot be read against itself. The interlocutor does not reach any further insight, but the narrator is further established in his truth by the exposure of the interlocutor's fault. The closing sentence has the tone of an accomplished mission hidden as a failure of speech: «io rimasi senza parole, ma nello smarrimento mi lampeggiò l'idea che il vino prima d'entrar nella botte passò sotto il torchio» (PR: 91). Further discussion in this chapter, will highlight how a meta-analysis can call the narrator, his ideology and his praxis of argumentation, into question when the nature of the text moves from satire to parody.

5. Bini suggests an intertextual connection between *Tristano* and the Preface to *La Persuasione e la Rettorica,* where «sia Michelstaedter che Leopardi, si rendono conto di ripetere cose già dette, perchè la verità è una ed è che la vita è dolore». Bini, 'Leopardi e Michelstaedter tra Autenticità e Inautenticità': 219. The same is affirmed by Paganelli in her interpretation of Michelstaedter as 'inattuale' (Paganelli, 'Il Sorriso Tragico di Carlo Michelstaedter': 56), introducing another level of comparison which exceeds the goals of our present chapter, but will be an important part of our final conclusions.

6. Bellucci correctly interprets the epigraph as having a canonical function, according to the systematization by Genette: «sottolineare indirettamente il significato del testo». Novella Bellucci, 'Riverberi Novecenteschi del Riso Leopardiano,' in *Il Riso Leopardiano. Comico, Satira, Parodia. Atti del IX Convegno Internazionale di Studi Leopardiani* (Firenze: Leo S. Olschki, 1998): 639. She continues, adding «per mezzo dell'epigrafe uno scrittore si autodefinisce, esibisce la propria appartenenza intellettuale» (ibid.: 640). The demonstration of the thematic parallels between the dialogue with the «grosso signore» and the *Palinodia,* exceeds the goals of our brief comparative notes. However, the epigraph which appears in the edited edition is a restoration from the manuscript A, absent in the final copy C. That said, I do not believe that there is evidence in the text which leads to a rejection of a Leopardian framework.

7. Ibid.

8. Campailla, 'Postille Leopardiane di Michelstaedter'.

9. This would imply a discussion inside the framework articulated by Severino: Emanuele Severino, *Il Nulla e la Poesia. Alla Fine dell'Età della Tecnica: Leopardi* (Milano: Rizzoli, 2005).

10. Bini, 'Leopardi e Michelstaedter tra Autenticità e Inautenticità'.

11. See for example the ambiguous relationship with the attempt to find «salvezza nell'arte» (ibid.: 224). Bini's interesting article on 'Leopardi e l'Ultrafilosofia' (Bini, 'Giacomo Leopardi's Ultrafilosofia') focuses on the poet's answer to the consciousness of the 'nulla'

and the poetic project derived from this nothing. Producing a poetry that this nothing signifies, seems almost a necessary counterpart to her interpretation of Michelstaedter. We will discuss this point below in our concluding chapter.

12. It will be clear in that context how the interpretation of Leopardi's nihilism as 'ontologic' is the most fruitful point of departure for this comparison. See for example Laura Sanò, *Le Ragioni del Nulla. Il Pensiero Tragico nella Filosofia Italiana tra Ottocento e Novecento* (Troina: Città Aperta 2005).

13. «Allora l'amor di sistema, o finto, o vero e derivante da persuasione, è dannosissimo al vero» (Zib, 948. But on this theme see 947-8. Giacomo Leopardi, *Zibaldone*, ed. Lucio Felici (Roma: Newton & Compton, 1997): 220-1. For a mapping of the topic in Leopardi's production, and a discussion of the relationship between «sapere sistematico» and «riso», see: Antimo Negri, 'Il Riso di Nietzsche e il Riso di Leopardi' in *Il Riso Leopardiano. Comico, Satira, Parodia. Atti del IX Convegno Internazionale di Studi Leopardiani* (Firenze: Leo S. Olschki Editore, 1998).

14. I am using the term 'satire' here in order to underline some features of the discourse on/of the 'grosso signore'. Firstly, the utterance is reproduced but not embodied in the narratorial voice, and thus discussed as something foreign to it; in this I am following a suggestion from Rose: «one major factor which distinguishes the parody from satire is the parody's use of the performed material of its "target" as a constituent part of its own structure». Margaret A. Rose, *Parody: Ancient, Modern and Postmodern* (Cambridge: Cambridge University Press, 1993): 81. In this sense, satire reveals itself as less ambivalent than parody (Rose, *Parody: Ancient, Modern and Postmodern*: 83). The structure of a dialogue with two characters and two clearly differentiated voices – together with the surprised reactions of the narrator after the man's utterance – fit with this definition. Furthermore, the deterministic link between physical appearances, culinary habits and moral values in the depiction of the interlocutor of the dialogue, reminds me (although shifted in context) of some considerations developed by Sibley, in the definition of *satura* in ancient Rome (tracing the link between habits/manners at the table and morality back to Plato's *Symposium* – one of Michelstaedter's sources). See: Gay Sibley, 'Satura from Quintillan to Joe Bob Briggs: A New Look at an Old Word' in *Theorizing Satire. Essays in Literary Criticism*, ed. Brian A. Connery and Kirik Combe (New York: St Martin Press, 1995): 61. There could be also an interesting field of possible comparison with Michelstaedter's production of caricatures, but this footnote is not the place for the development of such a complex point. On the topic of caricatures, see: Bini, 'L'Autenticità del Segno' (also in her monograph on the author). More generally, 'structured' definitions of satire, as for example in Frye («wit or humour founded on fantasy or a sense of the grotesque or absurd» together with an «object of attack». Northrop Fryre, *Anatomy of Criticism: Four Essays* (Princeton: Princeton University Press, 1957): 224-5), and the further reduction of this definition to an 'attack towards a social object', as discussed in Brian A. Connery and Kirik Combe, 'Introduction,' in *Theorizing Satire. Essays in Literary Criticism*, ed. Brian A. Connery and Kirik Combe (New York: St. Martin Press, 1995): 8-9, clearly fit the case we are discussing.

15. Both building and demonstrating: the narrator demonstrates the validity of his thought through an *ad hoc* stylization of Hegel's philosophy (and thus, he 'builds it').

16. Linda Hutcheon, *A Theory of Parody* (New York, London: Methuen, 1985): 6.

17. As may always be the case with genres, broad to the point of being questionable at its borders, in particular in its risk of overlapping with the concept of 'quotation'. Can a quotation be considered 'a repetition with a critical distance'? Can we really make the point that in a quote the distance from the source is 'non critical' or only 'implicitly' critical?

And does 'marking the difference' instead of the 'similarity' not belong to a vaste series of quotes? Hutcheon responds to the problem by discussing Deleuze's *Difference and Repetition*: «according to Gilles Deleuze, repetition is always by nature transgression, exception, singularity. Yet parody, while often subversive, can also be conservative; in fact, parody is by nature, paradoxically, an authorized transgression. It cannot be accounted for only in terms of *différance*, deferral» (ibid.: 101). However, 'finding' this *proprium* of parody, different from quotation, in a close reading of a text remains a rather complex task; for example, Hutcheon's definition of T.S. Eliot's poetry as 'allusive or parodic' (Hutcheon, *A Theory of Parody*: 2), reveals the complexity of definition in practice. Other critics would rather define the modern American poetry of Eliot and Pound starting from the pole of quotation/allusion. For Diepeveen, quotation, in its disruption, is repetition with critical (dialogic) distance (Diepeveen, *Changing Voices. The Modern Quoting Poem*). An interesting critique of the problematic vagueness of this definition can be found in Seymour Chatman, 'Parody and Style,' *Poetics Today* 22, no. 1 (2001): 33.

18. «Ironic versions of "trans-contextualization" and inversion are its major formal operatives, and the range of pragmatic ethos is from scornful ridicule to reverential homage» (Hutcheon, *A Theory of Parody*: 37); a common thesis, stressed by many scholars who are questioning the univocal burlesque nature of the genre, see for example the review in Rose, *Parody: Ancient, Modern and Postmodern*.

19. It resembles Genette's definition of 'strict parody' as a parody that follows the original as closely as possible. For Genette's mapping of the different types of parody, see: Gerard Genette, *Palimpsests: Literature in the Second Degree* (Lincoln: University of Nebraska Press, 1997).

20. Rose, *Parody: Ancient, Modern and Postmodern*: 8, discussing Quintilian on ancient parody. See also Hutcheon, *A Theory of Parody*: 32: «the prefix para has two meanings, only one of which is usually mentioned – that of "counter" or "against" [...]. However, para in Greek can also mean "beside", and therefore there is a suggestion of an accord or intimacy instead of a contrast». Elswere in Rose: «Householder describes it as "a narrative poem of moderate length, in epic meter, using epic vocabulary, and treating a light, satirical, or mock-heroic subject". Householder also comments this usage of "parodia" to an earlier use of the term, [...] to describe an "imitating singer" or "singing in imitation"» (Rose, *Parody: Ancient, Modern and Postmodern*: 7) The entire article by Householder is of great interest for reflecting on the ancient roots of the contemporary debate on the genre, see: Fred W. Householder, 'Parodia,' *Journal of Classical Philology* 39, no. 1 (1944).

21. At least for the implicit status given to the parodied text: conceiving a parody of an unknown text, or a work considered insignificant would be rather pointless. In Michelstaedter's case, the context of the rising 'crocianesimo' in Italy at the beginning of the twentieth century (as we discussed in our Introduction; see: Asor Rosa, 'La Cultura a Firenze nel Primo Novecento,') makes the figure of Hegel very poignant, and imediately recognizable by a potential reader in terms of its ramifications inside Italian culture.

22. In a satire, as we saw, this re-encoding at the level of style is not necessary. A satire could consist for example of a description of the grotesque, immoral habit of a person without an embodiment of this person's voice.

23. Michail M. Bakhtin, 'From the Prehistory of Novelistic Discourse' in *The Dialogic Imagination. Four Essays* (Austin: University of Texas Press, 1981): 51.

24. Bakhtin, *Problems of Dostoevsky's Poetics*: 210-12 et passim.

25. «Stylization stylizes another's style in the direction of that style's own particular tasks. It merely renders those tasks conventional» (ibid.: 193).

26. We approached this point in our previous chapter, discussing the embodiment of the Presocratics inside a Schopenhauerian framework.

27. «Der Staat ist die göttliche Idee, wie sie auf Erden vorhanden ist», is the narrator's quote from the *Philosophie der Geschichte* in his footnotes (PR: 92). Here is the key for a humoristic reduction, which could lead to a whole series of interesting considerations, both in terms of the interpretation of Michelstaedter's understanding of Hegel, and the possibility of deconstructing these structures of explanation and exemplarity. Unfortunately these tasks exceed the goals of our present analysis.

28. In the presence of parody: «the second voice, once having made its home in the other's discourse, clashes hostilely with its primordial host and forces him to serve directly opposing aims» (Bakhtin, *Problems of Dostoevsky's Poetics*: 193). Bakhtin will further discuss the sub-genre 'parodied stylization' in his interpretation of Dostoevskij's The Double (see above), insisting on analogous definitions: «As in any parodic stylization, there is an obvious and crude emphasis upon the basic characteristics and tendencies of Golyadkin's discourse» (Bakhtin, *Problems of Dostoevsky's Poetics*: 211).

29. The most important of which, emblematically crossed out from the final draft, is the prefatory paratext.

30. «Infatti è questo che l'uomo cerca, è così che crede giungere alla gioia – né può uscire di sé per vedere di più – soltanto egli paga l'ignoranza con l'oscuro tormento» (PR: 93).

31. See: Bakhtin, 'From the Prehistory of Novelistic Discourse' particularly section III: 68-83.

32. We could argue that the choice of stylization, instead of a full discussion/interpretation of the quoted philosopher, can be considered an attempt to avoid the 'rhetoric of interpretation' of a source, against which the critique of the narrator is often targeted. However, the same problems occur on a different level: in order to stylize one needs to have interpreted, if one's stylization does not come *after* a rhetorical understanding, then it is the rhetorical understanding. The substitution of the rhetoric of a genre with another is not the correct battlefield for the narratorial agenda; the possibility of a genre to question itself is a more crucial point on the possibilities to perform the 'way to persuasion'.

33. Rose, *Parody: Ancient, Modern and Postmodern*: 91. Rose seems to understand the meta-fictional property of parody as a possible yet unnecessary or insufficient feature: every meta-fiction is not necessarily a parody and vice versa. On this topic see also: Margaret A. Rose, *Parody//Metafiction* (London: Croom Helm, 1979).

34. Bakhtin, *The Dialogic Imagination. Four Essays*: 312.

35. Michel Foucault, 'Nietzsche, Genealogy, History' in *The Foucault Reader*, ed. Paul Rabinow (New York: Pantheon Books, 1984).

36. Ibid.: 93.

37. Ibid.: 94.

38. Ibid.: 94.

39. Gianni Vattimo, *Nietzsche* (Bari: Laterza, 1985): 47-8.

40. Roland Barthes, *S/Z* (New York: Hill and Wang, 1974): 45.

41. Michele Hannoosh, 'The Reflexive Function of Parody' *Comparative Literature* 41, no. 2 (1989): 116.

42. «Reflexivity is inherent to the definition of parody [...] and is demanded by the form itself» (ibid.: 113).

43. Ibid.: 113-4.

44. Ibid.: 116.

45. Ibid.: 113.

46. A 'playful critical treatment', thus a parody by definition: «a comical retelling and

transformation of another text» (ibid.: 113).

47. I think it useful to maintain the distinction between self-reflexive and non self-reflexive (or indirectly self-reflexive) parody in place, as for example in Chatman, 'Parody and Style'.

48. And starting from the same Bakhtinian 'dialogic' understanding of language.

49. Friedrich Nietzsche, *The Gay Science* (Cambridge, new York: Cambridge University Press, 2001) (Book 5, n. 370).

50. Ibid.: 226.

51. Harrison, 'The Michelstaedter Enigma' (electronic copy, no page numbers given).

52. PR: 93-4; 89; 96; 103; 117.

53. Furthermore, by defining the negative dialectic and at the same time giving a positive, objective and stable definition of 'persuasion', mathematical language demonstrates and performs its own inadequacy.

54. The same case could be made for the irony implied in the famous «esempio storico» (PR: 66-73). In the next chapter, however, in our attempt to demonstrate the dialectical mechanisms of Michelstaedter's text on different grounds, we will treat this passage as a myth of the origins of 'rhetoric'.

CHAPTER FOUR

Narrator as a Relativized Voice

Die Tieflademarke,
die mit uns sinkt, unsrer Last treu,
eulenspiegelt das alles
hinunter, hinauf und – warum nicht? wundgeheilt, wo-, wenn –
herbei und vorbei und herbei.

Paul Celan

The concluding page of *La Persuasione e la Rettorica* introduces a dramatic moment in the economy of the whole text. It is worth quoting the entire passage:

Così se ne facciano un uomo di scienza, avranno resa possibile l'*oggettività*. Infatti egli sarà abituato dalle fasce in su a sapere che altro è lo studio, altro è il giuoco. Così egli si potrà mettere a sciogliere problemi filosofici movendo i concetti che le norme scientifiche insegnano, e come insegnano, senza mai curarsi del loro valore: <altro è la teoria, altro la pratica>. <… Tu devi fare uno studio su Platone o sul vangelo> gli diranno <è perché così ti fai un nome, ma guardati bene dall'agire secondo il vangelo. Devi esser oggettivo, guardare da chi Cristo ha preso quelle parole o se *omnino* Cristo le abbia dette e se non meglio le abbiano prese gli Evangelisti o dagli Arabi o dagli Ebrei o dagli Eschimesi, chi lo sa … Naturalmente *parole* che valevano in riguardo all'epoca, adesso la scienza sa come stanno le cose, e tu non te ne devi incaricare. Quando tu hai messo insieme il tuo libro sul vangelo – *allora puoi andar a giuocare*>. – Come al bambino si diceva: <fai come dice il babbo che ne sa più di te, e non occorre che tu domandi 'perché', obbedisci e non ragionare, quando sarai grande

capirai>. Così si conforta il giovane a perseguire nel suo studio scientifico senza che si chieda che senso abbia, dicendogli: <tu cooperi all'immortale edificio della *futura* armonia delle scienze e sarà un po' anche merito tuo se gli uomini quando saranno grandi, un giorno *sapranno*>. Ma gli uomini temo che siano sì bene incamminati, che non verrà loro mai il capriccio di uscir della tranquilla e serena minore età (PR: 131).

It is the ultimate critique of objectivity and science in the form of a dismissal of the project of academia: concepts are 'moved around' without regard to their value or sense, and the aim of the academy – the building of the 'future harmony of sciences' – is presented as a future-oriented knowledge that is nothing more than an example of the inadequate affirmation of values, the *non entia coagito*[1] that defines 'rhetoric'. Thus, with one final stroke, Michelstaedter sweeps away the entire academic system, including his first interlocutors: the panel of professors who are going to read and judge his work.

On this final page, *La Persuasione e la Rettorica* seems to anticipate and reject its potential critics by setting its entire project on a different level: that of the 'coming of age'. In fact, in the dialogical section of the quote above, the addressee of the scientists' voice is so close to the writer of *La Persuasione e la Rettorica*, that the entire example can and should be read as self-reflexive: it is the conclusion of a work on Plato and Aristotle[2], which not only figures a series of quotes[3] and references from the New Testament, but presents Christ as one of the most important examples of 'persuasion'. The interlocutors of the dialogue, in offering a topic for study, are also offering a 'good' reason for undertaking the task ('fame', a 'career'), and a methodology for succeeding based on philology and historical contextualization. A reader who has reached the end of *La Persuasione e la Rettorica* should know that neither of these recommendations are followed or fulfilled in the text. Thus, the paragraph offers explicit evidence of the narrator's awareness – almost a truism in criticism – that his entire project is born under a wrong sign and for «motivazioni tutte esteriori»[4]: for it is the academy that requires his writing and its form, the rhetoric of a «tesi di laurea» (PR: 4). However, the dialogue presents a further level of conflict with the context in which the thesis is conceived. *La Persuasione e la Rettorica* is written 'despite itself' and 'against' an academic thesis, in the neglect of the scientific requirements listed in the passage. Michelstaedter seems to defend the coherence of his project against what 'men are set off for'. The adversative 'but', so crucial in the development of the argument on 'rhetoric'[5] appears again, and as in the opening lines of the chapter on 'La Rettorica' («[m]a gli uomini si stancano su questa via [of persuasion], si sentono mancare nella solitudine» PR: 53), the sentence that concludes the text marks an opposition concerning mankind: «ma gli uomini temo che siano incamminati» (PR: 131). *La Persuasione e la Rettorica* is moving elsewhere, and the coherence between theory and practice remains an explicit theme of Michelstaedter's work.

This final accusation/defence acquires a further dramatic charge when we consider its position in the text as the utterance preceding the beginning of the 'Appendici Critiche', the section where the comprehensive treatment of the philosophy of Plato and Aristotle occurs. More than any other section of the text, the 'Appendici' fulfil the academic requirements for a critical interpretation of their object through an accurate discussion of its sources, and thus, their position (directly after the anti-academic quote above) is potentially incoherent. In the text and manuscripts we have explicit evidence of this perceived threat, and an attempt to justify what follows.

The first consists of a note in the autograph manuscript (A):

– Perché le ha chiamate appendici 'critiche'?
– Secondo la definizione dell'ironia l'ironia è quel tropo per il quale diciamo con un concetto un concetto contrario al concetto [usitato][6]

Here, the dialogic form of question and answer puts the adjective 'critical' under a scrutiny that is further stressed through the use of inverted commas. 'Critiche' can be read as referring ironically to the systematic treatment of Platonic and Aristotelian sources, that is, as a dismissive comment on the 'rhetorical' (as opposed to 'critical') nature of the supposed exhaustive academic critical analysis of the object. This question thus suggests that the real critique occurs in the body of the text, while the 'Appendici' are a retreat into what 'men are set off for'. Reading the passage in this way implies sympathy for the argument of the body of the text. From that point of view the question in the passage is a legitimate self-reflexive moment.

However, if we consider the first readers of the thesis, its natural addressees, to be an academic panel, we can interpret the presence and role of the inverted commas in a rather different sense. The question 'why have they been called "critical"?' can be read also as a critique of the status of the 'Appendici', suggesting these as an element of the thesis that does not fit the requirements of academic argumentation. The interlocutor may have intended: 'why did you call them "critical", they are not "critical"!' After all, it is in the 'Appendici' that the Leopardian dialogue between an 'I' and his foot takes place. The appendices in fact deploy a problematic stylistic complexity that cannot be reduced to the paradigm of a 'retreat'. The multiple references to the body of the text, the reworking of themes, and the deployment of a variety of stylistic strategies in the punctuation of the academic critique of Plato and Aristotle show how this section can be considered part of a wider dialectic that encompasses the whole of *La Persuasione e la Rettorica*.

A further formulation of the problem of ambiguity and potential incoherence in the project of the 'Appendici' can be found in the quatrain chosen as the epigraph of the final manuscript (the copy C) :

Con le parole guerra alle parole / siccome aure nebbiose l'aria viva / disperde perché pur il sol risplenda – / la qual per suo valor non s'avvantaggia (PR: 131).

The statement 'with words, war against words' suggests a number of readings which account for the complexities stated above, and thus partake of the same self-reflexive preoccupation. We could assign to the first line a meaning which is internal to the program of the 'Appendici'. Here, the 'words' employed in the argument of the appendices are the tool used against some other 'words' in order to achieve what is forecast in the following lines of the quatrain. However this interpretation does not reveal anything about the status of the 'words' of the appendices. Is it a 'rhetoric' deployed against another 'rhetoric'? A 'rhetoric' against itself? Or are the appendices an attempt to substitute a 'rhetorical' word with an adequate one? The reading of the following lines helps to make sense of these points. The simile introduced by «siccome» outlines a difference in status between the two 'words'. The comparison of the dismissed one to a 'cloudy aura' to be 'cleared' by the other, the 'living air', could be read as a figurative illustration of the negative dialectic towards 'persuasion'. The lines that follow seem to corroborate this possibility; the activity of clearing the clouds in order for the sun to shine, and the lack of advantage gained through this achievement, offer clear parallels with the points already discussed: the infinite dialectic, the negation of the value of one's own dialectic achievements, the necessity of avoiding stopping to ask something for oneself (PR: 40), because «dare non è per aver dato, ma per dare» (PR: 42). If this is true, the 'Appendici critiche' cannot simply be dismissed as the carrying on of a contradiction for 'external reasons', no matter how self-conscious.

The goal of this chapter is to offer a concluding interpretation of the dialectic that takes place in the 'war with words against words'; the figurative representation of which is given in the quatrain. In doing so, we will use the results of our second and third chapter as a springboard. In those contexts, we outlined two ways in which the foundational status of the narratorial voice is undermined: the first takes place in the relation between theory/poetic and practice of signification; and we showed it through the ambiguity of the narratorial generalizations with regard to his theory of exemplarity. The second is a consequence of the juxtaposition of different sub-genres. The declension of these two levels in the context of the text results in a complex scenario. We have two macro-sections – the body of the text and the appendices – linked in a reciprocal interaction on theoretical and formal levels; and inside each of these parts an analogous net of re-formulations, confirmations, corrections, dismissals and juxtapositions emerges.

In order to address this complexity, we will enquire into the theory of adequate and inadequate affirmation expressed in the text. Once again, we will frame our problem as one of poetic and rhetoric. This preliminary theoretical definition of the concepts of 'persuasion' and 'rhetoric', this time declined in their linguistic properties as 'adequate' and 'inadequate' utterance, will offer us the basis for a double development of our enquiry. On the level of a strictly theoretical interpretation of Michelstaedter's poetic, we will have the chance to bring our argument on the links with a Kantian theory of genius and aesthetic judgement to a conclusion. We will show how Michelstaedter's 'adequate utterance' can be read as an original speculation on themes derived from romantic developments of Kantian aesthetics. Through the stylistic analysis we will demonstrate how the intrinsic impossibility of performing a signification that absolutely fulfils the requirements of 'adequacy' leaves the text in an irresolvable dialectic which we will understand under the category of 'repetition': if adequacy is impossible to achieve, what remains (in coherence with the philosophical presuppositions) is an infinite 'correction' always in need of further dismissal, of further relativisation, as inadequate. The demonstration of this process in the text will help us to trace how Michelstaedter, through the radicalization of romantic themes[7], reaches conclusions similar to the poetic of the Italian Novecento, and how *La Persuasione e la Rettorica* can be considered an application of these results.

4.1   Allegories, figures and stylistic dialectic

The first step in our analysis is a demonstration of the ways in which Michelstaedter's problem of adequate affirmation can be read through the theorization of the opposition between allegory and symbol, as developed in post-Kantian aesthetics. This dichotomy is linked with the problem of the aesthetic relationships between figuration and conceptualization[8], seen as multiplicity and univocity of interpretability. In order to approach this theme, we need to address an ambiguity in the treatment of ideologies. We will see how a series of dismissed 'rhetorics' and their vocabularies are elsewhere embodied in the text as part of a positive demonstration of a narratorial argument. This undermining implies an implicit negation of the epistemological value of these passages, and the need to read them as 'rhetorical', figurative illustrations. Here, we will outline how these illustrations work according to a particular definition of allegory.

4.1.1   Ambiguity in the critique of ideologies and their vocabularies

The first part of Michelstaedter's text is devoted to understanding the philosophical reasons for the choice of moving towards 'persuasion' or retreating into 'rhetoric', and concludes with the climactic pages which try to define the realm of the former[9]. The second part, relying on the previous results, focuses on an analysis of 'rhetoric', linking 'rhetorical language' with a critique of social conventions and ideologies on which the social system finds its foundation. Here, under the preliminary and all-encompassing image of the human who «porta l'Assoluto per le vie della città» (PR: 54), the argument against the «sapere accanto alla vita» (PR: 56) is introduced. In this passage, the man of 'rhetoric' is criticized for mistakenly dividing the «corpo, o una materia, o un fenomeno» from «un'anima, o una forma, o un'idea» (ibid.)[10]. This attack against conceptualization is specifically conceived with regard to the forms of modern science (in the chapter titled 'La costituzione della rettorica' PR: 74-88); objectivity[11]; philosophy (or better, the 'optimistic' philosophy which founds and justifies the modern system of society[12]); law as social foundation, and society in general, with its «organismi assimilatori» (PR: 121). In the realm of rhetoric, once the principle of self-perpetuation is in place, the struggle for safety (PR: 96) implies violence against nature and humanity (PR: 97). Society takes care of its own self-perpetuation through the building of ideologies, it is an «officina dei valori assoluti» (PR: 125). The acculturation of humanity to the 'objective values' of society perpetuates the system by providing both the possibility of satisfaction of needs and the 'rhetorical framework' to valorize that satisfaction. In this sense it offers the 'cover for the eyes', the material of the veil of Maya. In this context, where rhetorical objectivity implies the renunciation of individuality (ibid.), social institutions and their vocabulary become the means for the annihilation of the subject. Thus church, socialism, sociology, medicine (PR: 124-6), civil education (PR: 129), and so forth are all conceived as a finely tuned system of praise and condemnation[13], which at its extremes leads to an absolute mechanization of life. In the prophetic pages on 'rhetoric organized as a system' (PR: 118-9), the link between language and society is stated in its end-limits: «la lingua arriverà al limite della persuasività assoluta, quello che il profeta raggiunge col miracolo, – arriverà al silenzio quando ogni atto avrà la sua efficienza assoluta. [...] Tutte le parole saranno termini tecnici quando l'oscurità sarà per tutti allo stesso modo velata, essendo gli uomini tutti allo stesso modo addomesticati» (PR: 118-9). With a famous and fortunate motto, in the future «gli uomini si suoneranno vicendevolmente come tastiera» (PR: 119).

A vast number of critics have dealt with this part of Michelstaedter's thesis; not least those concerned with a re-evaluation of the thinker in the contemporary debate[14], or those deploying in various ways a Marxist framework[15]. However, our reasons for recollecting this critique of ideologies are different. What interests us is that, in apparently open contradiction, these dismissed modes of affirmation and their vocabularies not only survive in the text, but are adopted as positive tools of argumentation. It is worth exploring this contradiction between theory and practice, because it will take us to the core of the problem of the 'rhetoric' of the text.

Medicine is a case in point. The narrator asserts that the language and objective aims of medicine operate as a *locus* of social control because they suppress diversity by reading it as abnormality[16]. Only a few pages earlier medical language is deployed inside the narrator's argument to define the consequences of the development of society in terms of the atrophy of human capacities: «il corpo dell'uomo si disgregherà ... si verserà» (PR: 107) is the final statement on the alienation of the individual. Medicine is thus treated as a stable meta-language which can function as the basis for social critique, and not as a cause of corruption. It gives an objective account of a disease that has a social origin, that is a 'social invention':

[u]n principio di ciò, certo almeno un'invenzione sociale sono le

malattie degli arti, le malattie muscolari in genere per inerzia e atrofizzamento – e le malattie degli organi interni perché lavorano a vuoto […] o per ipertrofia; connesse a queste le malattie della circolazione del sangue: in generale il disturbo di quello che è l'affermazione d'esistenza di un organismo: l'assimilazione della materia alla propria forma: *le malattie del ricambio materiale*. Il segno di questo esser fuori di fuoco della vita sono i mali del sistema nervoso – dei quali la società sembra quasi menar vanto. – (PR: 107-8).

The rhetorical language of medicine of PR: 125-6 is positively embodied to diagnose the disease that medicine itself, as rhetorical systematization, creates and perpetuates[17].

A similar incoherence emerges in a slightly more indirect manner, in the discussion of oneiric experience and the language that gives account of it[18]. This case also appears in the last pages of the body of *La Persuasione e la Rettorica*, as an example of the inadequacy of the «parole convenute per ogni riferenza particolare» to communicate «le sensazioni del sogno» (PR: 111). In this critique, while dreams are considered a moment when humans are naked in front of their condition, «l'intima misura della vita» (ibid.), the experience of this state can only be given by means of an inadequate, 'rhetorical' language. This critique finds an immediate reference in the passage which was crucial for our opening argument in chapter 1. In fact, horrifying experience of lack of groundedness in nightmares is chosen by the narrator to describe the ontologic condition of 'nothingness' and human reactions against it. The depiction is similar to the section we are discussing, both in the image of 'nakedness'[19] («l'uomo si trova nuovamente senza nome e senza cognome, senza consorte e senza parenti, senza cose da fare, senza vestiti, solo, nudo, con gli occhi aperti a guardare l'oscurità». PR: 23-4), and in the shared aphasia, or failure to linguistically master the experience. That said, in reading the descriptions of the nightmares in this latter context, a question on the adequacy of the adopted language immediately arises: are the «forti contrasti e […] mutevoli velocità»[20] of these fictional and figurative sections – appreciated by Debenedetti and critics who defend the literary value of the work, or those who variously frame Michelstaedter inside the expressionist movement[21] – sufficient to avoid the rhetoric identified as a «parola conveniente per ogni referenza particolare»? Or does the dialectic between the philosophical concept and its illustration resolve in a rhetoric where the univocal objective affirmation of the concept is pursued? So as to give a plausible answer to this question – and now it should be clear how the answer will also answer our question regarding the positioning of the text in relation to its own project –a further passage needs to be analyzed.

4.1.2 Figurative language as allegory

In his important contribution[22] on the literary features of *La Persuasione e la Rettorica*, Aurelio Benevento identifies 'poetic elements' by grouping together various forms of figurative language: «ma gli elementi poetici sono da ricercarsi soprattutto nelle metafore, nelle similitudini e negli esempi o apologhi, cioè nei modi tipici del parlare figurato [...]. La rassegna delle metafore [...] attesta come il gusto del linguaggio figurato sia vivo in Michelstaedter e come in lui il ragionamento tenda a tradursi in immagine, il discorso filosofico in discorso poetico»[23]. Benevento does not differentiate the function and use of these three figures in the text; his focus on finding «tendenze alla descrizione e al racconto autonomo»[24] as evidence of the presence of 'artistic concreteness' leads him to put the figures in a ranking based on the «tendenza ad uno svolgimento narrativo autonomo»[25], starting with a discussion of metaphors, moving to similes, extended similes and apologues, and finally reaching the 'Esempio Storico' on Plato and Aristotle (PR: 66-73), which he interprets as «un documento evidente di come il pensiero di Michelstaedter si trasformi in favola e in poesia»[26]. While sharing an interest in figurative language and, more in general, in alternatives to the generalizing narratorial utterance, we tried to add a degree of complexity to the topic by reading the figures in their context and linking them to the surrounding narratorial frame. It is thanks to this approach that we were able to outline how a problem of the relation between conceptual and figurative language emerges, and threatens to reduce the 'poetic elements' to mere illustrative devices. A third example of the embodiment of different vocabularies in the text will lead us to a broader understanding of what is at stake here.

In the first chapter of the present volume, when we analyzed the dialogical and self-referential nature of the text through an enquiry into the shifting of the grammatical subject, we approached what we neutrally called a series of 'experiments', conducted by the narrator with the goal of outlining the dynamics and philosophical implications of the satisfaction of determinate needs. The 'example' of chloride (PR: 13-5), discussed then, has relevance also in the present context. First of all, it shares with the embodiment of medical rhetoric and depiction of oneiric experience the use of a language (in this case the scientific language of chemistry) elsewhere discredited as 'rhetoric'. Chemistry becomes the privileged standpoint for argumentation: «quando due sostanze si congiungono chimicamente, ognuna saziando la determinazione dell'altra cessano entrambe la loro natura, mutate nel vicendevole assorbimento» (PR: 13). It leads to an illustration of the behaviour of chloride and hydrogen: «per esempio il cloro è sempre stato così ingordo che è tutto morto, ma se noi lo facciamo rinascere e lo mettiamo in vicinanza dell'idrogeno, esso non vivrà che per l'idrogeno» (PR: 13-4). Following this, the narrator will introduce the philosophical concept of φιλοψυχία (PR: 17). The example contradicts the poetic of the text both because of its investment in a scientific language and the univocal translation of the example into a category – φιλοψυχία – which is the 'transparent' key for the interpretation. In this sense, philosophical and scientific language support each other, as if they were privileged standpoints for interpretation: something unacceptable according to Michelstaedter's theory.

This interpretation would, on a general level, complicate Benevento's argument, and bring us back to the aporia of Michelstaedter's project. What we are outlining here however, can be also understood through the debate around a particular rhetorical figure, something Benevento does not discuss, and which will give us a deeper insight into what is at stake in this stylistic choice and its 'artistic concreteness'. This figure is allegory: a *continua metaphora*, as pointed out since Quintilian[27], or a series of words taken in their literal meaning, yet referring obliquely to something else[28]. In pursuing a reading of the 'experiment' as allegory, we notice firstly that the passage in general terms is referring to one thing, while intending another – *aliud verbis, aliud sensu*[29] – and it does so through extending «beyond [...] the sentence and the discrete utterance»[30]. The oblique reference is rendered explicit: the human stomach, isolated as a single determination of will, is the vehicle of a simile, «lo stomaco è tutto fame, esso è l'attribuzione di valore al cibo [...]. Così, quando due sostanze si congiungono chimicamente [...]» (PR: 13). This reference is then immediately extended to indicate humans in general, by means of personification of the attributes of the chemical elements. In this movement a key feature of allegory is introduced:

> the staple of allegory is personification. By definition personification is a metaphoric, hence mixed, mode – something non human is endowed with human characteristics. This endowment results from the transfer of semantic features from a predicate normally associated with humans to a noun (typically functioning as a subject) that designates something non human[31].

In our passage this transfer is explicit: where chloride is depicted as «ingordo» and «tutto morto» (PR: 13), «la sua vita sarà unirsi all'idrogeno» in order to «soddisfa[re] l'amore» (PR: 14), thus, «il cloro nella lontananza dell'idrogeno si annoia» (PR: 15); hydrogen is the «*palpebra* all'occhio dell'atomo di cloro, che non vedeva che idrogeno», and «il loro amore non è per la vita soddisfatta, per l'essere persuaso, ma pel vicendevole bisogno che ignora la vita altrui» (PR: 14). The play on the terms «valore» and «valenza»[32] allows the comparison and possibility of comic effects. Hence, in the passage, the simile is widened; personification allows the comparison to be read not only with regard to the stomach (the original term), but to humans in general. If this reading is sound, the relationship of 'love' and 'boredom' between the two chemical elements can be taken as an allegory for human relationships, the spectrum of which will be covered in the development of *La Persuasione e la Rettorica*.

A third point, namely the relationship between the passage and the context in which it appears, displays a further feature of allegory, and offers the link between poetic and style. In our discussion on exemplarity and the use of parody and sarcasm, we have pointed out how the frame offered by the narrator, extra-diegetic and generalizing, works against the poetic of the text and towards the univocal affirmation of philosophical categories that work as the foundation of its system, generalizations, and the path to overcome its own rhetorical contradiction. This explanatory aim of the narrator has a crucial role in the context of the passage we are reading; it offers a univocal interpretation under the umbrella of a general concept, and thus reduces the experiment with chloride to a transparent exemplification of a theoretical argument. The general concept that is the basis of the passage is explicitly stated in a series of points that precede and frame the 'experiment', and that works as a series of definitions: «*1° Ma la volontà è in ogni punto volontà di cose determinate.* [...] *2° Determinazione è attribuzione di valore: coscienza.* [...] *3° Nessuna cosa è per sé, ma in riguardo a una coscienza.* [...] *4° La vita è un'infinita correlatività di coscienze*» (PR: 12-3). These preceding statements are nothing more than the general concepts of which the following passage is an illustration. Hence, the fictional paragraph on chloride and hydrogen, being an oblique illustration of a general concept[33], is by definition an allegory. This is particularly so if we intend the term inside the widespread[34] romantic sense which opposes allegory to symbol: «the symbol, as what can be interpreted inexhaustibly, because it is indefinite, is opposed to allegory, understood as standing in a more exact relation to meaning and exhausted by it, as art is opposed to non-art»[35].

If our analysis is correct, we can present a few concluding remarks. Firstly, a discarded vocabulary of 'objective' science is employed in what appears to be the demonstration of a theoretical point, and thus its value as evidence is intratextually undermined. Secondly, the passage's allegorical features make the example work as the illustration of a philosophical concept referred to humans in general, reducing the tale of chloride to a riddle whose key resides in the statements of the generalizing narrator. This practice results immediately in a conflict with the dictates of the hyperbolic way. Our methodological framework suggests, however, that we look for further evidence of an explicit theoretical treatment of these rhetorical points in the text, in order to read its stylistic manifestation in terms of the poetic/rhetoric relationship. In other words, what is evident in the case of the adoption of a scientific vocabulary for illustrative examples has to be verified at the level of the sub-genre 'allegory', and its relation with a pre-existent philosophical conceptualization which exhausts its interpretability. This analysis will lead us to the core of the problem that we are facing in this chapter: the question of the position of the text toward itself on the level of the dialogue between rhetorical strategies and sub-genres.

First of all, we need to map where in the text a discussion on the problem of illustration and conceptualization takes place. Secondly, we need to demonstrate if and how this theorization refers to the problem of allegory anticipated in this section. Only after this, will we be able to generalize our results to encompass the different figures outlined by Benevento and question how these cases can be located inside Michelstaedter's theoretical context. In this sense, we are coherently following the logical structure of the preceding chapters.

4.2 Allegory and symbol between Schopenhauer and the romantics

4.2.1 The dismissal of knowledge as generalization and false affirmation

The first 'Appendice Critica' is the place where we can find the most comprehensive and systematic treatment of the problem of 'rhetorical' language from a linguistic point of view. Here, 'rhetoric' – linked with the problems of self-perpetuation, time and alienating projections of one's needs and desires in the future – is considered in terms of the implications of linguistic affirmation through different modes and tenses of the verb. In the introductory section of this chapter, we have shown how the 'Appendici Critiche' are in many ways an integral part of *La Persuasione e la Rettorica*, and how their engagement with the body of the text exceeds the interpretative label of a 'retreat'. Indeed, in the first appendix, explicit reference to the body of the text[36] and the justificatory nature of the content serve as an expanded footnote, engaged in a close dialectic with the passages referred to[37]. Hence, the systematic presentation offered in the appendix dialectically completes and is completed by the relevant passages in the body of the text.

'Appendice I' opens with a series of statements that define speech as an act of illusory self-affirmation[38], a reification of reality outside the subject and an interpretation of the infinitude of every actuality through finite and arbitrarily limited concepts: «l'infinito d'ogni attualità è dato per finito, ogni *concetto arbitrariamente chiuso*». This is an inadequate affirmation of the self, because «il soggetto, in ciò che parla, si finge *Soggetto* assoluto. Ogni cosa detta ha un *Soggetto* che si finge assoluto» (PR: 135). Allegory, as the figurative illustration of a concept which works as the key to a riddle, can thus be the object of this critique of inadequacy. The allegory is entangled in a network of arbitrarily closed categories which arbitrarily inform the interpretation of an example, orienting and guiding it towards an univocal and inadequate interpretation[39].

The appendix further develops the point of the opening statements as a linguistic problem, demonstrating how all the modes of the verb cannot escape from inadequate affirmation. While through the «modo diretto», «con l'indicazione di un fatto [...] il narratore crea la presenza del fatto senza riguardo al tempo. – È un'attualità che il Soggetto si finge indipendente dal tempo» (PR: 136), under the «modo congiunto» all the affirmations of facts which are outside «l'attualità del soggetto» (PR: 138) are grouped. The subject can refer to these facts only through a reflection, a knowledge, a «rivivere sé stesso», on the basis of the affirmation that «so che questo è», in all its variants: negation, possibility, necessity, will, and so forth (PR: 138-9). Once again, both the dismissal of the value of a general statement outside the actuality of the subject, and the critique of a vocabulary which tries to give a general account of reality are in clear contrast with the mechanism of generalization and illustration proper to allegory. If the critique dismisses that «nella realtà del Soggetto ci sono ora le <*cose*> e il *pensiero* che con i suoi nessi le domina, la materia e la forma» (PR: 138), then the application of this dichotomy between matter and form in the allegory of chloride cannot be defended.

4.2.2 'Modo imperativo' as an alternative

If every affirmation based on an always inadequate general/generalizing knowledge has to be avoided (and consequently every rhetorical device that in some ways relates to this false knowledge), then the text's entire foundation on the categories of 'persuasion' and 'rhetoric' is shaken[40]. The extent of this problem becomes clear when a possible mode of adequate affirmation is outlined in the text: as 'rhetoric' is in logical opposition to 'persuasion', so are their linguistic declensions. Thus, the alternative to a 'rhetorical' utterance is a 'non-mode', the «modo imperativo» (PR: 141):

> *Non è realtà intesa, ma vita; è l'intenzione che vive essa stessa attualmente*, e non finge un'attualità *in ogni modo* finita e sufficiente: è reale tanto quanto è reale il Soggetto, perché appunto come questo non è finita nel presente, ma è *attuale come volontà d'una cosa. È il soggetto qui che invade con la propria vita il regno delle proprie parole: non fa parole, ma vive* (PR: 141-2).

The affinities between this passage as a linguistic declension of the features of 'pure possession' and earlier definitions of 'persuasion' are clear. However, this quote tells us a few more things about the 'persuaded utterance'. Firstly, such an utterance potentially exists and is somehow describable. In his notes on Parmenides, Michelstaedter states that «colui che è persuaso tace perché non ha nessun movente a parlare»; even if the possibility of a 'persuaded' word is here implied (he does not have a 'motive', but he does not lack the tool), this word is unknowable until it is possessed: «ma chi è angosciato dal mistero [...] tacerà finché non conoscerà la parola persuasiva»[41]. Elsewhere, at the beginning of the famous 'Esempio Storico', the exemplary Socrates is depicted as silent and indescribable (if not a Buddhist-like negation of opposites[42]): «né volò al sole – né restò sulla terra; – né fu indipendente né schiavo; né felice né misero; – ma di lui con le mie parole non ho più che dire» (PR: 66). In the passage we are discussing, however, the definition seems more immediately and also somehow more positively addressed. Despite the general inadequacy of the narratorial utterance, a definition is given, and it is closer to other examples we have encountered, such as Beethoven and Christ: not by accident, two examples from the artistic and the religious, as we are about to argue.

In the passage, the positive description of an adequate utterance emerges through a relatively small number of dichotomies[43]: 'life' versus comprehension of a reality, 'actuality' versus finitude in the present, 'invasion' of the realm of the word versus rhetorical word 'production'. The key to these dichotomies resides in understanding the role that conceptualization plays in their construction: the avoidance of reification and crystallization of words into an arbitrary finitude leads to an overcoming of 'rhetoric'. The apparent obscurity of this overcoming is further clarified in passages of the body of the text that directly refer to and develop this synthetic definition through reference to artistic language. More specifically, the last section to which 'Appendice I' refers (PR: 113-17), offers – inside an argument developed towards the prophetic dismissal of technical language as the ultimate achievement of 'rhetoric' and human alienation – a discussion on the adequacy of affirmation within the realm of aesthetics.

The *pars destruens* of these pages is a faithful application of the 'modo diretto' and 'modo congiunto' of the 'Appendice I' to the destinies of the «uomo ammaestrato» (PR: 113). His fallacious relationship with his own reality is opposed to the alternative synthesized in the Parmenidean motto: «portare vicine le cose lontane» (PR: 46)[44]. The example is well known: the «uomo ammaestrato» «s'avvicina alle cose lontane per vedere» (ibid.) in the same way that a 'bad painter' – «il semplice» (PR: 114) – wanting to paint two rows of trees of an alley, goes closer to them and paints them all the same size, same color, same shadows. On the contrary, the 'good painter' has «nell'occhio e nella mano parallele le linee dei due filari, quando le fa convergenti; e gli alberi della stessa altezza quando li fa digradanti; e tutti dello stesso colore quando li fa più velati d'azzurro» (PR: 113). This artistic faculty is interpreted as a «facoltà potente di sogno»: «l'artista [...] vede le cose lontane come le vicine e perciò le può dare così ch'esse appaiano nella loro reciproca relazione di vicine e di lontane » (ibid.).

The preceding comparison reveals first of all a positive investment in artistic language as a possible solution to the problem of adequate representation[45]. Art is described as a 'powerful faculty of dream', linked to the power that dream has to reveal the reality of existence beyond the veil of Maya.

In the context of the passage, the privileges of figurative art are soon expanded to incorporate poetry: «[b]ene dice Boccaccio: <Dante Alighieri son, Minerva oscura / d'intelligenza e d'arte ... / L'alta mia fantasia, pronta e sicura ...>» (PR: 113), and so the link with the example of the painter encompasses this language. The guilt of the 'simpleton' painter with regard to the object he represents is that «lo ha significato con quelle apparenze che ogni volta lo fanno riconoscere a chi l'abbia già visto» (PR: 114), while the artistic goal is «comunicare l'intimtà, la stessa natura dell'oggetto» (ibid.). In the case of linguistic signification: «così quando parla [il semplice] si trascina attraverso le relazioni elementari dei concetti e per più girar che faccia non più ne prende» (ibid.). In this sense, conceptualization equals recognition and thus false affirmation. The movement of this fall is described as a progressive 'crystallization': from a potential «pienezza delle referenze» and the 'life' which allows them to perform a multiplicity of determinations and connections, to a univocal, crystallized and finite determination through «elementari relazioni di tempo e [...] finalità» (PR: 115). Again, inadequate signification takes the shape of a corruption: «del resto il bell'organismo vivo di un periodo rivelatore, è ridotto al pesante seguito di proposizioni incolori come una catena di forzati, legati pesantemente coi <che>, coi <siccome>» (ibid.).

Further clues gathered through the reading of this passage can help us to integrate the 'Appendice I' into this argument, and offer a schematic synthesis of what is at stake in the alternative between inadequate and adequate affirmation. First of all, alongside the logical relation between the two words, the 'rhetorical' and the adequate, a parallel argument of 'originality' versus 'corruption' is added. This is presented both in the concept of a progressive 'crystallization' and 'reduction' of the revelatory sentence. If this is in some way implicit in the motto 'with words, war against words' – where 'fallen' language fights against itself in order to regain an original unity between subject and object[46] – identification of the original language with the language of art can be a springboard for a contextualization of Michelstaedter inside a Rousseauian and Leopardian line of thought. This theoretical connection ought to precede any attempt at an analysis of Michelstaedter's critique of technical language and mechanization based on a Marxist framework[47]. This parallel will be a crucial point of our concluding chapter: in the present context, however, it is discussed towards a comprehensive understanding of the problem of 'persuasion' in the realm of aesthetics, both theoretically and in its translation into strategies of signification.

A further point to be drawn from the preceding passage is that adequate language should embody the characteristics of what the narrator calls 'fullness of reference'. I read this as a degree of multiplicity in potential interpretations, against the univocal reference of the crystallized word. This multiplicity is obtained once again through an avoidance of conceptualization, time and causality. Adequate language should be immediate, as 'persuasion' is pure presence outside the *principium individuationis*. The adequate utterance has the prerogative of being 'revelatory' or of 'bringing close the things which are far': it does not imply the act of signification but the communication of an intimacy, of the «*stessa* natura dell'oggetto[48]» (PR: 114). In other words, the adequate affirmation is uttered from beyond the veil of Maya, and is revelatory both of the existence of the veil itself and the perlocutionary: it moves towards 'persuasion'.

The above conclusions take us back to the example of chloride, that now stands out for its incoherence with the prerogatives of the poetic of adequacy. We could argue, with Brianese, that examples of this sort are evidence of an investment in artistic language and are conceived in order to avoid an academic tone. And further, that the vocabulary drawn from chemistry should be intended as part of this fiction, and thus free from any slide into a positive adoption of scientific modes. However, two hurdles remain. Firstly, even inside a figurative frame, scientific knowledge and the laws of chemistry are adopted as part of a demonstration and further reinforcement of the argument of the narrator. To say that 'humans work like chloride' can only have a 'rhetorical' value. Secondly, by reading the example in the context of its appearance, we can see how it functions as a one to one illustration of a rule, anticipated in the framing narratorial utterance. This allegorical feature of the passage is clearly understandable within Michelstaedter's critique of inadequate affirmation. The discrepancy, if there is one, is in the adopted terminology; for the broadness of Michelstaedter's critique goes beyond allegory, encompassing any language that relies on conceptualization and reification, and allegory in this case looks like one of the fallacies which the text unavoidably incurs in its attempt to escape the boundaries of the philosophical academic genre. However our link with allegory has the merit of allowing some remarks on its adequate opposite.

As noted above in Gadamer's review of Romantic, post-Kantian aesthetics, a polarization between allegory and symbol takes place in nineteenth-century speculations. Furthermore, in the same context this opposition becomes synonymous with the dichotomy art/non-art. It is rather difficult to draw intertextual links that can give us direct evidence of Michelstaedter's familiarity with Romantic frameworks. However, our discussion already points towards a series of similarities – and some crucial philosophical differences – along with the treatment of aesthetic production in a certain source: Schopenhauer. The third book of *The World as Will and Representation* offers a series of parallels with passages of *La Persuasione e la Rettorica* and will allow us to precisely define the philosophical distance between the two authors. Moreover, the comparison will enable us to define the philosophical reasons behind Michelstaedter' investment in the aesthetic, and to make sense of the discrepancy in his stylistic adoption of illustrative, allegorical modes.

4.2.3 Michelstaedter's position towards Schopenhauer's idea of art

We can start by showing the similarities between the two philosophers, they include: the idea of the work of art as the product of genius that lifts itself above the *principium individuationis*; the subsequent definition of the extraneousness of conceptualization to artistic production; the lifting of the veil of Maya by both the artist/creator, and the audience that is moved by the work of genius. The first point is almost self evident: Schopenhauer's definitions of art are very clear in this sense: «what kind of knowledge is it that considers what constitutes to exist outside and independently of all relations, but which alone is really essential to the world, the true content of its phenomena, that which is subject to no change, and is therefore known with equal truth for all time? [...] It is *art*, the work of genius»[49]. The work of genius is beyond the principle of reason, its foundation is 'intuition': «such a subject of knowledge no longer follows relations in accordance with the principle of sufficient reason; on the contrary, it rests in fixed contemplation of the object presented to it out of its connexion with any other, and rises into this»[50].

Michelstaedter subscribes to these statements and radicalizes them. First of all, what in Schopenhauer is a temporary act becomes in Michelstaedter the endpoint of a journey of emancipation. While, for the German, what constitutes the genius is that his «power of knowledge is [...] withdrawn *for a part of his time* from the service of his will» (my italic)[51], in Michelstaedter the hyperbolic way implies, *ad infinitum*, a leap which coincides with the absolute: «il persuaso – il dio» (PR: 77). It is hard to imagine this as a temporary state, leading back to the humanity of finite relationships[52]. This is a radicalization in the sense that the Schopenhauerian paths of the saint, philosopher and artistic genius seem to merge into a singular path towards the absolute; and the language linked with this way will be declined in artistic and religious terms[53].

The second point, the extraneousness of conceptualization to art, is a consequence of the intuitive prerogative of the genius against the principle of reality. It is interesting to acknowledge how for Schopenhauer «the pure subject of knowledge and its correlative, the Idea, have passed out all these forms of the principle of sufficient reason. Time, place, the individual that knows, and the individual that is known, have no meaning for them»[54]. Michelstaedter, in his linguistic treatment of the problem, affirms instead that the crystallizations to be avoided as inadequate affirmations are only «tempo e finalità» (PR: 115). This leaves open the possibility for a theoretical distinction between a figure of speech based on time, such as allegory – where a time-bound relationship between the preceding concept and the following illustration is unavoidably present – and figures based on space, a distinction which is not to be found in this passage of Schopenhauer's work, but which develops throughout German Romanticism inside the dichotomization of allegory versus symbol[55]. What the two philosophers agree upon however, is the fact that «the concept [...] is eternally barren and unproductive in art»[56], specifically because it is *unitas post rem*»[57]. For Michelstaedter, this generalization from a subjective experience constitutes the very core of his argument against false affirmation and rhetorical language, and is a further radicalization which dismisses once and for all the pretences of philosophical systematic language. Muzzioli's statement that Michelstaedter cannot subscribe to the difference between the Saint and the Philosopher as proposed by the German, also finds here its linguistic demonstration, and shows not only that the *noluntas* is 'too passive'[58] and substituted with the 'activity' of Socratic dialectic, but that at the limit of this activity, the language of adequate affirmation is the language of the artistic genius.

It is time to highlight the prerogatives of this language. In his argument against conceptualization in art, Schopenhauer introduces his critique of allegory: «we shall not be able to approve, when a work of art is intentionally and avowedly chosen to express a concept; this is the case in allegory. An allegory is a work of art signifying something different from what it depicts»[59]. It is clear how a series of other rhetorical figures can be enclosed within this general definition, namely all the cases when the immediate representation that informs the work of art is reduced to an illustration based on a logic of temporality and reason. Schopenhauer himself acknowledges that fact when he moves from the aesthetic analysis of figurative art to that of poetry. However, in this movement, the figure of allegory comes to assume for him a positive value, one that constitutes the very basis for the distinction between the two arts. In fact, while «in plastic and pictorial art allegory leads away from what is given in perception, from the real object of all art, to abstract thoughts; but in poetry the relation is reverse. Here the concept is what is directly given in words, and the first aim is to lead from this to the perceptive, the depiction of which must be undertaken by the imagination of the hearer»[60]. This is the affirmation of a positive use of conceptualization, one that opens the way to a defence not only of poetic, but philosophical language. At the same time, this is precisely the distance that separates the German philosopher from Michelstaedter. In *La Persuasione e la Rettorica* there is not space for a justification of what in the text is called 'false affirmation'. We have seen how the critique of philosophical language[61], the representation of the 'way to persuasion' through the mathematical function of the hyperbole[62] and the linguistic treatment of inadequate affirmation do not allow any space for such a redemption.

If our reading is correct, it opens a number of points of discussion. Firstly, we need to ask something more specific about the positive, 'persuaded' language and its features, and outline the position of the 'persuaded' with regard to aesthetics, philosophy, and their generic languages[63]. Secondly, we need to address the problem of the apparent contradiction between what is stated theoretically by Michelstaedter and the presence of allegory in the textual production of the argument itself. In doing so, we need to demonstrate how the structure of allegory can be adopted as a framework to interpret the remaining rhetorical figures, and more in general, the dialectic between them.

4.2.4   One language: persuaded and persuading

«The striving on the part of the Romantic aestheticians after a resplendent but ultimately non-committal knowledge of an absolute has secured a place in the most elementary theoretical debates about art for a notion of the symbol which has nothing more than the name in common with the genuine notion»[64]. This synthetic and highly effective critique of the romantic notion of 'symbol' as opposed to 'allegory' by Walter Benjamin could in many ways be adapted to make sense of much of Michelstaedter's project of an adequate language. In his move away from Schopenhauer, Michelstaedter develops notions which are comparable with and indirectly refer to a Romantic notion of symbol, which constitutes the discriminant between the artistic work of genius and, in a development of the Kantian notion we encountered in our second chapter, representation based on rules. The 'thirst for absolute' that is the engine of *La Persuasione e la Rettorica* works towards a definition of adequacy which can be encompassed in Benjamin's critique. It is worth remarking on this parallel.

Many of the reasons that lead to the Romantic separation and opposition between symbol and allegory are comparable, if translated into the theoretical vocabulary of *La Persuasione e la Rettorica*, with the effort to define linguistic emancipation from 'rhetoric'. When Schelling, in his *Philosophie der Kunst*, affirms that «the demand of absolute artistic representation is: representation with complete indifference, so that the universal is wholly the particular, and the particular at the same time wholly the universal, and does not simply mean it»[65] he prepares, as Gadamer points out, the central place of symbol in aesthetic speculation[66], as a «coincidence of sensible appearance and supra-sensible meaning»[67]. Gadamer[68] traces this development from Kant, stressing the importance of the shift from the preponderance of the concept of aesthetic judgement to that of the concept of genius, seen as the only aesthetic paradigm, particularly in the works of Schiller[69], and the *Sturm und Drang*[70]. He does so by tracing the rise and development of the concept of *Erlebnis*, which comes to be defined as follows: «the structures of meaning which we meet in the human sciences [...] can be reduced to ultimate units of what is given in consciousness, unities which themselves no longer contain anything, alien, objective, in need of interpretation»[71]. Here we find, by implication, the contraposition of objective concept and life/experience and therefore the closed nature of the concept, against the irreducibly open nature of life: «the experience [*Erlebnis*] has a definite immediacy which eludes every opinion about its meaning»[72].

It is on this basis that the symbol becomes the privileged mode for the signification of what Gadamer calls *Erlebniskunst*, where its division from allegory embodies all the contrapositions outlined above: subjectivity versus objectivity; openness versus closure; immediacy versus conceptual signification which relies on temporality and, most importantly, the immediate presence of the universal inside the particular. Paul De Man, in his article on 'the rhetoric of temporality', offers two insightful definitions of these figures, inside a Romantic aesthetic framework:

> In the world of the symbol it would be possible for the image to coincide with the substance, since the substance and its representation do not differ in their being but only in their extension [...]. Their relationship is one of simultaneity, which, in truth, is spatial in kind, and in which the intervention of time is merely a matter of contingency, whereas, in the world of allegory, time is the originary constitutive category. [... I]t remains necessary, if there is to be allegory that the allegorical sign refers to another sign that precedes it. The meaning constituted by the allegorical sign can then consist only in the *repetition* (in the Kirkegaardian sense of the term) of a previous sign with which it can never coincide, since it is of the essence of this previous sign to be pure anteriority[73].

It is possible to show, at this point, how the features of adequate affirmation introduced in *La Persuasione e la Rettorica* fit with De Man's synthesis. The emphasis on avoidance of temporality and causality (PR: 115) implies an understanding of 'space' as the category through which to achieve simultaneity[74]. As a consequence, while rhetorical words «da individualità precise [...] diventano *partes materiales*» (PR: 114), adequate utterance is *pars formalis*, it communicates the 'same nature of the object' (ibid.). It is the representation of the pure possession of the object which does not differ from the act of possession, as described in the 'imperative (non) mode': «*è il Soggetto qui che invade con la propria vita il regno delle proprie parole: non fa parole, ma vive*» (PR: 142). This coincidence of life with word, further declined as 'unity of life and art' in many of Michelstaedter's descriptions[75], offers the link with the concept of *Erlebnis*, as the key alternative to conceptualization and science, and in this sense, the project of *La Persuasione e la Rettorica* can be contextualized as one of the developments of a Romantic aesthetic, in the sense outlined by Gadamer:

> Schleiermacher's appeal to living feeling against the cold rationalism of the enlightenment, Schiller's call for aesthetic freedom against mechanistic society, Hegel's contrasting of life (later, of spirit) with 'positivity', were the forerunners of the protest against modern industrial society which at the beginning of our century caused the words *Erlebnis* and *Erleben* to become almost sacred clarion calls. [...] The influence of Friedrich Nietzsche and Henry Bergson played its part, but also a 'spiritual movement' like that around Stefan George and, not least, the seismographical accuracy with which the philosophy of Georg Simmel reacted to these events are all part of the same thing. The life philosophy of our own day follows on its Romantic predecessors. The rejection of the mechanisation of life in contemporary society puts such obvious emphasis on the word that its conceptual implications remain totally hidden[76].

We can argue that Michelstaedter's speculations anticipate expressionist and existentialist themes, and modes proper to Italian Novecento as a result of taking a post-Romantic system to its extreme consequences.

In stylistic terms, we have seen how *Erlebnis* is linked with symbol. Symbol as the 'giving'[77] of *Erlebnis* is 'open', indeterminable and inexhaustible through conceptualization: it is what Michelstaedter's calls 'fullness of relationship'. Moreover, the word 'symbol' opens to an understanding of its nature through the realm of the religious, where it assumes an anagogic function: 'it leads up to the knowledge of the divine'[78]. Michelstaedter's recurrent use of the word 'revelation' («il bell'organismo vivo di un periodo *rivelatore*» PR: 115) works also on this level; it links the lifting of the veil of Maya and the perlocutionary role of the exemplary 'persuaded' with a religious vocabulary. According to De Mauro's dictionary[79], among the uses of the term 'rivelatore' we can identify the following ones: «che rivela ciò che è sconosciuto, in particolare ciò che è soprannaturale o divino; che costituisce il tramite umano alla rivelazione divina»; while 'rivelazione', «atto della divinità che comunica all'uomo verità inconoscibili dalla ragione» gives us the sense of emancipation from concepts with which adequate affirmation is concerned. Michelstaedter confirms this point in his definition of the word of Christ: «così Cristo parla denso e complesso ai discepoli e in parabole al popolo» (PR: 48). The total avoidance of the problem of the relation between parable and explanation in the New Testament affirms the idea of the 'persuaded word' as an aesthetic/religious one, and the figure of Christ therefore becomes exemplary.

4.2.5   Why an allegory, then?

Given this theoretical context, it is clear how a figurative strategy like the allegory of the chloride cannot be considered evidence of an investment in artistic/poetic/literary language that fulfils the requirements of adequacy. Reading the passage in its dialectic with the framing utterance threatens Benevento's theory and further confirms the idea that *La Persuasione e la Rettorica* is not written from the point of view of an achieved, positive state of 'persuasion'. In other words, it does not deploy a language emancipated from the problematic it is describing: it is not the word of 'revelation' but the word of 'repetition' («se io ora lo ripeto come so e posso» PR: 4). Logically, the 'persuaded expression', as well as the expression of 'persuasion' are entangled in a time-bound conceptualizing language, and can only be stated as an impossibility. Consequently, the text is exiled from its chimera of emancipation and finds its only coherent possibility in the dialectic of (self) negation[80].

In this sense, the notion of 'repetition' offers the chance to pursue a general interpretation of this fight, and some remarks on the links between allegory and repetition can illustrate the point. Because repetition can never be coincidence – or in Michelstaedter's words «si duo idem faciunt non est idem»[81] (PR: 62) – allegory orients itself towards the narratorial explicative frame at a certain degree of dialogism. The one to one interpretation that allegories and the generalizing narrator put in place is therefore never a perfect equation, and the 'gap' that this equation leaves is precisely the basis on which the voices of the text are relativized. Juxtaposition of genres is an interpretation; it is a continuous correction that shows/performs the impossibility of a final result. The high level of self-referentiality in the text is confirmed by a style that proceeds along the hyperbole of the negative dialectic[82]. This is what De Man in *Blindness & Insight* calls 'accounting for the rhetoricity of its own mode'[83], when he critiques Derrida's reading of Rousseau's philosophy of language inside the framework of a metaphysic of presence. It is not our task to offer the final word on the debate on Rousseau, nor on the difference between the two contemporary philosophers, but De Man's points on Rousseau's style help us to synthesize what we have discovered about the argumentative style[84] of *La Persuasione e la Rettorica*. According to De Man's reading, language, in an analogy with music, can be seen as a system of relations without a referent: it 'refers to the absence of meaning'[85]. Meaning is thus conceived not as a presence, but as a void[86]. A logical consequence is the problem of asserting a meaning about language through a language that can only witness its absence. De Man acknowledges the point as follows: 'as [the text] accounts for its own mode of writing, it states at the same time the necessity of making this statement itself an indirect, figural way that knows it will be misunderstood by being taken literally'[87]. This means a degree of literariness:

> diachronic structures such as music, melody, or allegory are favoured over pseudo-synchronic structures such as painting, harmony or mimesis because the latter mislead one into believing in a stability of meaning that does not exist. The elegiac tone that is occasionally sounded does not express a nostalgia for an original presence, but is a purely dramatic device, an effect made possible and dictated by a fiction that deprives the nostalgia of all foundation[88].

As a result, «with Rousseau [...,] a vocabulary of substance and presence is no longer used declaratively but rhetorically, for the very reasons that are being (metaphorically) stated»[89].

Our reading of *La Persuasione e la Rettorica* until this point has been devoted to showing how the text addresses the same problem of working with a language divested of its authority. It is clear that Michelstaedter's philosophical point of departure is different from that claimed by De Man for Rousseau; our author subscribes to a metaphysic of presence, and shows a nostalgia for the plenitude of meaning as original unity to be regained. Yet this lost fullness is conceived as the 'impossible' metaphysical endpoint of a dialectic which should at the same time state a philosophical program and negate the value of ('rhetorical') language as the *locus* of meaning. The text partakes of a similar problem: negating value to inadequate affirmation. The 'war with words against words' is Michelstaedter's way to account for the rhetoricity of his own words.

4. 3   Figures, sub-genres and conceptualization

Our discussion on allegory outlined the dialectic between the figure and the *logos* to which it refers. Furthermore, it took this mechanism as an example of a general dialectic that relativizes the voices and stylistic strategies juxtaposed in the text, and in doing so performs the consciousness of its 'rhetorical' nature. In this sense, we affirmed that *La Persuasione e la Rettorica* performs a level of fiction that is rather different from that outlined only through a decontextualized analysis of the figure. What we need to demonstrate now is how the structure of allegory works when other figures or sub-genres are involved. This generalization is necessary for our concluding interpretation, and will start with a discussion of the 'Esempio Storico' (PR: 66-72), the most extended fictional attempt to be found in the body of the text. This will offer us the opportunity to make some remarks on the use of simile, and thus exhaust the list of Benevento's evidence of 'concretezza artistica'. The discussion of this last figure is important not only because it confirms our reading, but because it shows how the conceptual system developed by the narrator ambiguously shares a vocabulary and method derived from the figurative illustrations. Once we have demonstrated that similes cannot be coherently invested with such an epistemological value, we will reach the conclusion that the entire text is consciously constructed as a rhetoric that withdraws from the pretence of adequacy and performs a continuing dialectic of negations.

4.3.1 'Un Esempio Storico' (PR: 66-72) as a myth

Nimis, in his work on simile in the epic tradition, offers a slightly different definition of allegory that is useful for clarifying our argument:

> [a]n allegorical text establishes a network of relationships among various conventional units [...] so that these conventional content-forms become expression-forms. The units are manipulated in such a way that signals to the addressee that the rule organizing the discourse is not the usual one governing these units [...] but some other non-explicit rule [...]. There is always the possibility that the reader will not 'catch on'[90].

My point is that in *La Persusione e la Rettorica* it is impossible for a reader not to 'catch on', because the rule governing the units is explicit, reiterated and expressed as an univocal interpretation of the figure. This is the case also in the 'Esempio Storico': a dramatization of Plato's philosophy and its corruption, and Aristotle's final betrayal through the tale of a trip on a hot air balloon led by Plato and his disciples. *Per se*, this would again be evidence of a direct investment in fiction, through an ironic take on Plato's 'second navigation' and a dismissal of Aristotle's philosophy in a concluding moralizing passage[91]. However, close analysis of the structure and content of the tale reveals also a myth of origins: in this case the origin of 'rhetoric' [92]. The Platonic use of myth as 'narration of the origins'; the setting in a past beyond historical evidence; the use of a protagonist who is an individual with a 'proper name', and the mix of real and fantastic geography all contitute the narrative of Michelstaedter's 'hot air balloon'. Surely the conception of this story has not only a moral, but a sarcastic intent, attempting to dismantle with witty stylization the speculations of the two philosophers (the original object of Michelstaedter's 'degree thesis'). Even so, however, the choice of fiction implies a moral and, in its avoidance of academic rhetoric, eikastic[93] aim; the latter confirmed in the many intertextual references to myth throughout *La Persuasione e la Rettorica*. Myth is consistently exploited as a positive figurative synthesis of an argument, thus performing a symbolic/eikastic function[94]. The narrator cannot afford to incur the contradiction of attacking Aristotle's rhetorical system through his own system of concepts, hence the language of the fiction seems to provide a first escape route. The literature on myth can help to analyze this investment, and draw a parallel with our analysis of allegory.

In interpreting this dismissal as a tongue-in-cheek myth, the contraposition between poetic/artistic and philosophical language which we discussed in this chapter is declined inside the Platonic opposition between myth and *logos*, intending the former as an «imaginative narrative without need of persuasive reasons», and the latter as «present[ing] putatively persuasive reasons in a rationalized progression»[95]. As Brisson states, this is the differentiation between narrative and argumentative, unverifiable and verifiable[96]. We know that in the argument of the second appendix, where the critique of Plato's republic is developed, Michelstaedter explicitly affirms that the expulsion of the poets from the republic is a sign of a defence, organized by a 'rhetorical' construct, against the 'truth': «Platone *teme* ora la verità che sommuove l'individuo dalle radici e scatena in lui la domanda d'un presente più pieno – che non venga a turbare i cerchi arbitrari delle sue finzioni di vita: – *egli non tollera più l'arte*» (PR: 149).

For Michelstaedter, the values of the opposition are inverted, and the artistic word – in coherence with our reading so far – is the positive pole which cannot find its place in the rhetorical language of the republic, simply because its function is to shatter such a construct. In other words, in Michelstaedter's text the 'benefit' and the 'usefulness' of poetic language is opposite from that which would allow the poet back inside the republic[97].

It is well known that the frequent presence of myths in Plato's own writing calls into question the theoretical dismissal of the poetic genre. Not only is the myth adequate for the realms of ethics and politics 'for the great majority of those who are not philosophers, and in whose souls the desiring part (epithum a) is predominant'[98] but its possibilities are fully exploited in crucial passages of philosophical speculation. Benitez, among others, interprets this investment as a sign of what he called a broadly agreed upon 'two-worlds view' of Plato:

> the phrase 'Two-Worlds' is sometimes read in a general and indefinite way, to refer to Plato's separation of the Forms, and sometimes in a narrow, theoretical way, to refer to an interpretation of Plato's epistemological distinction between knowledge and opinion according to which knowledge and opinion range exclusively over different kind of objects. [...] If I am right about Plato taking an aesthetic approach to the reality/appearance distinction, however, the separation of Forms does not have to take a *theoretical* or strictly *logical* shape; it can instead be mythopoietic[99].

According to this reading, myth gains an epistemological role in relation to the signification of reality. If fantasy is an illusory construct[100], eikastic myth – in opposition to fantasy – offers a solution to the problem of positive signification: if «the real world is not the "true earth" inside the myth, but rather one that lies beyond the myth, as reality lies *beyond* a picture. That world can only be apprehended by mind (*nous*)», eikastic myth can be read as «a picture that is *like* the way things are». Benitez concludes that within philosophy, myth is the 'positive' solution to a dialectic of negation: «*Aporiai* can only show how the real is not, they cannot show us as the real is [...]. Myth is required to give wings to the soul, and convey thinking upwards to the *noetic*»[101].

We are not in a position to draw conclusions regarding Plato's philosophy and style. Rather we are interested in how the embracing of fictionality, and in particular fictionality which is not a fantasy, offers Michelstaedter a tool which seems to be coherent with the requirements of adequacy of affirmation.

The 'Esempio Storico' comes at the end of the argument on 'rhetoric' (PR: 53), as a fictional representation of its origin and an explicative example of the «rettorica filosofico-letteraria»; the dismissal of which as a «vaneggiamento» (PR: 66) precedes the example. Despite being expanded to occupy several pages, it works as an illustration. Moreover, the fictional nature of the passage is explicitly acknowledged and justified through different devices. A footnote at the very beginning («Note giustificative: v. App. 2» PR: 66) links the passage with the second appendix, where the frame of the myth is reproduced in the most academic-like argumentation of the entire work[102]. Once again, the 'rebellious' efforts of artistic language are frustrated, and the critique of Aristotle ultimately becomes the critique of the process of conceptualization that is in place: «il regno delle parole è [...] così ben costituito che ogni ribellione rientra anch'essa nelle istituzioni preparate. A ogni obiezione è opposto un τόπος» (PR: 220).

Finally, open explanation of the potential misunderstandings of fiction excludes the possibility of a literal reading, and demands that the readers 'catch on':

> è per sé stesso chiaro, che come io non pretendo che davvero Platone abbia fatto l'aeronauta, così non voglio aver fatto congetture sulle relazioni con Aristotele come in fatti avvenissero. Ma certo che gli ultimi dialoghi e specialmente il *Parmenide* sono animati da uno spirito aristotelico e sembrano un preludio alle categorie e alla metafisica di Aristotele. [...] Il dissolversi del mondo delle idee nella infinita trama delle forme, – del quale questi dialoghi (*Parmenide*, *Sofista*, *Politico*) segnano un punto intermedio [...] è una necessità che pur sotto altre apparenze si ripete ogni qual volta degli uomini seguendo materialmente la via d'un uomo migliore, s'affaccendino coi concetti per loro ormai privi di valore (PR: 72-3).

4.3.2 Similes as illustration of a logos

The 'Esempio Storico' is evidence of a first degree of generalization of the mechanisms of allegory. Inside the same order of problems, we will now read the presence and treatment of simile, in order to develop our point towards its conclusion.

The motto «*Si duo idem faciunt non est idem*» (PR: 62) includes an account of the problem of temporality in repetition. Furthermore, it is coherent with theories on simile which see the role of the vehicle as more complex than a simple reduction to the common principle, the *tertium comparationis*, between the two semantic domains of tenor and vehicle[103]. Addison, for example, faithful to a grammatical definition of simile, opts for a non analytic reading which interprets the similarity marker[104] ('like', 'as') as a link based on resemblance, rather than equality and coincidence[105]. In this, she confirms the importance for simile of a framework which (as Ricoeur – in order to give an account of its paradox – developed in his seminal work on metaphor) avoids the dichotomy sameness/difference[106]. This leads to a series of remarks concerning interpretation: the impossibility of 'closing' a simile[107] through a mono-dimensional reduction to its *tertium comparationis*, which highlights the common attribute between the two compared terms, thus focusing exclusively and reductively on similarity[108]; the constructive role of the simile in '*creat[ing]* similarities and connections between categories'[109]; and the particular epistemological, poetic, rhetorical and pedagogical role that simile comes to assume in this sense. It is with regard to the latter that Bridgeman speaks of metaphor and simile as «having the same perlocutionary force: they ask the listener/reader to compare»[110]. 'Perlocutionary' is a term that assumes a crucial role in our understanding of Michelstaedter's idea of adequate utterance. It is in this sense that the motto «*si duo idem faciunt non est idem*» gives an account also of a particular intention that should be at the basis of the adoption of simile.

However, on another level, if the perlocutionary feature of simile is coherent with the poetic of *La Persuasione e la Rettorica*, the figure poses a problem which we can identify in the role of the *tertium comparationis*, or in the *logos* that is communicated and which the figure helps to discover/illustrate: simile can also 'convince' – both inductively and deductively – of the objective validity of a general thesis, which works as the foundation for the comparison. If, as Bridgeman states, simile can cease to be part of a truth functional semantics[111], the existence of similes that are strictly anchored to a single and generally agreed upon key to interpretation[112] is evidence that we can identify a rhetorical use of the figure which is blind to the problem of the failure of repetition and the open/inexhaustible nature of the comparison: the figure is adopted as evidence of an underlying hypothesis. In the language of *La Persuasione e la Rettorica*, we can translate this point by saying that as there is a 'correct' use of simile as perlocutionary, on the other hand, simile is 'rhetoric' – it is inadequate pedagogy, inadequate affirmation of a falsely objective rule[113].

Our point here is two-fold. Firstly, we can confirm how the structure of allegory as illustration works in the text, and how similes are closely bound with their underlying *logoi*. Secondly, and more crucially, we can demonstrate how the vocabulary adopted in the similes (often of a scientific nature) is emptied of its epistemological value by a critique and dismissal of science as 'rhetoric'. At this point, we will be able to show how the different semantic domains of the simile's tenor and vehicle are permeable, and how a linguistic exchange takes place. The movement of figurative terminology inside the conceptual will offer final evidence of the self-conscious literary/figurative status of the argumentation, and justify the dialectic dynamics of the 'words against words'; that of the 'rhetoric against itself'.

At the end of the chapter on the 'Illusion of Persuasion' (PR: 11-30), where the concept of φιλοψυχία is introduced, we encounter four similes that develop in conspicuous paragraphs, all opening with the similarity marker «come». Each is conceived as the illustration of a preceding statement, in which the reasons for interpreting violence as the result of a fight between two different entities longing to fulfil their will of affirmation, where this affirmation does not imply reciprocal satisfaction, are offered: «quando il dente dell'una ruota piccola o grande non vada nel vacuo dell'altra e viceversa, la violenza inimica si fa manifesta: ché dove l'una s'afferma l'altra non può affermarsi, e se non soccombono entrambe nella lotta, convien che l'una ceda o soccomba. E allora insieme si fa manifesta l'impotenza della minor potenza»[114]. (PR: 28) In the deployment of similes we find a conclusive link with a further tenor which, while repeating the theme of adaptation and the necessity to succumb, reveals the *logos* which is at the basis of all the comparisons: «*così nella vita il debole s'adatta*. E a questo lo guida il *dio*[115] della φιλοψυχία» (PR: 29). Φιλοψυχία is the *tertium comparationis* and works as a general category that invests the similes by limiting the openness of their interpretability. The generalizing aim of the narrator is in place and he is working to establish himself and his message as the centre of the text. If this is true, and if 'love for life/cowardice' is the 'guide' – logically speaking the reason – for the adapting action of the 'weak', then the question is: why is there a need for a series of similes which 'stand out of the text'[116]? If the simile is there in order to support the argument, on which basis does this support take place?

In general terms, the similes provide a degree of difference from the simple reiteration of the concept of φιλοψυχία, and in ways which seem to show a further expansion of the reasons for the adaptation of the weak. The first simile interprets the sculptural group of the satyr and hermaphrodite from the Uffizi in Florence (PR: 28). The description focuses on the weakness of the satyr, and rather than describing the reasons behind his submission to φιλοψυχία, describes the moment in which φιλοψυχία falls short, against the «oscurità di una potenza che lo trascende» (ibid.) that is in the eye of the hermaphrodite. In this sense, the simile embraces the entire dynamics of the experience of horror, the escape from horror and the consequent building of 'rhetoric' which the term φιλοψυχία embodies[117]. But in doing so, it chooses a particular case of this process, namely one in which the incomprehensible horror is experienced through a relationship with another person, the 'strong'. The 'weak' would like to affirm himself «nella sua consueta relazione di fronte a chi è più forte di lui» (ibid.), but is petrified by what he does not understand, and in defence he becomes terrified. It is, in this case, something very close to the failure to interpret a 'persuaded' word: one specific declension of the manifestation of φιλοψυχία[118].

The second simile widens the dichotomy 'strong' versus 'weak' to encompass the animal world: the dove in the claws of the hawk is the 'weak' that becomes 'matter' for the life of the other (ibid.). The horror of the discovery of the impossibility of affirming one-self is, in this animal world, completely absent. So is representation of the possibilities of an active choice for or against φιλοψυχία : here there is no consciousness, and the affirmation of the strongest against the weakest is mechanical, it is a 'law of nature'. This difference is indirectly stressed in the following simile, where the object is the wider and more accurate sense of perception that pertains to the 'strong' hunter because of his more vast consciousness: «nella coscienza più vasta la stessa cosa è più reale, perché riflette quella coscienza più vasta» (PR: 29). Here the relationship between tenor and vehicle is limited to a definition of the reason beyond 'weakness' and 'strength', which leads to the violence of affirmation and submission: 'consciousness' is the *tertium comparationis* of the 'weak' «tiratore inesperto» and the «cacciatore». 'Adaptation' seems to be an implicit consequence, under the necessities of a limited perception: the 'weak' would shoot after guessing, thus he will not get the animal, and necessarily adapt. This implication becomes explicit in the last simile, where a 'strong' chess player is able to predict a wider range of possible moves, while for the 'weak' «le mosse dell'altro gli sono una incomprensibile contingenza per la quale via via si vede scalzati i suoi piccoli piani ed è necessitato, ogni volta alla nuova situazione adattandosi, a ricominciarli» (ibid.). This is the final comparison, which allows the simile to become 'closed', focusing on the interpretation of the verb 'to adapt', which is repeated in the tenor: «così il debole s'adatta» (ibid.).

This cluster of similes confirms the underlying mechanism we outlined in this chapter, but it does more than that: it outlines an entire system of philosophical categories. Firstly, will to affirmation is a cause of violence where there is a 'weak' and a 'strong' who strive for the same fulfilment; the difference in strength results in adaptation or defeat of the weak. In the natural world this mechanism is automatic because animals cannot have consciousness of it; in humans, on the contrary, different degrees of consciousness discriminate between 'strong' and 'weak'. Furthermore, the discovery of one's weakness (itself a form of consciousness), as in the case of the satyr, does not open in the weak a path towards a deeper understanding, but freezes him in horror and need of protection – an implicit reference to the 'cover for the eyes', to 'rhetoric'. That said, φιλοψυχία, the preservation of one-self, is, in strict terms, the basis for the development of this rhetoric which guides adaptation.

The above system of categories underpins the logical structure of the similes and their juxtaposition. The investment in this link is so evident that other similes in the body of *La Persuasione e la Rettorica* have the same structure, are concerned with the same problems and draw on the same system and similar imagery. In this sense, «gli uomini, che nella solitudine del loro animo vuoto si sentono mancare, s'affermano inadeguatamente fingendosi il segno della persona che non hanno», and they are «come il bambino nell'oscurità [che] grida per farsi un segno della propria persona, che nell'infinita paura si sente mancare» (PR: 58). This simile implies φιλοψυχία and comparison with a being who shows a lower degree of self-consciousness; in fact, like children, humans «si stordiscono l'un l'altro» (ibid.) with the words of inadequate affirmation. Elsewhere this sort of 'ranking of consciousness' is explicitly formalized: «i ricercatori di verità che per la paura dell'oscurità si fingono una vita assoluta nell'elaborazione del sapere [...]. La loro coscienza non è più un organismo vivo, una presenza delle cose nell'attualità della propria persona, ma una memoria: un aggregato inorganico di nomi legato coll'organismo fittizio del sistema. In questo modo l'uomo per la sua rettorica non solo non procede ma ridiscende la scala degli organismi e riduce la sua persona all'*inorganico*. Egli è meno vivo di qualunque animale» (PR: 65). The 'inorganic' relates to the fate of the weight that opens the text (PR: 7-8) and chloride (discussed above).

In this last example we witness the movement of vocabulary from the simile to the philosophical theory. The final point of this process takes place with the introduction of a category for interpretation of φιλοψυχία called «assenso inorganico»: «e *guardare* vuol dire procurare all'occhio la vicinanza che risvegli il *suo assenso*: non come occhio che serve al mio corpo ma come *occhio*, come *insieme di lenti: l'assenso inorganico*» (PR: 78). Here, the figurative language of the similes merges into the realm of the theory, as if simile could be invested with an epistemological role. If in general this is the case, than the theoretical context of *La Persuasione e la Rettorica* rules out the possibility of attaching any positive value to the process. If it is true that the similes explicitly refer to a foundational *logos*, then it is a logical consequence that they partake of 'rhetorical' false affirmation. Hence, the simile on the 'searchers for truth' (PR: 65) quoted above, should be read against itself, as self-addressing. In synthesis, induction, deduction or the more open relationship of abduction[119] – in the measure in which they imply generalization – are banned from the poetic of the text; a contradiction between theory and practice that empties the similes of their 'scientific' epistemological value. If similes are engaged in outlining a relation of causality then they fall into the 'rhetoric' of science: «gli scienziati portano [...] via via a ricavare dalla contemporaneità o dal susseguirsi d'una data serie di relazioni una presunzione di causalità: un'ipotesi modesta, che diventi teoria o legge» (PR: 84). In the case of the satyr and the hermaphrodite the same is declined inside the realm of the aesthetic. The simile is shaped as a comment on a work of art, conducted in order to outline a series of rules which establish possibilities of comparison. We analyzed this in our second chapter in relation to Michelstaedter's philosophy of art – the fruition[120] of art and its production[121] – and found that there is no space for such a mechanism[122].

Furthermore, the adoption of a language derived from a scientific realm (chemistry, biology, zoology, medicine, and so forth) immediately divests the figure of any authority, precisely because scientific language is the object of attack. In this sense the shifting of vocabulary demonstrates how the generalizing narrator is also invested with the same order of problems. If scientific/philosophical epistemology is ruled out, both simile and generalization lose their grounding foundation. And if this is true, what the literature on simile tells us is that what remains of the simile is its rhetorical (not in Michelstaedter's sense), non analytic, entymemic and not syllogistic[123] perlocutionary role[124] – which dramatizes the mode of the learning process[125] and moves the reader, rather than proving things to him[126]. This is precisely the level on which *La Persuasione e la Rettorica* embraces and performs its own fictional nature[127]. Consequently, a different aesthetic from the one we outlined in this chapter takes place, an aesthetic which refuses the illusion of adequacy. When Benitez states that Plato's separation of Forms can be mythopoietic, he offers a point which could fit with our conclusions: Michelstaedter's theoretical stand, given his investment in religious-aesthetic language, can be considered figurative, or mythopoietic inside an aesthetic world-view. This achievement however, is not yet the language of 'persuasion'; it does not '*immediately give the complexity of relationships*', but is the most extreme result of a dialectic which, *ad infinitum*, must undermine itself. The entire text has lost a privileged language, and the argument can be interpreted as a dialogue between sub-genres and stylistic strategies conceived as a reciprocal relativization and a repetition-correction of a perlocutionary message. In other words, as much as there is not 'art' in the sense given in the text, there is no literal meaning[128].

4.4   Dialogue, repetition and irony

At the beginning of the present chapter we quoted a brief dialogue from the manuscripts of *La Persuasione e la Rettorica*, and introduced an ironic reading of the title 'Appendici Critiche':

> – Perché le ha chiamate appendici 'critiche'?
> – Secondo la definizione dell'ironia l'ironia è quel tropo per il quale diciamo con un concetto un concetto contrario al concetto [usitato][129]

The conclusions we have reached throughout this chapter allow us to imagine that this exchange could have been referred to the entire work, and the opening question would have to be taken rather seriously: 'why did you call it a degree thesis?'

In the first chapter of the present enquiry, while discussing the importance of a study of the narrator and the orientation of his utterance with regard to other voices of the text, we stated that according to a Bakhtinian framework, academic writing is monologic: if a dialectic is present, it is so in order to build an argument through undermining other positions and offering the 'correct' point of view on the object. In the course of the same chapter, we demonstrated that the generalizing, external, academic narrator, following the representation of the experience of the horror beyond the veil of Maya, is in fact directly involved in an attempt to orient himself 'on the path to persuasion'. This path implies the adoption of a particular dialectic that in the text is defined as Socratic, and its movement is exemplified through the figure of the hyperbole. We have demonstrated how this movement should have been present in the style and argumentation of the text, and has to embody, by definition, a process of continuous negation of any stop, any rest. In this sense the 'you' of the text, introduced through the most crucial question («Questo che fai, come che cosa lo fai? Tu ami questa cosa per la correlazione di ciò che ti lascia dopo bisognoso [...] [o] *sai cosa* fai?» PR: 31) is also a self-referential you, around which the entire text revolves.

Our second and third chapter, devoted respectively to exemplarity and parodic and sarcastic undermining strategies, offered us two levels of undermining: that of the contradiction between theory/poetic and practice of signification/style, and that of the dialogue between sub-genres. In the first case, the scheme of the narratorial structure of the text develops as follows.

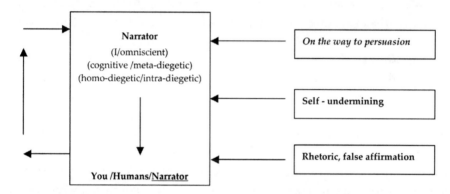

The scheme we offered in chapter 1 is basically confirmed. The narrator undermines an ideology or a point of view as 'rhetorical', but in doing so, he shows that the practice of signification, the style and the vocabulary that he is using, is itself an ideology which, if compared with the poetic of the text, shows its own rhetorical status. The following scheme represents the dynamics of dialogue between sub-genres and rhetorical strategies:

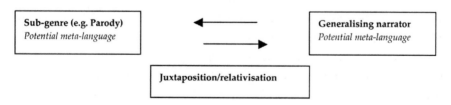

Here, as in the case of parody (but also in the case of the 'Esempio Storico'), two sub-genres with the potential to claim a meta-linguistic status – and thus an appropriate affirmation – in their reciprocal orientation run into a process of relativization, leaving the text without a stable linguistic foundation.

Furthermore while the argument in the text develops logically (from the simple to the complex, from experience to language), the sub-genres are not explicitly linked in a logic of induction or deduction, but work as repetition, which always implies a difference, and thus perform a perpetual correction which never achieves the status of a meta-language because neither conceptualization nor figuration remain disengaged from this mechanism. In his text on early expressionism, Thomas Harrison offers us important material for a concluding comparison. In his interpretation of Arnold Schoenberg's *Erwartung* (1909), he quotes Anton Webern: «there is not a single bar in this score which does not display a completely new tonal picture», while «a unity of sound is created, in spite of everything»[130]. In regard to this unity Harrison comments, «the question Schoenberg raises [...] is [...]: can unity be found in strife itself?»[131] In the case of *La Persuasione e la Rettorica*, the 'dissonance' of the juxtaposition is the negative strife that resolves in a unity only *ad infinitum*: the 'persuaded' language, as we will see in our concluding chapter, is only evoked or announced.

The points synthesized above offer us the chance to interpret the text also through a different, and for our goals more poignant, definition of irony. The negative dialectic and the demonstrated self-consciousness of the related commitment towards 'persuasion', means that the text consistently reveals its own 'rhetoric' and lays bare its own mechanisms: it is a 'permanent parabasis'. This is Friedrich Schlegel's definition of irony[132], explained by De Man as «the author's intrusion that disrupts the fictional illusion»[133]. The ways in which *La Persuasione e la Rettorica* is devoted to the fulfilment of this task should be evident by now. De Man's further speculation, defines irony as: «the permanent parabasis of the allegory of tropes. [...A]ny theory of irony is the undoing, the necessary undoing, of any theory of narrative [...] always be undone by the ironic dimension which it will necessarily contain»[134]. This is in many ways close to our review of the debate on parody, irony, and sarcasm in our third chapter, and confirms this reading. We have shown how allegory – and by extension all the actors in the dialectic of the text – partake of this ironic laying bare.

Our concluding remark borrows a quote from Luigi Pirandello on Michelstaedter, in an interview for 'Termini'[135]:

la vita ha pur da consistere in qualche cosa se vuole essere afferrata. Per consistere le occorre una forma, deve darsi una forma. D'altra parte questa forma è la sua morte perché l'arresta, l'imprigiona, le toglie il divenire. Il problema è questo per la vita. È qui tutto il tragico dissidio della storia della libertà. Nietzsche, Weininger, Michelstaedter, vollero far coincidere assolutamente, ad ogni istante, forma e sostanza, e furono spezzati e travolti[136].

This quote reminds us how at the bottom of the struggle of the negative dialectic, at the 'infinite' goal of irony, there is 'persuasion', which in its being 'life' outside 'rhetoric' is indeed a (classical) coincidence in every moment between 'form' and 'substance'. This reminds us of a comment on Schlegelian irony by Peter Szondi, criticized by De Man yet clearly applicable to Michelstaedter's project: «he nostalgically aspires towards unity and infinity [...] What he calls irony is his attempt [...] to change his situation by achieving distance toward it. [...] The knowledge of his own impotence prevents the ironist from respecting his achievements: therein resides his danger. Each achievement becomes in turn inadequate and finally leads into a void: therein resides his tragedy»[137].

All in all *La Persuasione e la Rettorica* is conceived as a struggle to regain a unity, an absolute possession. In its being written from the point of view of the non 'persuaded', it stylistically deploys the dialectic that would – so is the belief – lead to this unity; this implies a loss of centre and a relativisation of the pretences of the narrator-hero which are Michelstaedter's original contribution to the poetic of Italian literary Novecento.

Notes

1. PR: 61.
2. Where one of the main concerns is to recuperate a certain Socrates of the early dialogues (as opposed to a Platonic Socrates of the later dialogues), leaving the discussion of the philosophical reasons for the hypothesis of this Platonic betrayal entirely to the 'Appendici Critiche' (see 'Appendice II. Nota alla Triste Istoria', particularly: 171-4 et passim).
3. For example, in chapter 1 we discussed the ones from Saints Luke and Matthew, PR: 10.
4. Asor Rosa, ''La Persuasione e la Rettorica' di Carlo Michelstaedter': 265. We discussed this point in our introduction.
5. See the section 'Delle Particelle Avversative' O: 708-10. See also the introduction to the present volume.
6. It is a small note that precedes the manuscript: FCM III 3d.
7. Together with a lack of investment in the fictional language of art. This is a theme we will discuss further in our concluding chapter below.
8. Raschini confirms our reading, when she argues that, in Michelstaedter's interpretation of

Socrates «la scoperta del concetto diventa per lui un'attribuzione posteriore, con la quale Aristotele avrebbe tradito l'autentica aspirazione dell'Ateniese, traducendo in schemi logici la dialessi vivente del suo pensiero». Raschini, *Michelstaedter*: 156.

9. We will discuss this further later in this chapter, reading the dense use of figurative language in the 'description' of 'persuasion' in relation to the widespread use of allegory.

10. Implicitly alluding and therefore attacking the framework of the Platonic 'second navigation', an attack that the second of the 'Appendici Critiche' will explicitly undertake. On the topic of the 'second navigation' in relation with the earlier Plato, see, for example: Giovanni Reale, *Per una Nuova Interpretazione di Platone. Rilettura della Metafisica dei Grandi Dialoghi alla Luce delle 'Dottrine non Scritte'* (Milano: Vita e Pensiero, 1991), Giovanni Reale, *Storia della Filosofia Antica*, 3 vols., vol. 2 (Milano: Vita e Pensiero, 1976), Sarri, *Socrate e la Nascita del Concetto Occidentale di Anima*.

11. It is in the first of the 'Appendici Critice' and its references to the body of the text that the problem of inadequate affirmation is fully discussed. We will dedicate a section to the critique of objectivity, its space inside Michelstaedter's philosophy of language, and the consequences for a possibile identification of a 'persuaded language'.

12. The system-building 'optimistic' philosophy of Hegel, which we discussed in our Chapter 3.

13. «E questo è sempre stato; tanto che per esser diverso dalla norma comune, essere *anormale* significa esser pazzo» (PR: 126).

14. See, for example, Giovanna Taviani, 'Lettura (Attuale) di 'La Persuasione e la Rettorica' di Carlo Michelstaedter' *Annali della Facoltà di Lettere e Filosofia*, no. 17 (1996); Taviani, 'Attualità di Michelstaedter'. An interesting area to be developed is the comparison between Michelstaedter and contemporary theorists concerned with the themes of 'post-historical condition'. Agamben's *The Open*, for example, with its framework that moves from Kojève's reading of Hegel and the fate of the human after the completion of the movement of history, and its post-Heideggerian development, could be a fruitful starting point. Giorgio Agamben, *The Open: Man and Animal* (Stanford: Stanford University Press, 2004). However this excedes the goals of our present enquiry.

15. On this, see our introduction, but also: Benussi, *Negazione e Integrazione nella Dialettica di Carlo Michelstaedter*: 47-59.

16. See above, and PR: 125-6.

17. Similar conclusions could be drawn from the pages preceding our quote. For example see the account of the skin's 'natural' reaction to sunlight as a standpoint for a critique of technical progress which «instupidisce per quella parte il corpo dell'uomo» (PR: 104): «Per neutralizzare gli effetti dannosi della luce del sole, la pelle esposta s'abbronzisce, messa a riparo ridiventa chiara. La pelle della faccia e delle mani esposta sempre alle variazioni si colorisce subito e subito perde il colore. – La pelle del corpo quando eccezionalmente è esposta tarda a colorirsi e mantiene il colore anche quando è al riparo. Questo ritardo della reazione produce generalmente pericolose scottature di sole» (PR: 105). The example here is given through the objectivity of physiological/medical knowledge and observation, and it is used as evidence for 'normality' versus the abnormality of 'clothing' and 'artificial heating' (ibid.) which leads to atrophy.

18. The case of mathematical language that we anticipated in the preceding chapter fits with this discussion as well.

19. Of Platonic derivation, as we will further see in this chapter.

20. Muzzioli, *Michelstaedter*: 170.

21. On Michelstaedter and expressionism see our introduction, and also: Cerruti,

Michelstaedter: 146; Sergio Campailla, 'Espressionismo e Filosofia della Contestazione in Michelstaedter' in *Scrittori Giuliani* (Bologna: Pàtron, 1980).

22. Important, as acknowledged in our introduction, because it is one of the few articles entirely devoted to a discussion of rhetorical figures in the text, thus stressing the relevance of argumentative style in *La Persuasione e la Retorica*, and its link with the argued philosophy. Perna's recent article links Michelstaedter's predilection for fictional narration to his Jewish background and Hasidic parables. Our argument will show how the requirement of the poetic expressed in *La Persuasione e la Rettorica* are not fulfilled by the simple presence of narratives and fictional sections, and their importance can be highlighted only in the dialectic with the framing narrator. In this sense, my discussion of Benevento's article can be referred also to Perna's framework (Perna, 'Dal Libro alla Parola').

23. Benevento, ' 'La Persuasione e la Rettorica' di Michelstaedter e la 'Concretezza Artistica'': 122.

24. Ibid.: 123.

25. Ibid.: 122.

26. Ibid.: 124.

27. *Institutio Oratoria*, IX, 2, 46. Quintilian, *The Institutio Oratoria of Quintilian*, trans. H. E. Butler (London: Heineman, 1969-77).

28. Ibid., VIII, 6, 47.

29. Mortara Garavelli, *Manuale di Retorica*: 259.

30. Janet Martin Soskice, *Metaphor and Religious Language* (Oxford: Clarendon Press, 1985): 55.

31. Samuel R. Levin, 'Allegorical Language' in *Allegory, Myth and Symbol*, ed. Morton Bloomfield, W. (Cambridge, London: Harvard University Press, 1981): 24. Obviously I am not arguing that every allegory implies an explicit personification, but rather stressing that personification gives a key for allegorical reading. More on this topic in: Morton Bloomfield, W., 'A Grammatical Approach to Personification Allegory' *Modern Philology* 60, no. 3 (1963).

32. «La valenza è il correlato del valore» (PR: 14).

33. This closed 'one to one' relationship between concept and illustration takes place in the text also in cases where the argument seems to develop inductively from example to rule, as in the case of the so-called 'apologo del peso' (PR: 7-8), discussed above in our chapter 1. Further in our discussion, we will demonstrate how the prerogative of the allegory of chloride can be extended to most of the figurative language of *La Persuasione e la Rettorica*.

34. Hans Georg Gadamer, *Truth and Method* (New York: Crossroad, 1982): 54-5.

35. Ibid.: 67. See also Paul De Man, 'The Rhetoric of Temporality' in *Interpretation. Theory and Practice*, ed. Charles Singleton (Baltimore: John Hopkins Press, 1969): 174.

36. «Per ciò che è detto a pagg. 16, 18-21, 56-7, 113-17» (PR: 135).

37. Genette, in his study on paratext, considers footnotes part of the body of the text, reinforcing our conviction on the importance of this appendix in the general stylistic discussion on the reciprocal orientation of sub-genres and rhetorical strategies. See: Gerard Genette, *Paratexts. Thresholds of Interpretation*, trans. Jane E. Lewin (Cambridge, New York, Oakleigh: Cambridge University Press, 1997): 325; 328.

38. These statements are a reworking of PR: 56, the third section to which the appendix refers.

39. Which implies the 'absolute Self' of the generalizing narrator, as we pointed out in our passages on the treatment of exemplarity. It should sound obvious, at this point, that the stylistic efforts of the text should move in the opposite direction.

40. Until the limit-point in which we could argue that the pages of 'Appendice I' are written in

a language that is open to the same critique that it expresses. We will come to a full understanding of this aporia at the end of this chapter.

41. PEE: 26. It is interesting to note how the chosen term in this latter quote is not 'persuasa' (persuaded), yet 'persuasiva' (persuasive). This implies in any case an interlocutor: if this is addressed to one-self, and persuasive is intended as self-persuading, this would imply a reificaton which is in contrast with what we discussed above. If the addressee is someone else, the persuasive function is closest to the definitions which gather around a religious and prophetic understanding of the persuaded, under the example of Christ (already discussed; see Chapter 2). This second hypothesis will emerge again in our argument.

42. See the 'Riflessione su Temi Buddisti', now in PPA: 115-21, and Franchi's editorial comments.

43. Even if we demonstrated how the opposition between 'persuasion' and 'rhetoric' does not work as a dialectic and the description of 'persuasion' as the other of 'rhetoric' is a necessity dictated by the non-persuaded status of the utterer, who can know 'persuasion' only through negative data. It is clear that the polarization of two opposites in this description is open to a deconstructive critique. Futher in this chapter, when we will define this 'word of persuasion' through German romantic poetics and a Schopenhauerian reading of Kant's genius, we will point out how the investment in the figurative language of symbol and metaphor calls for a critical deconstructive reading in the wake of Derrida's *White Mythology* and De Man's *Rhetoric of Romanticism*: Jacques Derrida, 'White Mythology: Metaphor in the Text of Philosophy' *New Literary History* 6, no. 1 (1974); De Man, *The Rhetoric of Romanticism*.

44. Diels, B, 4. Parmenides of Elea, *Fragments*.

45. We could further exploit this point and ask ourselves which kind of figurative art Michelstaedter has in mind as a 'positive' example and question if and how the rules of perspective and light inform a particular poetic. The passage offers a critique of mannerism: «un altro semplice s'accontenta di protestare che non capisce niente [of the alley painted by the simple ...]; ma il critico dice: <l'idea c'è, la scuola gli manca>» (PR: 114). However, following this thread, which could have some merit for a contextualization of the author, would imply conceiving an entirely different enquiry from the one I am undertaking; one which should take into consideration the figurative production of Michelstaedter (for example asking the question about the contextualization of caricatures as proto-expressionist or linked to an earlier tradition: see on this Bini, *Carlo Michelstaedter and the Failure of Language*: 211-29), its sources, its techniques, its development, and so on.

46. On this topic, of great interest is the article by Giorgio Brianese, 'Il Silenzio e i Richiami. Per una Rilettura de 'I figli del Mare' di Carlo Michelstaedter' *Studi Goriziani*, no. 65 (1987).

47. See our introduction to the present volume.

48. The italicized «stessa», 'same', in Michelstaedter's framework could be intended as referring to the nature of the object beyond rhetoric, and thus emancipated from the category of time and space. It could also refer more explicitly to the Schopenhauerian concept of art as rising to the realm of ideas: «[art studies] the inner nature of the world, always appearing the same in all relations [...], in other words the Ideas of the world» (Schopenhauer, *The World as Will and Representation*: 274).

49. Ibid.: 184.

50. Ibid.: 178.

51. Ibid.: 188.

52. See for example the descriptions of Tolstoj (O: 650-4).

53. The latter will be the topic of our next chapter.
54. Schopenhauer, *The World as Will and Representation*: 179.
55. From Winkelmann use of the terms as synonyms, to Goethe's choice of the symbol, as traced in: Gadamer, *Truth and Method*; De Man, 'The Rhetoric of Temporality'.
56. Schopenhauer, *The World as Will and Representation*: 235.
57. Ibid.
58. Muzzioli, *Michelstaedter*. See our introduction to the present volume.
59. Schopenhauer, *The World as Will and Representation*: 237.
60. Ibid.: 240.
61. Chapter 2.
62. Chapter 1.
63. Religious language will be treated in our next chapter.
64. Walter Benjamin, *The Origin of German Tragic Drama* (London: Verso, 1998): 159.
65. Friedrich Wilhelm Joseph von Schelling, *The Philosophy of Art*, ed. Douglas W. Stott (Minneapolis: University of Minnesota Press, 1989). Also in Gadamer, *Truth and Method*: 69.
66. Gadamer, *Truth and Method*: 69.
67. Ibid.
68. For a historical review of the aesthetic of symbol, see also Tzvetan Todorov, *Theories of the Symbol* (Ithaca: Cornell University Press, 1982).
69. See: Frederick Beiser, *Schiller as Philosopher. A Re-Examination* (Oxford: Clarendon Press, 2005). Particularly chapter 4.
70. Gadamer, *Truth and Method*: 50-3. Taste as a 'levelling' concept that subordinates genius to the mediocrity of a common judgement is coherent with Michelstaedter's idea of the singularity of the path to 'persuasion'.
71. Ibid.: 59.
72. Ibid.: 60.
73. De Man, 'The Rhetoric of Temporality': 190.
74. In partial difference with Schopenhauer, as we pointed out.
75. Such as Tolstoj, as quoted above.
76. Gadamer, *Truth and Method*: 57. The relevance of this quote, both on the level of conceptual content and intertextual references, shows us the extent to which Michelstaedter's speculation is rooted in a Romantic aesthetic. This offers some explanation for the reading of Michelstaedter's poetic production inside a Romantic framework, as in Kanduth, 'Dal Tu all'Io nella Poesia di Carlo Michelstaedter'. The contrast between *La Persuasione e la Rettorica* and the poems, which often emerges in the criticism, can be smoothed by our reading, offering the ground for a more comprehensive and somehow unitarian interpretation of the author.
77. I use this term to stress the modalities of representation proper to the Romantic idea of symbol, namely atemporality and unity with the whole.
78. Gadamer, *Truth and Method*: 66. According to Gadamer's reading of Pseudo Dionigi, Symbol and Allegory are in place because it is impossible to know the divine if not through something related to our senses; however, symbol has a 'metaphysical background' (ibid.) in its avoidance of reference to something else. We will touch briefly on the problem of the sensual appreciation of the divine in our discussion on the use of similes in *La Persuasione e la Rettorica*. In any case, Michelstaedter's heavy reliance on a *logos* as a starting and end point of a rhetorical use of the figure will circumscribe our discussion of the topic to what is relevant for our goals.
79. Tullio De Mauro, ed., *Grande Dizionario Italiano dell'Uso* (Torino: Utet, 1999-2000).

80. At this point, the rendition of Socratic experience at the beginning of the 'esempio storico' can finally show all its importance: «[Socrate] consunta insieme la speranza della libertà e la schiavitù – lo spirito indipendente e la gravità – la necessità della terra e la volontà del sole – né volò al sole – né restò sulla terra, – né fu indipendente né schiavo; né felice né misero; – ma di lui con le mie parole non ho più che dire» (PR: 66).

81. See our chapter 2, where we also discussed how 'Michelstaedter's words' are linked in a network of complex and revealing intertextual references. A further definition of the consequences of 'repetition' is given by De Man in his reading of Rousseau: «repetition is a temporal process that assumes difference as well as resemblance. It functions as a regulative principle of rigor but asserts the impossibility of rigorous identity, etc. precisely to the extent that all interpretation has to be repetition, it also has to be immanent», see: Paul De Man, *Blindness & Insight: Essays in the Rhetoric of Contemporary Criticism* (New york: Oxford University Press, 1971): 109. The void showed by the mechanisms of this repetition is precisely the undermining of 'rhetoric', the (again rhetorical) evocation of that which is 'beyond the veil' that is Michelstaedter's dialectic aim.

82. At the end of this chapter we will end up calling this process 'ironic', after a De Manian definition of the term.

83. De Man, *Blindness & Insight: Essays in the Rhetoric of Contemporary Criticism*: 136.

84. We shoud write 'rhetorical' but, again, we adopt the term 'stylistic' to avoid confusion with Michelstaedter's own philosophical category.

85. De Man, *Blindness & Insight: Essays in the Rhetoric of Contemporary Criticism*: 131.

86. Ibid.: 127.

87. Ibid.: 136.

88. Ibid.: 132-3.

89. Ibid.: 138-9.

90. Stephen A. Nimis, *Narrative Semiotics in the Epic Tradition* (Bloomington, Indianapolis: Indiana University Press, 1987): 151. The possibility of a 'literary' reading of the allegory is a well known point in the definition of the figure. See for example: Umberto Eco, *Semiotica e Filosofia del Linguaggio* (Torino: Einaudi, 1974): 249-51. In regard with the impossibility of literal interpretation of metaphor, which those pages assume (ibid.: 249), and which should bring to light the category under which a difference between allegory, simile, symbol and metaphor could be drawn, I should acknowledge here that the debate is rather more complex, and too wide to allow us a detour. However, see for example David E. Cooper, *Metaphor* (Oxford: Basil Blackwell, 1986) and his reading of Davidson's theory as given in Donald Davidson, 'Truth and Meaning' *Synthèse* 17 (1967); Donald Davidson, 'What Metaphors Mean,' in *On Metaphor*, ed. Scheldon Sacks (Chicago: The University of Chicago Press, 1979). On this topic, see also: Soskice, *Metaphor and Religious Language*, in particular chapter 5: 67-96.

91. «E il pubblico era felice di poter dire che la merce veniva dal cielo e di potersene servire proprio come se fosse stata merce di questa terra. Quell'uomo era Aristotele. Il suo sistema […] ancora vive fra noi» (PR: 72-3).

92. On these points in Plato, see: Luc Brisson, 'The Role of Myth in Plato and its Prolongations in Antiquity,' *The European Legacy* 12, no. 2 (2007) Particularly: 141-4.

93. I draw this term from Beinitez' reading of Platonic philosophy as a 'two world-view', to which are related two different uses of myth, the eikastic being one representing an image of the world beyond appearances. See: Eugenio Benitez, 'Philosophy, Myth and Plato's Two-World View,' *The European Legacy* 12, no. 2 (2007). We will briefly return to the point later in this section.

94. Plato's *Gorgia*, for example, is the source for the myth of the 'naked souls', first encountered

in La Persuasione e la Rettorica as a concluding aphorism: «persuaso è chi *ha in sé la sua vita*: l'anima ignuda nella isole dei beati» (PR: 10). The original Greek quote follows, together with a loose reference «(Gorgia)» (PR: 10). In chapter 2 we interpreted the passage and discussed the role of these features inside the broader argument on aphorisms and exemplary quotation. After this, the symbol of the 'naked soul' becomes part of the vocabulary of the argument on the dialectic movement towards 'persuasion', and embodies its moral instances. See PR: 148; 171.

95. Benitez, 'Philosophy, Myth and Plato's Two-World View': 226.

96. Brisson, 'The Role of Myth in Plato and its Prolongations in Antiquity': 143. The argument on the development of the term 'myth' in Plato and its interpretation in opposition to argumentative language is fully discussed in: Luc Brisson, *Plato the Myth Maker* (Chicago: University of Chicago Press, 1998). The discussion of this argument in some depth would be of absolute interest, but unfortunately is outside the goals of our present enquiry. Therefore, we limit our exposition to the few relevant points for an interpretation of the presence of and reference to myth in *La Persuasione e la Rettorica*.

97. «Effettivamente, sarebbe per noi tutto un guadagno se la poesia risultasse non solo dolce, ma anche utile » (Rep X, 607 E), «di vantaggio alla società e alla vita dell'uomo» (Rep. X, 607 D). Platone, *Tutti gli Scritti*: 1317. The development of this argument regarding the role of poetic voice in Plato can be found in Evanthia Speliots, 'Image, Myth and Dialectic in Plato' *The European Legacy* 12, no. 2 (2007).

98. Brisson, 'The Role of Myth in Plato and its Prolongations in Antiquity': 144.

99. Benitez, 'Philosophy, Myth and Plato's Two-World View': 231.

100. Ibid.: 229.

101. Ibid.: 233. Similar conclusions are reached for example by Jacob Howland, 'Plato and Kirkegaard: two Philosophical Stories,' *The European Legacy* 12, no. 2 (2007) E.g.: 177.

102. «Abbandono della via socratica» (PR: 143), «il macrocosmo» (PR: 144), «il riflesso del sole» (PR: 166), «la decadenza» (PR: 174), «il discepolo» (PR: 199).

103. The terms 'tenor' and 'vehicle' come from the seminal work of Richards, who used them to refer to the two terms of a metaphor: see I. A. Richards, *The Philosophy of Rhetoric* (Oxford: Oxford University Press, 1936). They are also appropriate to simile, even more so given that in this case the two subjects are clearly separated, both formally and grammatically. On the grammar in the structure of simile, see: Ziva Ben-Porat, 'Poetics of the Homeric Simile and the Theory of the (Poetic) Simile' *Poetics Today* 13, no. 4 (1992): 738; Catherine Addison, 'From Literal to Figurative: An Introduction to the Study of Simile' *College English* 55, no. 4 (1993): 404; in the case of metaphor, particulary in the case of catachretic uses, the distinction can be more problematic. This is a point made by: Soskice, *Metaphor and Religious Language*.

104. As Ben-Porat names the formal connector between tenor and vehicle. Ben-Porat, 'Poetics of the Homeric Simile and the Theory of the (Poetic) Simile': 738.

105. Addison, 'From Literal to Figurative: an Introduction to the Study of Simile': 404; 406.

106. Paul Ricoeur, *The Rule of Metaphor: Multi-Disciplinary Studies of the Creation of Meaning in Language* (London: Routledge & Kegan Paul, 1978). While in a metaphor of the type 'John is a tree' the paradox and the problem between sameness and difference is clear and based on an explicit claim of identity between the two terms, Addison affirms that the same problem emerges with simile, with both rhetorical and epistemological consequences.

107. Closed simile is defined as a comparison between one single attribute of vehicle and tenor, for instance in the case of 'his blood is red like the petal of a rose'; where the color is the

compared attribute and its explicit presence avoids the question of the incongruence between the two semantic fields which 'his blood is like a rose' would have implied. For a brief taxonomy of the different types of simile, metaphor and analogy, see: Joseph Margolis, 'Notes on the Logic of Simile, Metaphor and Analogy' *American Speech* 32, no. 3 (1957); for 'closed simile', see: 187.

108. Between the others, this is the argument of Ben-Porat. His interest in the epic simile, where both tenor and vehicle «are expanded in ways that rarely attain a one-to-one matching» (Ben-Porat, 'Poetics of the Homeric Simile and the Theory of the (Poetic) Simile': 742) clearly shifts the priority to a reading of the possible reasons for this expansion.

109. Teresa Bridgeman, 'On the 'Likeness' of Similes and Metaphors (With Special Reference to Alfred Jarry's 'Les Jours et les Nuits')' *The Modern Language Review* 91, no. 1 (1996): 69. The focus of Bridgeman is on 'polysemic and ambiguous simile' (ibid.), and is concieved in order to explore the poetic importance of the figure, and widening the range of interpretation to intertextual and contextual references.

110. Ibid.: 65.

111. Ibid.: 67.

112. This is what Ben-Porat calls '(over) used simile', as a parallel with 'dead metaphor' (Ben-Porat, 'Poetics of the Homeric Simile and the Theory of the (Poetic) Simile': 746).

113. For a conceptualization and a history of the problem of the relationship between *logos* and simile, see for example: Nimis, *Narrative Semiotics in the Epic Tradition*.

114. The presence of figurative strategies in this passage should itself be thematized, but I think that the complexity of our examples will give account also of this case.

115. The appellation 'god', given to φιλοψυχία also deserves some space. In our discussion, I hope to show how φιλοψυχία, as a foundational philosophical concept, enters into a dialectic which implies a degree of irony. It is deployed in a way which relativizes the status of philosophical vocabulary and, as a consequence, loses its centre without replacing it, leaving to its message a perlocutionary and rhetorical (not in Michelstaedter's sense) aim. In this sense, more than just being employed against the cowardice of humans, more than being extended to the role of society as a vehicle for the satisfaction of relative needs, the 'god of φιλοψυχία' can be also referred to the metaphysical status that the term assumes in the philosophical interpretation given in the text. It is itself an ironic statement about the 'inadequate affirmation' that language imposes as a generalization.

116. Richard H. Lansing, *From Image to Idea: A Study of the Simile in Dante's «Commedia»* (Ravenna: Longo Editore, 1977): 43.

117. As we discussed in our chapter 1.

118. This interpretation is coherent with the footnote that comments on the simile, where the «tranquilla sicurezza» (ibid.) of the hermaphrodite is compared with Tiziano's Christ who looks at Judas (ibid.).

119. A concept which we introduced earlier in this chapter. See again: Umberto Eco, 'The Theory of Signs and the Role of the Reader' *The Bulletin of the Midwest Modern Language Association* 14, no. 1 (1981), and, for its application to simile, Nimis, *Narrative Semiotics in the Epic Tradition*.

120. Which lead to the discussion of the Kantian Genius and the correct way to follow an example, see chapter 2.

121. See above, particularly the discussion of symbol and allegory.

122. The dismissal of the art critic who, in front of an artist's painting, explains it through a series of generalizing categories drawn from a technical vocabulary («viene il critico e dice: 'che primi piani! Che secondi piani! Che linea, che luce, che aria, che colorito!'» PR: 114)

can be as easily applied to the narrator of the simile. We encountered this passage earlier in this chapter while discussing the poetic value of artistic language in the text.

123. Nimis, *Narrative Semiotics in the Epic Tradition*: 159.

124. Bridgeman, 'On the 'Likeness' of Similes and Metaphors (With Special Reference to Alfred Jarry's 'Les Jours et les Nuits')': 65.

125. Lansing, *From Image to Idea: A Study of the Simile in Dante's «Commedia»*: 44.

126. Nimis, *Narrative Semiotics in the Epic Tradition*: 159. In this sense, it is true that the hermeneutic process involved in the interpretation of the figure 'creates an intimacy' between the utterer and the reader, as Cooper affirms in his article on metaphorical truth (Cooper, *Metaphor*. See in particular: 153-78). This intimacy in Michelstaedter should not be based on the shared discovery of a set of underlying rules, but rather in the sharing of an always individual orientation on a path towards 'persuasion'.

127. In this sense, the dialectic between theoretical affirmation and figurative illustration which took us to this point reveals itself as a juxtaposition of narrations. 'Repetition' performs in Deleuze's terms, «transgression or exception, always revealing a singularity opposed to the particulars subsumed under laws»; see Gilles Deleuze, *Difference and Repetition* (London, New York: Continuum, 2004): 6.

128. We could, in fact, read Michelstaedter's critique of 'rhetoric' as a critique of the existence of a literal meaning in language, following the steps of theorists such as Derrida; see Jacques Derrida, 'White Mythology: Metaphor in the Text of Philosophy'. In fact the language of the 'persuaded human' as we discussed above, is itself 'open' and metaphorical.

129. In the Fondo Carlo Michelstaedter of the Biblioteca Statale Isontina this manuscript is labelled: FCM III 3d.

130. Harrison, *1910. The Emancipation of Dissonance*: 51.

131. Ibid.: 49.

132. «*Eine permanente Parekbase*». Friedrich Schlegel, *Kritische Ausgabe*, quoted in De Man, 'The Rhetoric of Temporality': 200.

133. Ibid.

134. Paul De Man, *Aesthetic Ideology* (Minneapolis, London: University of Minnesota Press, 1996): 179.

135. Luigi Pirandello, 'Pirandello Parla di Pirandello' *Termini* 2 (1936).

136. Ibid., today also in Taviani, *Michelstaedter*: 123.

137. Peter Szondi, *Satz und Gegensatz*, quoted in De Man, 'The Rhetoric of Temporality': 201. This view, referred to Michelstaedter, is similar to the reading of the aporia of language by Daniela Bini in: Bini, 'Carlo Michelstaedter: the Tragedy of Thought'.

CHAPTER FIVE

Not Enough of an Artist?

WIR LAGEN
schon tief in der Macchia, als du
endlich herankrochst.
Doch konnten wir nicht
hinueberdunkeln zu dir:
es herrschte
Lichtzwang.

Paul Celan

In his article on Kant's examples, David Lloyd points out how the necessity of overcoming the pedagogue is implicit in Kant's theorization of the genius, and can be derived from an analysis of the inadequacy of the exemplary status of the pedagogue with regard to the exemplary status of the genius:

> «it becomes clear that the [Kantian] "perfect" pedagogue [...] would
> be as imperfect an example as would be the pedantic pedagogue whose
> practice is limited to the inculcation of rules and regulations by rote.
> For it is the force of the example to fall short of the ideal toward which
> it gestures, just as it is the proper procedure of the pedagogue to point
> out this shortcoming of the example with regard to the ideal»[1].

In this sense, the incommensurability between the example and the ideal is at the core of the relationship between pedagogue and pupil: «the student's disappointment in the master, itself a crucial moment in the aesthetic education, is the fulfilment of a process of exemplification, whose goal is to produce autonomy of judgement in the student»[2]. In the case of *La Persuasione e la Rettorica*, we have seen how this negation of the pedagogical

177

role is performed both through an explicit rejection of its value and a dialectic mechanism which, while undermining the central role of the generalizing academic narrator, places the fictional and the figurative at the core of the text and its perlocutionary aim[3]. It is the inadequacy of the narrator/pedagogue that works as the key to the movement from 'imitation' of the exemplary to its original/individual 'following'. While Kantian speculation develops inside the realm of a rule-bound pedagogy of taste, for Michelstaedter the entire process of negation works towards an emancipation from rules, that is, towards genius.

The 'way to persuasion' can also be thought of as a progressive negation of rules and rule-bound language, and as an embracing of artistic language. The education to 'persuasion' is, in its pedagogical goals, an 'education through art' (the exemplary sources) which is also an education 'to art' (moving the pupil to find his/her own 'way to persuasion')[4]. The pedagogue himself is engaged in the same process of emancipation, where paradoxically only the undermining of his own pedagogical role and the language attached to it can put the 'persuasive' word in reach: the mediation of the example by the pedagogue is negated and ultimately it is only from a position of exemplarity that the 'moving' word can be uttered («non può *fare* chi non *è*, non può *dare* chi *non ha*» PR: 42).

Socratic dialectic is revealed once more as a process that is addressed from both a logical-philosophical and linguistic point of view. On the on hand, pedagogy and its concept-based language are ruled out by the dialectic movement of negation; on the other, the language of conceptual assertion must be relativized and lose its linguistic centre in order to fulfil the requirements of the dialectic. At the extreme and infinite point where the hyperbole leaps onto the line of justice – the 'pure present' – there is an absence of time-bound, linear or hyperbolic progress. The language of the 'persuaded' utterance should be consistent with this change: a dialectic/allegorical strategy of argumentation is overcome by a word which is able, in every moment, to give 'fullness of reference', that is, an open word which is able to «muovere il cuore di ognuno» (PR: 4).

The problem that remains for us in this concluding chapter is to locate as precisely as possible the position of *La Persuasione e la Rettorica* on the 'way to persuasion', and the implication that this position has for the possibility to fully represent 'persuasion' itself. In other words, we need to read the text against its positive formulation. Before beginning this task, we need to offer a few further theoretical remarks on both 'negation' and 'adequate affirmation'.

5.1 Self-negation

Discussing the importance of negation in Michelstaedter's idea of 'persuasion', Thomas Harrison offers a fruitful comparison with Max Stirner:

> while scholars are right to distinguish Michelstaedter from the most extreme philosopher of individualism, Max Stirner, few lines are more reminiscent than Stirner's 'I am the creative nothing, the nothing out of which I myself as creator create everything'. Thus does objective nullity provide the foundation for plenitude. And subjective plenitude, in turn, restores the value of objective, historical being[5].

The parallel between the two philosophers is conceived around the definition of the subject as a negative *locus*. The will to possession expressed in Michelstaedter as a state of contingency, turns 'inwards' and becomes the fulfilment of the 'know thyself'; a process which turns out to be the discovery of the nullity of the subject, as Harrison confirms: «but when this process is taken to the extreme – or when the faith in outside knowledge is so broken that nothing appears to be real but the self – then one discovers that even this "self in itself" is nothing. It is nothing whatsoever outside its objective relations. It is speechless and can attain no self-knowledge»[6]. Deleuze also discusses this ultimate point of negation (and negation of the self) in Stirner and Nietzsche, offering further points useful to our analysis. Deleuze sees Stirner as «the dialectitian who reveals nihilism as the truth of the dialectic»[7], who «makes use of the question "which one?" but only in order to dissolve the dialectic in the nothingness of the EGO»[8]; for him, «State and religion, but also human essence are denied in the EGO, which is not reconciled with anything because it annihilates everything [...]. Overcoming alienation thus means pure, cold annihilation, a recovery which lets nothing which recovers subsist»[9]. The parallels between these definitions and the endpoints of Michelstaedter's dialectic are of much interest; Michelstaedter's implied negation of the meta-language on which the negative process is based – the negation of the value of one's own pain – is the ultimate annihilation, the extreme nihilism, the 'pessimism'[10] which destroys any positive foundation but paradoxically moves towards its own overcoming. By defining Michelstaedter's work inside Deleuze's framework we stress an important theoretical difference with Schopenhauer.

If the comparison we outlined is accurate, Michelstaedter's 'extreme nihilism'[11], as Deleuze defines Stirner's, is rather different from the 'negative nihilism' of Schopenhauer. Deleuze adopts the definition 'negative nihilism' in his account of the relationship between higher values and depreciation of life: 'values superior to life [God, essence, the good, truth] are inseparable to their effect: the depreciation of life, the negation of this world». It is in this sense that the Nietzschean critique of Schopenhauerian 'nothingness of the will' should be intended, as a 'will to nothingness': in this sense «nihilism signifies the value of nil taken on by life, the fiction of higher values which give it this value and the will to nothingness which is expressed in this higher values»[12]. As outlined in the introduction to the present study, this 'will to non will', is also at the core of the aporia under which the philosophical project of *La Persuasione e la Rettorica* is born, as noted by Cacciari[13]. In a way it is moulded on Nietzsche[14], and assumed by Michelstaedter as a self-conscious impossibility. However, the extreme self-negation required by the hyperbole towards 'persuasion', and performed as a stylistic practice in the text, implies the negation also of the will to nothingness and thus of the hyperbole itself. Therefore, instead of moving towards the higher values which found ascetic life, it moves deeply into what Harrison names «the hole called the soul»[15]. Here the difference with Schopenhauer emerges; it is as if Michelstaedter overcomes the German by taking to the extreme what at the start looks like a similar framework. This hypothesis implies a crucial interpretive decision: the choice of reading Michelstaedter's philosophical system under a metaphysics of presence, or rather, as a pre-expressionist destruction of the belief in a self-constituting realm of subjectivity[16]. In other words, the problem here is to give an account of the ways in which the longing and striving for 'presence' leads to the affirmation of an 'absence'. An obvious consequence of this choice is the interpretation of the state of 'persuasion' either as an 'higher value', a postulated 'impossibility' or an overcoming of human nature which does not have any dialectical link with a subject; that is being something else: god (PR: 77).

5.2 Representing affirmation: re-appropriating, overcoming, dissolving the subject

In a letter to Iolanda De Blasi dated 25th of April 1907 (E: 201-4)[17], Michelstaedter offers a brief interpretation of Stirner's philosophy[18], and sketches similarities and differences from his own developing thought. The letter presents a problematic object for an intertextual comparison with *La*

Persuasione e la Rettorica, because its date precedes by a year the first evidence of an interest in eloquence and 'persuasion'[19], and because its genre and addressee introduce variables which, while having relevance in the tone and the content of the message, fulfil an agenda which is other than a strictly philosophical examination[20]. However, we can at least define a certain movement from nihilism to a positive existential project, which if not in the specific content, at least in the general structure remains inside the framework of *La Persuasione e la Rettorica.* Firstly, the letter moves from a critique of Stirner's 'fixed ideas' to a reading of these ideas a product of a Schopenhauerian type of 'will to live'[21]; secondly, Michelstaedter logically introduces the themes of consciousness and pain – «chi esce da questa illusione sente immediatamente il peso del giogo, sente il disperato dolore della schiavitù» (E: 203) – which are potentially overcome in the realm of the aesthetic: «voglio e potrò foggiarmi la vita come un'opera d'arte, sentire in ogni cosa l'infinita bellezza della natura [...] e sfuggire alla necessità delle cose, idealizzandole, impadronendomene idealmente» (ibid.).

It would take some time to outline the differences between this 'positive' project and the final definition of the concept of 'persuasion', and this effort would not in any case be relevant for the goals of the present discussion. Nevertheless it is important to acknowledge that in relation to Stirner's approach, Michelstaedter stresses the necessity to come to terms with nihilism in a process which would lead to existential fulfilment. In the case of *La Persuasione e la Rettorica,* this state is 'persuasion'; and we now need to read it against this extreme nihilism, in order to come to a definition that will help us to make sense of the achievement of the text in the context of its own self-defined struggle. We will discuss three relatively different critical interpretations of 'persuasion' by highlighting the passages in the text on which these positions are grounded, asking ourselves the reasons for such apparently contrasting representations. In doing so, we will demonstrate how these different representations and their textual references share a common feature, which we will define as a unitary idea of 'persuaded language' as mono-directional. Defining this nature is for us the key to confirming the results of our enquiry, locating the pragmatic stylistic strategies of the text and providing a platform from which the rest of Michelstaedter's production can be interpreted.

5.2.1 *Figures and the unfigurable*[22]

From the opening pages of *La Persuasione e la Rettorica,* 'persusasion' is described as an experience of absolute possession of the object («Colui che è per sé stesso non ha bisogno d'altra cosa che sia per lui nel futuro, ma possiede tutto in sé». PR: 9), and as a fulfilment of a will to possess that is always frustrated («Ben son alto sulla pianura e sul mare; e vedo il largo orizzonte che è della montagna; ma tutto ciò non è mio: non è in me in quanto vedo, e per più vedere non mai <ho visto>». PR: 8). Reading the argument that follows in Michelstaedter's text under this introductory umbrella would imply understanding not only 'rhetoric', but also 'persuasion' as a form of dominion, a pure form of dominion which eliminates all contingencies and contains the object immediately in itself. This is the core of Brianese's interpretation, from which he derives a series of cosequences. The 'essential solidarity'[23] between 'persuasion' and 'rhetoric' implies that 'persuasion' is not an overcoming of the violence, but rather a «*negazione violenta della violenza*»: «[la persuasione è la] forma di dominio massimamente efficace che, mettendo in gioco la totalità stessa, è in grado di non parlare più di violenza solo nella misura in cui ha già violentato la totalità violentabile, non lasciando sussistere più nulla oltre la propria affermazione totalizzante. *Il persuaso non partecipa più alla lotta tra le determinazioni solo perché è rimasto l'unico a potersi affermare*»[24]. Furthermore, if at the core of 'persuasion' there is the absolute fulfilment of a will, its immutable status outside the flux of time becomes problematic to defend; «*un divenire vitale che vuol essere immutabile*» is a questionable solution for an «eterno ritorno del volere» which in its being a 'return' can never be of 'the same'[25]: «bisogna che il ritornante stia»[26]. According to this framework and the textual evidence on which it is based, the status of 'persuasion' is considered as the fulfilment of a metaphysic of presence, where the demystification and denial of rhetorical life ultimately leads to a re-appropriation of a pure presence of the object to the subject. The «voler e non voler per più volere» of the poem *Nostalgia* (P: 58- 60)[27] is read as a negation of life in the name of higher values: what Deleuze calls 'negative nihilism'.

A second interpretation of the state of 'persuasion' is conceived around the negation of violence that the 'persuaded' performs in any of his relations with his neighbor: a possibility that Brianese negates[28]. The most relevant pages to support this interpretation are at the at the end of the chapter on the 'way to persuasion' (PR: 31-49) and refer to 'persuasion' with the famous motto: «il coraggio dell'impossibile» (PR: 43). Here, the activity of the 'persuaded human' is represented through three different and interwoven movements. Firstly, the 'eradication of violence' (PR: 43) is seen as a process of negation[29], which in its description matches the infinity of the hyperbole: «*ora egli deve affermarsi non per continuare, deve amarlo [l'altro] non perché esso* sia necessario al suo bisogno, ma per ciò che esso *è*» (ibid.); and further: «ma questo tutto non è mai tutto e l'affermazione è sempre un cedere, poiché infiniti sono i travestimenti della φιλοψυχία. [...] Egli deve avere il *coraggio di sentirsi ancora solo*, di guardar ancora in faccia il proprio dolore, di sopportarne *tutto il peso*» (PR: 44). Secondly, on this substratum, which still implies a contingency in time, the action which negates violence is conceived as a «*dare non* [...] *per aver dato, ma per dare*» (PR: 42), so that «*dare è fare l'impossibile: dare è avere*» (PR: 43). In this sense, the overcoming of determinations is conceived as a paradoxical 'giving' of the subject to the other, breaking the bi-directional status of the relationship; if «non può fare chi non è, non può dare chi non ha, non può beneficare chi non sa il bene» (PR: 42), the subject who reaches this ultimate point of resistance to determination can 'possess', or 'have' the other, only in the measure in which he gives without asking something for himself: «deve darsi tutto ad esso per averlo: poiché in esso egli non vede una relazione particolare, ma tutto il mondo» (PR: 43). Hence this absolute act of giving implies also an absolutization of what should have been a determination: the problem of violence is overcome by postulating a paradox. This place of a gift that contravenes the reciprocity of the gift[30] is further specified in two different ways: firstly, as a representation of the 'perlocutionary utterance', and secondly as a series of metaphors regarding the place of the 'persuaded' and its positive, creative production. In regard to the first case, the section titled «il dolore parla» (PR: 46-9) offers the clearest description: «allora il *dolore muto e cieco* di tutte le cose che in ciò che vogliono essere non sono, *avrà per lui*, che ne avrà presa la persona, *la parola eloquente e la vista lontana*» (ibid.). The extreme embodiment of pain, in becoming absolute, universal, allows an utterance that gives an adequate account of this same pain, reveals it and moves the listener on the path to 'persuasion' (PR; 47). The 'persuaded' utterance that, as we discussed in the last chapter, «porta vicine le cose lontane» (PR: 45), is further described: «parlando la voce del proprio dolore egli parlerà loro la voce ad essi lontana del loro stesso dolore» (PR: 46), because «come questo dolore accomuna tutte le cose, in lui vivono le cose non come correlativo di poche relazioni, ma con vastità e profondità di relazioni»[31] (PR: 47).

In this context, the images adopted to represent this 'persuaded' state appear as a double figuration of both the process of 'resistance' in solitude and the ultimate moment of overcoming, the *kairos* coinciding with the leap away from a movement tied to temporality[32], synthesized as follows: «*facendo la propria vita sempre più ricca di negazioni, crear sé e il mondo*» (PR: 45). Firstly, this work «*nel vivo del valore individuale*» (ibid.), is expressed in relation to its audience, stressing both the exemplary status of the 'persuaded', and the elegance and equilibrium of his actions in comparison with the inadequate: «[a]lla fragile imbarcazione in mezzo all'uragano, la grande nave è un porto sicuro» (PR: 47); «le cornacchie nel loro volo pesante, ad ogni levar d'ala s'abbassano col corpo e non più il corpo leva le ali che le ali non abbassino il corpo, ma il falco nello slancio del suo volo, stabile il corpo, batte le ali, e si leva sicuro verso l'alto» (ibid.)[33]. Interestingly enough, this metaphor and comparison are conceived either from the point of view of a 'non persuaded', as in the first case, or from that of an external observer of the two different birds, and therefore as an interpreter of their actions. This chosen point of view is practically the same as that of the narrator of the text, who is dealing with a series of inadequate ('rhetorical') and adequate ('persuaded') affirmations, the latter defined both through exemplary quotes and philosophical, theoretical analysis. The problems of this figuration, namely the question of how a 'non persuaded' could recognize and furthermore define the state of 'persuasion' (in this case in terms of 'equilibrium' and 'sureness') is therefore similar to the discussion on exemplarity we provided in our second chapter and revolves around the theme of the 'perlocutionary': «è la luce che rompe la nebbia davanti a cui cadono i terrori della morte e il presente divien *vita*» (PR: 43). Secondly, in these pages the moment of resistance is given through metaphors of the 'solitude in the desert' (finally overcome in the positive construction of a world) and the final 'burning' in a single point of time (absolute, atemporal presence). «Egli si deve sentire nel deserto fra l'offrirsi delle relazioni particolari, poiché in nessuna di queste egli può affermarsi tutto» (PR: 44); the negation of determinations is in this sense not in contradiction with the adequate utterance, on the contrary, it is the 'utterance of this negation' that carries the revelatory and perlocutionary weight. However, this desert is still conceived as a temporal happening until the final moment: «e s'egli è solo, il mondo gli deve esser un uomo che dice sempre <no> a ogni suo atto, ad ogni sua parola, finché egli non abbia da sé riempito il deserto e illuminata l'oscurità» (PR: 45). Only at the extreme point does the human «solo nel deserto [...] vive una vertiginosa vastità e profondità di vita» (PR: 49), and the linearity and measurability of time fall into crisis because «ogni suo attimo è un secolo della vita degli altri» (PR 49), until time vanishes: «finché egli *faccia di sé stesso fiamma* e giunga a consistere nell'ultimo presente» (ibid.)[34]. This 'last present' and 'burning' of oneself deserve some further remarks. According to the framework we presented in this enquiry, this is in fact the impossible and infinite moment at which the hyperbole of 'the way to persuasion' is abandoned and the 'line of justice' is reached; it is not therefore incorrect that the chapter from which we are quoting has been named «Via alla Persuasione» (PR: 31): in fact it is only at the extreme point of the negative activity that the leap into peace is achieved[35].

There are two features of this leap which can be outlined from the above quotes. The first is related to the dynamics of negation: the act of saying 'no' to determinations goes hand in hand with the practice of a perlocutionary utterance conceived as an act of mono-directional giving. What the subject does is give voice to (his own) pain, thus revealing the human condition and the path of overcoming. The singular and individual utterance is at the same time universal and open: to be followed. In this process however, what is at stake is not the possession of the object, the interlocutor, or the absolutization of the relative determination in the name of a will which is becoming absolute and absolutely violent; rather the movement towards 'persuasion' seems to be away from determinations, as a negation and avoidance of their value which leads to extreme solitude. The solution to contingency is in this sense desired and performed within the boundaries of the 'know thyself' (PR: 46): the inward search, which at its extreme moments will face the nullity of its own pain. The second feature, which is linked to the first in its attempt to avoid falling into a new series of contingent determinations, is the depiction of the ultimate moment of 'persuasion' as an impossible, divine, atemporal and subjective creation. The act of 'filling the desert by oneself', and 'illuminating obscurity' are conceived under a radical transformation, an instant of 'becoming flame' which creates light. Here, the determinations are not somehow re-possessed, subsumed inside the subject and re-gained at an absolute level, they are simply non-existent because the act of appropriation is instead an act of creation. By becoming flame the 'persuaded' 'brings the light', and his utterance 'creates': it is (once again) original and originating.

This transformation into something that does not in any way resemble the features of a subject or its utterance constitutes the basis for a third possible interpretation of the link between nihilism/pessimism and 'persuasion'. Harrison synthesizes this reading by stressing the impossibility of the 'persuaded position': «even if it seems to achieve a type of mystical self-transformation at the height of persuasion, affirming the unspeakable reality of each of its historical experiences, it still loses its features. It dissolves into the arena of pure objectivity, where all "essences" are momentary and fleeting appearances, and no subject can be distinguished from object»[36]. Further, «if persuasion means self-possession, the self is now impossible to characterize in positive terms. It is not equivalent to its needs, it is not what the mind says it is, it is not the sum of its achievements or satisfaction. It is a mere dream of itself»[37]. Hence, if 'persuasion' is non human, it is not conceived inside an idea of the subject, not even as something that we could call pure subjectivity; it is not a form of overcoming nor a way for re-appropriation, therefore what remains is the extreme nihilism which denied the value of any project based on a stable subjectivity[38]. This is the basis on which Harrison can contextualize Michelstaedter as a pre-expressionist 'liberator of dissonance', stating that «after expressionists, artists no longer even believe in self-constituting realms of subjectivity»[39]. These same conclusions could be reached by stressing the coincidence between the 'mystical self-transformation' and the prerogatives of a god, namely the atemporal point of pure creation we quoted above. In fact, if the 'persuaded' is god, or – as in the representation of Socrates in the text – cannot be described by human words if not by the negation of human possibilities (PR: 66), then, and this is the third possible interpretation of 'persuasion', it is something postulated outside the realm of the subject, and in no way linked to it through a conceivable dialectical movement.

5.3   Persuasion as mono-directional utterance

The above section has shown how different critiques of the way in which 'persuasion' is conceived and represented all – despite their differences – find evidence and support in Michelstaedter's text. At this point, given the framework of our enquiry, and the discussion on dialectic and dialogue conducted in the fourth chapter, it would be rather straightforward to read the different sections on 'persuasion' through an argument on the impossibility of signifying the absolute from a relative standpoint. In fact, we opened our research by presenting the aporia under and against which the entirety of Michelstaedter's philosophical enterprise is conceived, and now we have reached the point in which this aporia emerges in the most explicit manner[40]: the 'persuaded' 'does the impossible' because there is no possibility through human actions or language to gain the postulated absolute, namely because it is outside the definition of the human and conceived as its logical opposite. However, such a discussion would lead us to a mapping of the stylistic strategies employed to address the 'persuaded' absolute, for example metaphor and description in negative terms, to name two encountered in the above quote, and their catachretic role[41]. This would further develop in a close reading of the single depictions, which would unavoidably highlight ways in which these attempts are entangled in a dialectic that, while attempting a representation of the absolute, also depicts the very impossibility of the attempt itself. This happens in ways which are similar to the dialectic between sub-genres outlined above in chapter 4[42], and such a reading would offer further evidence of the position of *La Persuasione* with regard to its own philosophical project.

Such a discussion would have the undoubted merit of confirming our previous results. However, we want to follow another interpretive path, and complete the analysis of 'persuaded language' begun above, in our previous chapter. This has the value of offering a unifying view of the different interpretations of 'persuasion' based on an underlying common idea of the adequate, a-rhetorical utterance. In this sense it implies reading the text against its positive formulations instead of inside its negative.

Different representations of 'persuasion' (as an absolute manifestation of the will of a re-unified subject; as the one that sees 'persuasion' as a perpetual negation, and as the extreme nihilism implied in the reading of the leap into the absolute as an impossibility beyond the subject-object distinction) can be seen as three declensions of a single idea of an absolute, mono-directional language which is the logical opposite of a human contingent, dialogical utterance. In other words, if human language is intrinsically 'adversative' because «l'uomo per affermare come <suo> un pensiero *non ha altro mezzo* che quello d'opporlo al pensiero degli altri» (O: 710), the language of the 'persuaded human' is beyond this dialectic, it is, *strictu sensu*, a creative language, and a language of creation. It is clear how this can be intended as a pure affirmation of a subject, and in our fourth chapter we provided a quote in support of this view when we introduced the 'modo imperativo' as the adequate mode of linguistic affirmation: «*è attuale come volontà di una cosa. È il Soggetto qui che invade con la propria vita il regno delle proprie parole: non fa parole, ma vive*» (PR: 142). This 'invasion' of one's own world is in fact the destruction of the object 'inside' a willing subject become absolute. In this sense, it is mono-directional; it is the logical opposite of other modes of affirmation, which are all based on a false absolutization of a contingent determination and imply therefore the annihilation of the object, as Brianese notes, or alternatively, the pure subjective creation emancipated from any determination («*non è realtà intesa, ma vita; è l'intenzione che vive essa stessa attualmente*» PR: 141). However we interpret this passage, the implied language is not entangled in a discourse, it relates to human discourse only as a moment of origin. The utterance, from this absolute standpoint, is 'life' outside determination, yet because uttered it enters into human discourse as an object of interpretation, and therefore as part of a successive determination which does not have any further implications for the 'persuaded human': it has no feedback. The 'non persuaded' might interpret this word, thus crystallising it inside a 'rhetoric' which inadequately objectifies it; however this objectification is totally irrelevant for the utterer. In this dynamic it is not difficult to see the mechanism that we discussed in chapter two with regard to the relationship between exemplarity and its interpretation.

The mono-directional nature of the 'persuaded utterance' can be explained also through the second interpretation discussed above: that is, as an uttering that does not ask anything in exchange, a pure giving. The pages on 'the way to persuasion' stress the intentionality of this giving as part of a complex project of emancipation. In the encounter with his neighbor, the human on the path to 'persuasion' offers an utterance which is not conceived in order to establish a relationship of contingent determination or reciprocal violence, but avoids it and eradicates the need for others: «parlando la voce del proprio dolore egli parlerà loro la voce ad essi lontana del loro stesso dolore» (PR: 46). The utterance is produced as a process of self-representation by the subject, as an inward looking 'know thyself' that finds the common sub-stratum of the human condition. Again, this utterance does not imply a feedback, and its truth is described as being independent from contingent determination. However, the determination takes place: we are 'on the way to persuasion' yet entangled in contingency, in a place where every occurrence of this contingent determination provides the occasion for a further movement towards negation. In encountering the other the human on the path of 'persuasion' «soffirà nello stesso punto della propria deficienza e della loro» (ibid.), so that every determination is resolved in an emancipation, a negation of its affirmative value substituted by the revealing power of the word on/of pain: «l'uomo nella via della persuasione [...] non teme mai il dolore ma ne ha preso onestamente la persona. Egli lo vive in ogni punto. E come questo dolore accomuna tutte le cose, in lui vivono le cose non come correlativo di poche relazioni, ma con vastità e profondità di relazioni» (PR: 47). In the emancipation from the inadequacy of a single determination, language stops being bi-directional and becomes at its extreme limits a mono-directional revealed word: «egli sarà apparso a loro come l'aurora di un nuovo giorno» (ibid.).

The act of 'giving' that belongs to the revelatory word does not ask anything in exchange because whatever it might receive would be taken as a chance for further negation. Only at the extreme point of this solitude, at its infinite and impossible point, is the mechanism overthrown and negated, and from the solitude of the desert the persuaded 'fills the obscurity' and 'becomes flame', or, in Harrison's terms, something which is other than a subject takes his place. This overcoming of the subject/object differentiation is described in the text as becoming 'god' (PR: 77) or becoming 'god to oneself' (PR: 62)[43]. Also in this sense, and this is the third of our hypotheses on 'persuasion', the 'persuaded utterance' would be once again mono-directional, a light for humanity which does not come as a result of human modes of determination: «egli sarà apparso loro come l'aurora di un nuovo giorno. Liberati da ciò ch'essi credono indispensabile, [...] vedranno che non c'è niente da temere, niente da cercare, niente da fuggire, che la fame non è fame, e il pane non è pane; poiché in altro modo avranno sentito la loro fame e altro pane sarà stato loro offerto» (PR: 47). If in this quote we find allusions to religious imagery (that of the New Testament), the structure of its language replicates that of the *logos*, which is outside determinations and time; it is at the same time a language which overcame negations, a pure language of creation. Michelstaedter's later predilection for the New Testament is well documented[44]; the alternative preface to *La Persuasione e la Rettorica* discussed above in the first chapter of the present volume, with its re-telling of John 1.1. is, in this sense, further evidence of a general investment in the source and its language. This alternative preface, whatever its importance might be, at least shows the logical possibility of a relationship between *logos* and rhetoric in the sense we are outlining here.

In the pre-lapsarian context of the 'word of the creator', the 'persuaded' word should be immediately convincing, and the reason for it not being so must be the result of an originary lapse of the creator himself: «certo la persuasione è il fine d'ogni parola [...] – e l'impossibilità della persuasione è causa che gli uomini parlino e ancora e senza fine parleranno. Ché se il primo verbo l'avesse convinto Adamo sarebbe muto e non si sarebbe curato né d'Eva né del serpente né dell'albero della scienza»[45]. In the post-lapsarian state, however, where humans are already born into 'rhetoric', what the 'persuaded word' communicates is not an immediate unity, but the intimate necessity of moving on an emancipatory path where the unity is regained at an infinite point.

The religious component of 'persuaded' language merges with the idea of 'creation' as a prerogative of the artistic language deployed by the genius. Both of these understandings of 'persuasion' – what of 'persuasion' is communicated – share the features of mono-directionality, fullness of reference and avoidance of conceptualization, and share as their common basis the knowledge, acceptance and embodiment of the horror of the experience 'beyond the veil'; a progressive path of which they are the ultimate, incommensurable accomplishment. Here, knowledge is the foundation of the negative dialectic, and the hyperbolic epilogue opens to a final meta-knowledge, a knowledge of the nullity of knowledge that is the springboard for the leap into absolute: a problematic absolutisation/overcoming/impossibility of the subject.

On the other hand, on the side of the fruition of the word, understandings of 'persuaded language' in religious or artistic terms disclose the same coherence. They enter into human discourse as examples and in both cases the problem of interpretation is resolved inside a dichotomy between rhetorical crystallization and a dynamic individual movement springing from the perlocutionary power of the example. In this context, the possibility to be moved towards the individual way of the 'know thyself' constitutes Michelstaedter's very personal Gnostic path towards the *logos*[46].

With this definition – or with these definitions – of 'persuaded language', and with the further acknowledgement that what is at stake in the theoretical relationship between 'persuasion' and 'rhetoric' is the very definition of Michelstaedter's pessimism, we can finally complete the comprehensive discussion on the position of *La Persuasione e la Rettorica* 'against itself'. The point we must highlight here is how the style of the text as we defined it can be considered with regard to the positive affirmation of the 'persuaded word', and if and how this positioning affects the idea of subjectivity as a dialectic process of narratorial undermining.

5.4   Pessimism and announcement

While the negative dialectic performs this path, it evokes at the same time the void, the unspeakable, that which 'rhetoric' – the constituent of the veil – can only show through its own failure (the unavoidable gaps of the dialectic of 'repetitions'). The moment of 'persuasion', which overcomes this nihilism, can be considered in this context as the necessary implication at the core of the will. In fact, «chi vuole la vita veramente, rifiuta di vivere in rapporto a quelle cose che fanno la vana gioia e il vano dolore degli altri [...]. La sua vita è il rifiuto e la lotta [...] e non disperdendosi nell'atto delle continue correlazioni (possessi illusori) si afferma e prende forma e si crea da se stessa: *questa è l'arte*» (O: 705). This positive attitude towards pain is the discriminant between the so called 'imperfect pessimist' and the 'true pessimist' (O: 706); the latter «prende la persona di questo dolore in atto: onde la vera attività che porta alla salute, all'inerzia» (ibid.), while the former «volgendosi ogni tratto a veder il proprio profilo nell'ombra <[è] pres[o] dalla vertigine>» (ibid.), thus «sono inerti nel dolore, vogliono riposare, perciò sono malati: vanno alla <pazzia>» (ibid.)[47]. While the allusion to Plato's myth of the cavern constitutes a further formulation of the state of distress brought by the consciousness of the inadequacy of rhetorical knowledge, the concept of 'activity' versus 'rest' shows how the attitude that is at the core of the movement towards 'persuasion' is the «non adattarti» (PR: 62). This 'do not adapt yourself' implies a struggle against the existential condition and thus a belief in an 'other' than the condition against which one is fighting.

To understand how 'persuasion', this absolute endpoint, is treated, and how Michelstaedter's text locates itself with regard to 'persuasion', we will interpret the theoretical presentation of the matter, so as to provide material for a comparison with our results on style and strategies of argumentation.

5.4.1 Representing the announcement

In regard to the first point, 'persuasion' is presented in the text through modalities that can be grouped and understood as forms of annunciation. The first mode of this annunciation is, in line with what we have said above, to be found inside the discussion of its (im)possibility. In this sense, the positive word is embodied in the striving for the re-achievement of that same word, as an individual, subjective self-possession, outside the rhetoric of inadequate conceptual interpretation and explanation (crystallization). This movement is not at all paradoxical. If we consider the 'persuaded utterance' as a self-sufficient, religious/artistic mono-directional affirmation, we should also read it as something outside human, relative discourse, and by extension outside of any dialectical attempt to move towards it, to re-achieve it. The text is written in a relative, historical, time-bound discourse that interprets the exemplary word; and it moves from this point of view toward an attempt at re-achieving this *logos* through the deployment of Socratic dialectic. As a consequence, the text necessarily fails to repeat or interpret the original word of 'persuasion'. It can only announce the original word of 'persuasion' through its infinite failure: it is the perlocutionary force which moved the narrator that originates his path and is the final target of his struggle:

> [Il persuaso] a loro metterà vicina una *vita*, per la quale essi vedranno sciogliersi la trama di ciò che li preme [...]; si troveranno a esser stabili senza la paura dell'instabilità, si vedranno ad un tratto strappate le

pareti della piccola stanza della loro miseria, e il loro piccolo lume impallidire, nel punto che fuori l'oscurità non sarà più a premerli col suo terrore, ma egli sarà apparso a loro come l'aurora di un nuovo giorno. Liberati da ciò che credono indispensabile [...] essi assaporeranno nell'impossibile, nell'insopportabile, la gioia di un presente più pieno. Vedranno che non c'è niente da temere, niente da cercare, niente da fuggire, che la fame non è fame, e il pane non è pane; poiché in altro modo avranno sentito la loro fame e altro pane sarà stato loro offerto. Non avranno più freddo e stanchezza [...] ma sentiranno nel presente raccolta la loro vita, poiché in un punto saranno fatti partecipi d'una vita più vasta e più profonda (PR: 46-7).

This passage gives an indirect account of the place of the narratorial utterance. The insistence of the future tense coincides here with the description of the effect of the perlocutionary word in all its revelatory powers. If we read this description against the text itself, we have firstly a confirmation of the project of 'persuasion' as an infinite striving for a future utterance; a time-bound and therefore rhetorical tragic movement against oneself, towards atemporality. Secondly, and most importantly, this passage represents a further implicit admission of the rhetorical, non-perlocutionary nature of the utterance of the text. To decline the perlocutionary in the future and yet represent its effects is a practice shows how the 'adequate utterance' can only be conceived as an announcement, or as the preaching of 'another' word revealed to the narrator[48]. It is always interpreted, always reduced inside a determination against which the text cannot produce anything positive but its own undermining. In other words, the pedagogy in which the text is engaged does not transform into an adequate example of what it is inadequately teaching: it can only perform the void of its continuous negation.

The restoration of the original *logos* by means of a rhetorical language which is not revelatory, but only moved by a revelation, is very close to some remarks offered by Kelber in his reading of the New Testament. For Kelber, the problem is that «the "Saviour's" discourses are by no means as unambiguously lucid as one might expect them, since they are meant to be "open", revelatory communications», but «insofar as the revelation discourses are not fully comprehended by Peter and James, they oblige the readers to involve themselves in the act of interpretation. And interpretation once again problematizes any claim to "open", unmediated revelation»[49]. The alternative preface to *La Persuasione e la Rettorica* posits the problem in similar terms. Moreover, Kelber stresses the problematic relationship between John's Gospel and the embodiment of the revelatory word, interpreting it as a recontextualization of the genres of sayings and parables inside a framing narrative[50]. This has the consequence of reducing the *logos* to a singular epitome of the metaphysics of presence, which must be deconstructed in order to restore the complexity and openness of the revelatory word, outside the «archaeology of human spirit which always places *arche* (or *telos*) above discourse»[51]. It is from this perspective that Kelber reads the Fourth Gospel as performing a series of rhetorical strategies oriented towards 'decentering the Logos', with the consequence of «administrat[ing] deconstruction of its own onto-theological origin»[52]. Our analysis of Michelstaedter's attempt can be easily compared with Kelber's conclusions. What needs to be stressed however, is that in *La Persuasione e la Rettorica* this process of 'deconstruction' does not immediately coincide with one's own re-achievement of the original *logos*; the motto «con le parole guerra alle parole / siccome aure nebbiose l'aura viva / disperde perché pur il sol risplenda» (PR: 134) can be interpreted in this context as a process of 'clearing' which does not imply 'becoming the sun', but allows the shining of the adequate word. The 'openness' and displacement derived from Socratic dialectic does not coincide with the 'openness' of the 'persuaded word' and its fullness of reference; the logic of the former is a critique of discourse from inside its relativity and the latter is outside/before any human discourse[53].

5.4.2 Style with regard to the announcement

Giorgio Brianese, in his article on Michelstaedter's poem *I figli del Mare* (P: 79-84)[54], convincingly outlines the position of the subject on the 'way to persuasion' with regard to its final target. Brianese shows how the movement of the two protagonists of this myth, Itti[55] and Senia (the stranger), is circular in type. Firstly, from the sea of their origin, the «pace del mare lontano» (l.1) in a «silenzio senza richiami» (l. 4) they wake up on a «suolo triste» (l. 6) «dei mortali a viver la morte» (l.9). This is interpreted by Brianese as a movement from origin and authenticity to 'rhetoric'[56]. After a process of rhetorical socialization (second verse), and a growing consciousness of their existential situation (third verse), Itti expresses to Senia the alternative of a way towards a «mare senza confini» (l. 86): a second and opposite movement «dalla terra al mare»[57]. This second step however, is not conceived as a return home, as the fulfilment of nostalgia, nor as a 'peaceful'[58] resolution, but as the final verse states («Senia, il porto è la furia del mare, / è la furia del nembo più forte, / quando libera ride la morte / a chi libero la sfidò»), this is a different sea:

[Michelstaedter] si pone, inconsapevolmente, da un punto di vista che *si identifica con il Caos del divenire* e che abbandona ogni pretesa di verità definitiva, assoluta; non c'è, infatti, un porto stabile cui il navigante debba giungere o nel quale si trovi, ma il senso del navigare è dato da null'altro che il suo stesso errare nella furia del mare: [...] l'Essere resta sempre di nuovo al di là dei tentativi che vengono messi in opera dalla volontà per raggiungerlo[59].

This interpretation of the impossibility and insufficiency of the subject against the absolute is almost entirely coherent with our line of argument, except for two points. Firstly, we would not subscribe to the 'unconscious' nature of Michelstaedter's definition, given what we have pointed out regarding the explicit consciousness of the impossibility of the position of the 'persuaded'. Secondly, the 'chaos of becoming' expressed by the fury of the sea does not coincide with the 'wandering' of the subject[60], but with a struggle against the fury towards 'resistance' (PR: 42-5): «alla fragile ibarcazione in mezzo all'uragano, la grande nave è un porto sicuro» (PR: 47). In any case, the parallel between this poem and *La Persuasione e la Rettorica*[61] offers us the chance to present some concluding remarks on the matter of style and 'rhetoric'. This means focusing on the ways in which the style of the text (at this point we could unambiguously write, its 'rhetoric') relates to the announcement of 'persuasion', and the philosophical consequences of this position.

In order to do so, some further points of comparison need to be stressed. The first is between Itti, the protagonist who gives voice to his longing for the sea, and the narrator of *La Persuasione e la Rettorica*. In the poem, once Itti and Senia learn to live on the earth they experience the voice that calls towards something else as «lontano dolore» (l. 46) and «voce del mistero / per l'ignoto lontano amore» (l. 47-8), because «la vasta voce del mare / al loro cuore soffocato / lontane suscitava ignote voci» (l. 57-9). The reaction to this experience of pain and the unknown brings Senia the wish for her own death (l. 70). But it is Itti who embodies this experience and through the description of his vision[62] of the 'other sea' (l. 85), exhorts Senia to resist the call of the rhetoric of the «domestico focolare» (l. 105) and to follow him on the path towards this sea[63], a path described in terms which are clearly coherent with the requirement of the negative dialectic: «il coraggio di sopportare / tutto il peso del dolore» (l. 150-1), «il coraggio di non sostare / nella cura dell'avvenire» (l. 154-5), il coraggio di non languire / per godere le cose care» (l. 156-7). Like the narrator of *La Persuasione e la Rettorica*, Itti represents the subject who faces obscurity and orients itself on the path of 'persuasion'; furthermore he is engaged in an attempt to represent and communicate his vision, the revelation of the 'other sea'. Given the position from which this vision is uttered, it is clear how it shares with *La Persuasione e la Rettorica* all the problems of definition of the absolute. Here, for the same reasons, 'persuasion' is announced. Indeed, in the myth the two protagonists are at the shore (l. 49) or looking «con l'occhio all'orizzonte / dove il ciel si fondeva col mare» 138-9), and it is from this position that both Senia's and Itti's words are uttered but not fulfilled through action. While Senia's only utterance is in the conditional («vorrei morire», l. 70, 141), Itti ultimately conceives his plan in the future («più forte saprò navigare» l. 164 and most clearly «giungeremo al nostro mare» l. 165)[64].

In chapter 4 above we have seen how in the 'Appendice I' the future tense and conditional mode are treated as examples of inadequate affirmation. Those conclusions would put Itti's project under exactly the same order of problems that the narrator of *La Persuasione e la Rettorica* is facing, in his attempt to define a theory of a way to 'persuasion' and deal with the 'rhetoric' that this implies. However, the narrator's word, as we demonstrated, is not uttered from 'the shore', but from the extreme point where the negative dialectic deployed in the text addresses itself, the point at which every affirmation dialectically resolves in a questioning of its own achievement. In *I figli del mare* we still have a 'well rounded' subject who is positively defining the *iter* of his will; his project, as a rhetorical systematization conceived to define and convince (himself and Senia), enters into a series of complicated ambiguities with the 'negative dialectic', as if the 'know thyself' – strangely linked here with the exploitation of a determinate relationship («se t'affidi senza timore / ben più forte saprò navigare» l. 162-3) – would lead to a process of reinforcement of the subject itself («giungeremo al nostro mare» l. 165) instead of being shattered by the ultimate negation. This point would be coherent with Brianese's reading: resistance to the temptations of φιλοψυχία coming from outside the subject (l. 106-33), becomes an 'infinite repetition' which does not ultimately develop into self-negation, but fights the fight 'against the waves' as a reinforcement of the will. Brianese might be therefore correct to interpret 'persuasion' on this basis as a form of 'will to power', where the subject in an act of absolute will destroys the object in absolutely possessing it, in reducing it to himself, as we discussed above in this chapter.

However, the object of our enquiry is not an interpretation of Michelstaedter's poetic language, or the question of whether his poetic language can be considered a coherent attempt at the 'adequacy' that artistic language is called to achieve. Nor is our intent to discuss whether the metaphoric process displayed in the poem is an adequate answer to the problem of 'persuasion' and signification[65]. Rather it is important to stress how all our efforts in this enquiry have been focused on demonstrating the peculiarity of *La Persuasione e la Rettorica* with regard to the fate of its narrator. The narrator of *La Persuasione e la Rettorica* embarks on a process which defines in different terms the aesthetic value of his text. In fact, the process of negation, relativization and loss of the linguistic centre of the text is, as we demonstrated in our fourth chapter, alien to any positive resolution. If every statement, every sub-genre and every ideologically charged vocabulary is engaged in the mechanism that we defined as a dialectic of repetition – time-based and open to evoke the void that every positive affirmation inadequately covers – we can affirm that the text is reaching the ultimate self-negation: the destruction of its own project. This failure implies the performance of an extreme nihilism that reaches the point of undermining the postulate on which it could itself take place. If this is true, as discussed in the case of the principles of Socratic dialectic (which we interpreted as a meta-language in need of the ultimate negation), it is true also for the positive definition of 'persuasion'. While Itti's announcement, problematic as it is, is left untouched and thus works as a sort of 'evocation'[66] of a future state, every definition of 'persuasion' in Michelstaedter's philosophical text is embodied in a dialectic of undermining that does not spare anything. Paradoxically, all the logical presuppositions that are indispensable for proceeding along the path towards 'persuasion' are undermined by the same path they allow: a path which does not admit a hiatus, not even to affirm its own value. In other words, on the level of practice, the attempt at adequate signification in *La Persuasione e la Rettorica* does not perform any stable positive representation of itself or of its positive goal, and does not stop its mechanism of negation allowing the presence of non-critiqued language which we could interpret as the example of a 'positive' investment.

This absence of a non-relativized utterance locates the text inside the context of the European 'crisis of language' sketched above in our introduction, by performing its own inadequacy, its own 'failure'[67]. Furthermore, in its implied idea of subjectivity, as Harrison suggested[68], *La Persuasione e la Rettorica* performs the inwardness of the 'know thyself' to the ultimate point of the negation of itself, which is a negation of the Self: the failure of the investment in the will of the subject is performed as an undermining of the subject as a stable centre. Bini considers death as the only possible fulfilment of the 'path to persuasion'[69] and links it with the biography of Michelstaedter and his suicide: what we can certainly say is that the path performed in *La Persuasione* leads to the death of the (stable) subject.

5. 5   Not enough of an artist?

The 'extreme nihilism' in which *La Persuasione e la Rettorica* finds itself implies a further negation: an implicit critique of artistic language as the preferential way towards adequate utterance. Because the dialectic of the philosophical text is never overcome by an utterance that does not itself enter into the mechanism of negation, there is no space for an investment in an untouched positive formulation: even the various embodiment of lines from the original poems[70] enter into the dialectic, casting a shadow on the effective position of this literary genre inside the existential project of their author. In other words, if Beethoven, in the famous letter to Paula, is the genius who after having experienced the nullity of his own pain is able to concieve the positive expression exemplified by the *Ninth Symphony*, Michelstaedter, in *La Persuasione e la Rettorica*, stops a step before.

In regard to this topic, some remarks by Daniela Bini offer us the chance to outline a concluding point. Bini's article on Leopardi and Michelstaedter gives the following interpretation: «anche Michelstaedter tenterà di trovare la salvezza nell'arte – ci proverà sia con la poesia che con la pittura. Ma non ci riuscirà, perché non accetterà mai l'impossibilità di superare realmente il limite ontologico, perché non accetterà mai il valore della finzione»[71]. In support of this statement, Bini engages in a comparison between the Leopardian *Infinito* and Michelstaedter's *Risveglio* (P: 69-70), showing how the parallels between the two poems reinforce the importance of one crucial difference, namely the absence of a positive investment in fiction: «manca in 'Risveglio' il nucleo essenziale dell''Infinito': il 'fingo' dell'io poetico; quell 'fingo' per Carlo ancora troppo pieno di risonanze retoriche, ma grazie al quale è data l'ultima salvezza»[72]. In another contribution, Bini develops her reading of Leopardi, stating that «before Nietzsche [...] Leopardi realizes the necessity of fiction»[73] and furthermore, in his late production «poetry [...] no longer stands in opposition to [his] nihilistic philosophy but, as a creator of appearances, it represents the very activity of nature»[74]. The complexities of the relationship between Michelstaedter and the Leopardian sources exceeds the goals of our present discussion[75]. Yet the specific comparison between *Risveglio* and *Infinito*, given Michelstaedter's theoretical investment in the adequacy of artistic language to overcome rhetoric, implies a definition of poetic 'fiction' in terms which are very close to a reading of the poetic *inventio* as the privileged tool for overcoming linguistic and existential finitude. We have seen how this idea is present in Michelstaedter as a development of Romantic aesthetics[76], a reading confirmed in the literature on his poetic production[77]. Therefore, we should read the problematic avoidance of the 'fingo' in *Risveglio* under this umbrella. In this sense, Margaret Brose's reading of the *Infinito* as an example of romantic sublime which aims at the «*production* of the experience of the sublime by means of contrast between the *finito* and the *indefinito*» resolving in a «substitution» of the «visual» with the «imaginative» field[78], with the consequence of a «de-reification»[79] and performance of a poetic word which is «an illusion – a rhetorical sleight of hand, but one which provides in the textual actuality of the poem the presence and plenitude that life denies»[80], offers an important contribution. It is this attempt at 'bringing close the things which are far' that Michelstaedter refuses to accept in his *Risveglio*; the poem is thus a Romantic idyll that states its own inadequacy: the poetic 'I' states that «volo per altri cieli è la mia vita …» (l. 24), and yet after asking «e la mia vita / perché non vive, perché non avviene?» (l. 25-6) he ends with the acknowledgement of his failure, because «la natura inimica ora m'è cara / che mi darà riparo e nutrimento, / ora vado a ronzar come gl'insetti» (l. 46-8)[81].

This mechanism of negating one's own presuppositions is precisely what constitutes the achievement of *La Persuasione e la Rettorica*. Its metaphysical starting points – the idea of a subject as a stable centre and *locus* of a will; the positive investment in this will; the investment in a logic that derives 'persuasion' as an external 'opposite' of rhetorical contingency,; the belief in a language that could utter this 'other than rhetoric' – are taken to an extreme point, inside the stylistic attempt at coherence, and here they cannot help but represent nothing more than their own inadequacy. Socratic dialectic itself, deployed in the ways that our enquiry has been committed to demonstrating, reaches the place of extreme pessimism, and in doing so negates the value of its own project, without any alternative, or leap into a positive resolution.

Ultimately, *La Persuasione e la Rettorica* is the representation of the fulfilment of a tragic understanding of life, a light in which Michelstaedter posited the entire text, starting from the opening epigraph (PR: 1)[82]. Peter Szondi, in his analysis of Simmel in *An Essay on the Tragic*, offers a quote that, in this sense, can work as our conclusion:

The destructive powers directed toward a being arise from the deepest strata of this very being and, with its destruction, a fate takes place that is moored in the being itself and, so to speak, is the logical development of the very structure with which the being constructed its own positivity[83].

The coherence with which the style of *La Persuasione e la Rettorica* represents this tragic process is its major contribution to the literature of the Italian Novecento.

Notes

1. Lloyd, 'Kant's Examples': 264.
2. Ibid.: 264-5.
3. It is interesting to acknowledge in this context how Kantian examples can also be read as revelatory of a dependency on the side of trascendental philosophy; as Caruth states: «Kant is concerned [...] with the fact that transcendental philosophy, as a purely formal structure, [...] depends on something outside of the concept, of "examples", for its "meaning"», see: Cathy Caruth, 'The Force of Examples. Kant's Symbols,' in *Unruly Examples. On the Rhetoric of Exemplarity*, ed. Alexander Gelley (Stanford: Stanford University Press, 1995): 283. Further comparisons would be interesting but would lead us too far from the goals of this chapter and our enquiry in general.
4. This comment is borrowed from Gadamer's reading of Schiller's *Über die ästhetische Erziehung des Menschen*: «an education to art comes through an education by art» (Gadamer, *Truth and Method*: 74). However, while in Schiller: «in place of the true moral and political freedom, for which art should prepare us, we have the culture of an "aesthetic state"» (ibid.), Michelstaedter outlines an individual, singular religious/aesthetic process: an incitement to 'become a genius'.
5. Harrison, *1910. The Emancipation of Dissonance*: 157.
6. Ibid.: 158.
7. Gilles Deleuze, *Nietzsche and Philosophy* (London, New York: Continuum, 2006): 153.
8. Ibid.: 154.
9. Ibid.: 152.
10. In Michelstaedter's vocabulary, the crucial category is 'pessimism': see the pages that dismiss «l'imperfetto pessimista» (O: 705-6) as someone who rests on his own pain, while the true pessimist «prende la persona di questo dolore in atto: onde la vera attività che porta alla salute» (O: 706).
11. Deleuze, *Nietzsche and Philosophy*: 153.
12. Ibid.: 139.
13. See our introduction. Cacciari, 'La Lotta 'su' Platone': 104.
14. «We can no longer conceal from ourselves what is expressed by all that willing which has taken its direction from the ascetic ideal: [...] *a will to nothingness*, an aversion to life, a rebellion against the most fundamental presupposition of life; but it is and remains a *will!*...», see: Friedrich Wilhelm Nietzsche, 'On the Genealogy of Morals' in *Basic Writings*

of *Nietzsche* (New York: Modern Library Edition, 1992): 598-9.

15. This is the title of the third chapter of his: Harrison, *1910. The Emancipation of Dissonance*:139-81.

16. Ibid.: 180.

17. See also O: 632-3.

18. Max Stirner, *The Ego and Its Own* (Cambridge: Cambridge University Press, 1995).

19. In the famous letter to the father dated 31st of May 1908 (E: 320-22). See also: Bini, *Carlo Michelstaedter and the Failure of Language*: 4.

20. We know that Michelstaedter had a romantic relationship with Iolanda, which had its epilogue in Carlo's proposal and the opposition of both families; *La Persuasione e la Rettorica* was written in the turmoil of this period. More in general, for the problem of genre, philosophical formulations and comparison I am indebted to Anne Freadman, in particular the theoretical framework set out in: Anne Freadman, *The Machinery of Talk: Charles Peirce and the Sign Hypothesis* (Stanford: Stanford University Press, 2004).

21. E: 202-3.

22. For this title I am indebited to: Alfonso Cariolato and Enrico Fongaro, 'Figure dell'Infigurabile' in *Parmenide ed Eraclito. Empedocle* (Milano: SE, 2003).

23. Brianese, *L'Arco e il Destino. Interpretazione di Michelstaedter*:31.

24. Ibid.: 37.

25. In chapter 4 we read this as the impossibility of repetition.

26. Brianese, *L'Arco e il Destino. Interpretazione di Michelstaedter*: 31.

27. Also quoted inside Brianese (ibid.: 30).

28. Ibid.: 37.

29. More than two dozens of «non» fill the most crucial pages of the 'positive' description of 'persuasion' (PR: 42-7); more generally, the entire section is constructed in a tight opposition with 'rhetoric', thus defining 'persuasion' as a logical (not necessarilly dialectical) opposite.

30. See the seminal: Marcel Mauss, *The Gift: The Form and Reason for Exchange in Archaic Societies* (London: Routledge, 1990). For a review on the theme and the interpretation of gift in 'modern societies', see also: Jacques T. Godbout, *The World of the Gift* (Montreal & Kingston, London, Ithaca: McGill-Queen's University Press, 1998).

31. In the vocabulary that we introduced in our preceding chapter, we could say that he becomes symbol of adequate affirmation.

32. On the instant as *kairos*, see: Raschini, *Michelstaedter*: 159.

33. The investment in the metaphor of the hawk is testified also by its presence in the poem *Risveglio* (P: 69).

34. The interpretations of the image of the flame are various, and a recollection of them exceeds the goals of this chapter. See at least: Bini, *Carlo Michelstaedter and the Failure of Language*: 40-1; Gianni Carchia, 'Linguaggio e Mistica in Carlo Michelstaedter' *Rivista di Estetica* 9 (1981); Carmela Demichele, 'La Via Luminosa' in *Il Maestro del Deserto Carlo Michelstaedter*, ed. Antonia Acciani (Bari: Progedit, 2005).

35. 'Through activity to peace' (PR: 49) is the concluding motto of the section on 'persuasion'.

36. Harrison, *1910. The Emancipation of Dissonance*: 158-9.

37. Ibid.: 159.

38. This is confirmed by Raschini's interpretation of Michelstaedter's reading of Socrates and the concept of 'soul': «Michelstaedter avanza un'interpretatione ben diversa da quella che [...] vede Socrate introdurre nel mondo occidentale il concetto di anima come forza unitaria spirituale e autonoma, centro di coscienza. [...] L'anima è [...] presa di coscienza di questo radicale mancamento, concetto affatto negativo». Raschini, *Michelstaedter*: 152.

39. Harrison, *1910. The Emancipation of Dissonance*: 180.

40. Here, at the moment of exhaustion of all possibilities and attempts, Bini's argument that the only way to partake in the absolute is through death, takes shape. (Bini, *Carlo Michelstaedter and the Failure of Language*: 41; Bini, 'Carlo Michelstaedter: the Tragedy of Thought'). If we consider death a possible example of an alternative to human contingency, then her analysis of the idea of subjectivity expressed in *La Persuasione e la Rettorica* is coherent with what we called extreme nihilism. What remains to be interpreted is Bini's reading of the relationship between subject, will and suicide, particularly with regard to the argument against suicide in the *Dialogo della Salute*; this however exceeds the goals of our present work. We will have the chance to discuss Bini in regard with pessimism and artistic production further in this chapter.

41. Soskice, *Metaphor and Religious Language*: 61-4.

42. It is interesting to notice how the 'perlocutionary' is a feature implied also in this attempt: the group of different figurations and their reciprocal links offer a degree of complexity and openness to be filled by the reader and potentially orient her/him towards the individual path of 'persuasion'. However, the ways in which these features (openness, perlocutionary intent) emerge from a dialectic grounded on a lack of 'persuasion', are intrinsically different from the 'fullness of meaning' of the 'persuaded' word, as discussed in this and our previous chapter. We will further acknowledge this point in our discussion on the status of *La Persuasione e la Rettorica* as an 'announcement'.

43. We discussed this point in the example of Christ above in the second chapter of the present volume.

44. Campailla, *A Ferri Corti con la Vita*: 101-2; see also Michelstaedter's letter to his family dated 27th of May 1909 (E: 381).

45. FCM III 3 – 37: 2 recto.

46. For an enquiry on the links between the 'know thyself' and the history of Gnostic perspective, see: Gilles Quispel, 'Hermes Trismegistus and the Origins of Gnosticism' *Vigiliae Christianae* 46, no. 1 (1992); for a definition of Gnosticism as 'mythical expression of Self-experience through the revelation of the Word' and its consequences, see: Gilles Quispel, 'Gnosticism and the New Testament' *Vigiliae Christianae* 19, no. 2 (1965): 73.

47. The very topic of the *Dialogo della Salute*.

48. «il muto dolore a me ha parlato» (*Alla Sorella Paula*, P: 72). See also PR: 34.

49. Werner H. Kelber, 'In the Beginning Were the Words: The Apotheosis and Narrative Displacement of the Logos' *Journal of the American Academy of Religion* 58, no. 1 (1990): 81.

50. Ibid.: 89.

51. Ibid.: 90. Kelber interprets Christ's utterance through the Heideggerian category of *Gleichspruenglichkeit*, seeing the original *logos* as a series of *logoi*, all claiming the status of originality without a prescribed time-based hierarchy. The discussion of possible parallels with Michelstaedter – for whom on the one hand the 'plenitude of speech' of the 'persuaded' could be interpreted as a metaphysics of presence, and on the other, the different utterances of the exemplary persuaded are not organized into a system that implies an *arche* – would be outside the goals of our research. What counts in this context is that the general relationship between revelation and its interpretation-communication is comparable in the two cases, allowing us to draw further conclusions.

52. Ibid.: 92.

53. On this point, Raschini states: «per Michelstaedter [...] il momento 'costruttivo' del metodo socratico è l'ironia, in quanto frantuma le false pretese di ciò che non è, mentre la maieutica

[si dà] nella volontà del singolo che ha *vissuto* il calvario dell'ironia» Raschini, *Michelstaedter*: 154.

54. Brianese, 'Il Silenzio e i Richiami. Per una Rilettura de 'I figli del Mare' di Carlo Michelstaedter'.

55. The name is a reference to the interpretation of Christ as 'saviour of himself' as discussed in PR: 61-2. See our introduction and chapter 2 above.

56. Brianese, 'Il Silenzio e i Richiami. Per una Rilettura de 'I figli del Mare' di Carlo Michelstaedter': 12. For the importance of the sea as metaphor for 'persuasion' and for the possible sources of this figuration, see also: Campailla, 'Michelstaedter Lettore di Ibsen'; Sergio Campailla, 'Il Terzo Regno' in *Poesie* (Milano: Adelphi, 1994) .

57. Brianese, 'Il Silenzio e i Richiami. Per una Rilettura de 'I figli del Mare' di Carlo Michelstaedter': 12.

58. «Δι' ἐνερΥείας ἐς ἀρΥίαν» is the motto in PR: 49.

59. Brianese, 'Il Silenzio e i Richiami. Per una Rilettura de 'I figli del Mare' di Carlo Michelstaedter': 21.

60. Brianese's choice of the verb 'errare' is very poignant, in its double sense of 'to wander' and 'to err'.

61. To the point that the former can be adopted by Brianese as the object from which to derive some generalizations on Michelstaedter's philosophical speculation.

62. «Ho veduto un altro mare» (l. 85), «vedo il mar senza confini» (l. 86), «vedo il sole che non cala» (l. 90).

63. «Se t'affidi senza timore / ben più forte saprò navigare, / se non copri la faccia al dolore / giungeremo al nostro mare» (l.162-5).

64. In this sense, the interpretation of the poem as «il tempo in cui l'autore è pervenuto a fare <in un punto di sé stesso fiamma> » (Campailla, 'Il Terzo Regno': 26) should be read more in the context of the development of Michelstaedter's poetry in relation with his own biography, a perspective from which Campailla offered crucial contributions.

65. More than any other reading this would introduce a series of methodological problems related to the fruition of a potential 'persuaded' language inside the rhetoric of relative interpretation, as Bini correctly pointed out in Bini, *Carlo Michelstaedter and the Failure of Language*: 30-3. For the hermeneutic problems inherent in the fruition of the originality of the Kantian Genius' utterance, with interesting parallels to be drawn with the 'persuaded', see: Timothy Gould, 'The Audience of Originality: Kant and Wordsworth on the Reception of Genius' in *Essays in Kant's Aesthetics*, ed. Ted Cohen and Paul Guyer (Chicago & London: The University of Chicago Press, 1982).

66. Bini, *Carlo Michelstaedter and the Failure of Language*: 10. A reading of this 'evoking' as a rhetorical form of 'explaining' (how Bini identifies what we called 'conceptualization') would be of some interest, but it exceeds the goals of our chapter.

67. As Bini chooses for the title of her volume.

68. See above.

69. Bini, *Carlo Michelstaedter and the Failure of Language*: 6, 41.

70. As editor of *La Persuasione e la Rettorica*, Campailla accurately points out the presence of references to Michelstaedter's poems. A full interpretation of the intertextual links between the academic prose and the poems would imply a research focused on discovering the correct direction of the borrowing, from poem to prose and vice versa, and the role of eventual consistencies in the variants and developments of the passsages inside the different genres. This would open to a broader discussion on the dialectic between genres and its role inside Michelstaedter's philosophy. However this would be alien to both the

methodology and the object of our research. For an example of intertextual references in the case of *I Figli del Mare*, see PR: 11, 35, 44, the latter being amongst the crucial pages devoted to a positive definition of 'persuasion'.

71. Bini, 'Leopardi e Michelstaedter tra Autenticità e Inautenticità': 224.

72. Ibid.

73. Bini, 'Giacomo Leopardi's Ultrafilosofia': 53.

74. Ibid.

75. On this topic, see: Campailla, 'Postille Leopardiane di Michelstaedter'; Cacciari, 'Leopardi Platonicus?' (for the embodiment of Leopardi's thought in Michelastadter's philosophical framework); Luigi Preziosi, 'Una Giovinezza Spezzata (Echi Leopardiani in Michelstaedter)' *Studi Goriziani*, no. 66 (1987); Paganelli, 'Il Sorriso Tragico di Carlo Michelstaedter'.

76. See chapter 4, but also: Antonio Piromalli, *Michelstaedter* (Firenze: La Nuova Italia, 1968): 17-8.

77. See at least: Kanduth, 'Dal Tu all'Io nella Poesia di Carlo Michelstaedter'; Bini, 'Leopardi e Michelstaedter tra Autenticità e Inautenticità'; Vittorio Enzo Alfieri, 'Michelstaedter Poeta' *Letterature Moderne* 12, no. 2-3 (1962): 135-7 et passim.

78. Margaret Brose, 'Leopardi's 'L'Infinito' and the Language of the Romantic Sublime' *Poetics Today* 4, no. 1 (1983): 59.

79. Ibid.: 53.

80. Ibid.

81. After our discussion, in chapter 4, of the fictional ladder from inorganic to organic and human proposed in *La Persuasione e la Rettorica* as a re-formulation of the hyperbolic way to 'persuasion', the image of the insect assumes here all its poignancy as one of the lowest levels of determination, and thus as human failure.

82. See above, the introduction to the present volume.

83. Simmel, quoted in Peter Szondi, *An Essay on the Tragic* (Stanford: Stanford University Press, 2002): 44.

Conclusions

In his article on 'Michelstaedter's enigma', Thomas Harrison states: «we find that Michelstaedter's poetry as a whole rarely *embodies* persuasion (as art presumably would, in a classical unity of form and content); it speaks around it – and less persuasively, I believe, than does his prose»[1]. Our enquiry was devoted to providing a precise mapping not only of the 'persuasive speaking around persuasion' deployed in *La Persuasione e la Rettorica*, but also of the ways in which the text 'embodies' the project of 'persuasion'. The starting point for this project was our interest in finding possible reasons behind the stylistic and rhetorical peculiarity of this text: the contradiction between the critique of academic ideology, the presuppositions of science, the initial self-dismissal that the crossed-out preface seems to affirm, and the complexity of the strategies of argumentation that are so distant from the genre of a university dissertation, showed an investment in the act of textual production that could not be exhausted in an interpretation of *La Persuasione e la Rettorica* as the unwilling accomplishment of a social duty. In response to this puzzling problem, we demonstrated a level of self-reflexivity in the text and interpreted the stylistic effort in the light of the theorized 'way to persuasion'. As a consequence, we developed a coherent methodology of research.

This approach produced results on different levels. Firstly, it allowed us to concentrate on the links between the theory of 'persuasion'/'rhetoric' and the parallel philosophy of language developed in the text. We showed how these two main categories can be understood inside a problem of adequacy of utterance, and how the movement towards this adequacy is comparable with the ethical and existential striving for the absolute of 'persuasion'. In this sense, we understood the infinite movement of negation of the Socratic dialectic as something to be sought also in a linguistic, stylistic practice. This constitutes, in our understanding, the first part of the poetic expressed in the text. We further outlined how the language of art is posited as a possible way to regain the adequacy of utterance through the immediacy of the complexity and fullness of reference that poetic and artistic language in general – supposedly – allow.

Secondly, our approach led us to verify the poetic of 'persuasion' in the stylistic practice of the text, in its rhetoric. This allowed us to further develop our analysis and reach two important conclusions. We demonstrated how the frequent appearance of fictional sub-genres, no matter how extended or developed, was not sufficient *per se* to support the interpretation of an anti-rhetorical investment in artistic language. The presence of the generalizing narrator, with his monologic aim that so much resembles the construction of a philosophical system, creates a context in which fictional sub-genres and more in general, figurative language enter into a dialectic in which both sides engage in a reciprocal relativization. We interpreted this juxtaposition as a 'repetition' which is a continous 'correction', thus indirectly asserting the inadequacy of any of the affirmations. In this sense, the stylistic complexity of the text should not be interpreted as a 'positive' investment in a particular language, but rather an attempt to fulfil the requirements of the negative dialectic: a continous undermining which is at the same time a self-undermining.

This result allowed us to come back to the theory of 'persuasion' with the evidence that the text does not embrace any linguistic illusion of overcoming contingency. In this sense, we had some material for a case that, in coherence with explicit statements in the text, sees 'persuasion' as an impossibility. If «non può *fare* chi non è, non può *dare* chi non ha» (PR: 42), and if *La Persuasione e la Rettorica* is not written from the point of view of 'persuasion' but from that of one who is a 'lacking and willing subject' (PR: 7), then the text, as a matter of coherence, is unable to offer a positive description of 'persuasion' or adequately address the 'persuaded word'. In this sense, the perlocutionary word of the 'persuaded' is an external exemplary utterance at the beginning of the subject's journey, that moves him towards the path of emancipation, and an unfulfillable postulate beyond dialectic. In other words, 'persuasion' is beyond the possibility of the subject, and the 'persuaded' is no subject at all. In coherence with this point, the dialectic of the text demonstrates in practice how every position that the subject holds is inadequate and thus the text loses its linguistic foundation.

If language 'fails', as Bini affirms in the title of her monograph, our research demonstrates that *La Persuasione e la Rettorica*, inside this unavoidable failure, in many ways succeds. It succeeds in performing the 'extreme nihilism' that remains to a subject conscious of its existential status, and it does so through the ultimate questioning of the value of this consciousness itself. It succeeds in being exemplary of the negative dialectic. It is not, in this case, the perlocutionary example of the 'persuaded', but the extreme attempt at coherence, the extreme 'spit' of the «sorba» (PR: 3) that shows the terms under which a fight within and against 'rhetoric' is possible.

In the introduction to the present volume, we quoted Cacciari's interpretation of Lukacs' idea of the 'essay' as a genre: «La verità è *l'idea* del saggio. Esso pertanto non 'fingerà' composizione, unione, ma dovrà compiutamente mostrare proprio l'insuperabile distanza che separa dalla verità – con ciò stesso *custodendone l'idea*. Il saggio [...] *mostra* la verità, ma precisamente come assenza»[2]. Now that we are at the end, we can finally affirm that in the context of Michelstaedter's philosophy *La Persuasione e la Rettorica* fulfils the same task: it can only evoke 'persuasion' as something that is infinitely beyond itself; its dialectic is irony not only because it undermines, but also crucially, because in its movement it 'speaks about something else', something unspeakable.

Notes

1. Harrison, 'The Michelstaedter Enigma' (electronic copy, no page numbers given).
2. Cacciari, 'Interpretazione di Michelstaedter': 24.

Bibliography

Abruzzese, Antonio. *Svevo, Slataper, Michelstaedter: Lo Stile e il Viaggio*. Venezia: Marsilio, 1979.

Adamson, Walter. *Avant-garde Florence: From Modernism to Fascism*. Cambridge, Mass.: Harvard University Press, 1993.

Addison, Catherine. 'From Literal to Figurative: An Introduction to the Study of Simile.' *College English* 55, no. 4 (1993): 402-19.

Agamben, Giorgio. *The Open: Man and Animal*. Stanford: Stanford University Press, 2004.

Agosti, Stefano. *Enunciazione e Racconto. Per una Semiologia della Voce Narrativa*. Bologna: Il Mulino, 1989.

Alfieri, Vittorio Enzo. 'Michelstaedter Poeta.' *Letterature Moderne* 12, no. 2-3 (1962): 133-47.

Arbo, Alessandro. *Carlo Michelstaedter*. Pordenone, Padova: Studio Tesi, 1997.

———. 'La Persuasione Beethoveniana. Riflessioni su un Tema di Carlo Michelstaedter.' *Studi Latini e Italiani*, no. 3 (1989): 247-61.

Asor Rosa, Alberto. 'Introduzione. Ritratto dell'Intellettuale da Giovane.' In *L'Arte di Persuadere*, edited by Giuseppe Prezzolini, 9-22. Napoli: Liguori, 1991.

———. 'La Cultura a Firenze nel Primo Novecento.' In *Intellettuali di Frontiera. Triestini a Firenze (1900-1950)*, edited by Roberto Pertici, 39-53. Firenze: Olschki, 1985.

———. ''La Persuasione e la Rettorica' di Carlo Michelstaedter.' In *Letteratura Italiana-Le Opere. Volume Quarto, Il Novecento. 1. L'Età Della Crisi*, edited by Alberto Asor Rosa, 265-332. Torino: Einaudi, 1995.

Austin, J. L. *How to Do Things with Words*. Oxford: Clarendon Press, 1975.

Bakhtin, Michail M. 'Forms of Time and Chronotope in the Novel.' In *The Dialogic Imagination. Four Essays*, 84-258. Austin: University of Texas Press, 1981.

———. 'From the Prehistory of Novelistic Discourse.' In *The Dialogic Imagination. Four Essays*, 41-83. Austin: University of Texas Press, 1981.

———. *Problems of Dostoevsky's Poetics*. Edited by Caryl Emerson. Manchester: Manchester University Press, 1984.

———. *The Dialogic Imagination. Four Essays*. Translated by Caryl Emerson and Michael Holquist. Austin: Univerity of Texas Press, 1981.

Barthes, Roland. *S/Z*. New York: Hill and Wang, 1974.

Bastianelli, Giannotto. *La Musica Pura, Commentari Musicali e Altri Scritti*. Edited by Miriam Omodeo Donadoni. Firenze: Leo S. Olschki Editore, 1974.

Beiser, Frederick. *Schiller as Philosopher. A Re-Examination*. Oxford: Clarendon Press, 2005.

Bellucci, Antonella, and Andrea Cortellessa, eds. *Quel Libro Senza Eguali. Le Operette Morali e il Novecento Italiano*. Roma: Bulzoni, 2000.

Bellucci, Novella. 'Riverberi Novecenteschi del Riso Leopardiano.' In *Il Riso Leopardiano. Comico, Satira, Parodia. Atti del IX Convegno Internazionale di Studi Leopardiani*, 631-

53. Firenze: Leo S. Olschki, 1998.

Ben-Porat, Ziva. 'Poetics of the Homeric Simile and the Theory of the (Poetic) Simile.' *Poetics Today* 13, no. 4 (1992): 737-69.

———. 'The Poetics of Literary Allusion.' *PTL: A Journal for Descriptive Poetics and Theory of Literature* 1 (1976): 105-28.

Benevento, Aurelio. 'L'<Epistolario> di Michelstaedter.' *Esperienze letterarie* XV, no. 4 (1990): 73-88.

———. "La Persuasione e la Rettorica' di Michelstaedter e la 'Concretezza Artistica". *Otto/Novecento* XV, no. 1 (1991): 119-28.

Benitez, Eugenio. 'Philosophy, Myth and Plato's Two-World View.' *The European Legacy* 12, no. 2 (2007): 225-42.

Benjamin, Walter. *The Origin of German Tragic Drama.* London: Verso, 1998.

Benussi, Cristina. 'La Persuasione e la Rettorica: Autobiografia e Scrittura.' In *Eredità di Carlo Michelstaedter*, edited by Silvio Cumpeta and Angela Michelis, 71-81. Udine: Forum, 2002.

———. *Negazione e Integrazione nella Dialettica di Carlo Michelstaedter.* Roma: Edizioni dell'Ateneo, 1980.

Bianchi, Ugo, ed. *Le Origini dello Gnosticismo: Colloquio di Messina, 13-18 Aprile 1966.* Leiden: E.J. Brill, 1967.

Bini, Daniela. *Carlo Michelstaedter and the Failure of Language.* Gainesville: University Press of Florida, 1992.

———. 'Carlo Michelstaedter: The Tragedy of Thought.' *Differentia: Review of Italian Thought*, no. 2 (1988): 185-94.

———. 'Giacomo Leopardi's Ultrafilosofia.' *Italica* 74, no. 1 (1997): 52-66.

———. 'L'Autenticità del Segno.' In *L'Immagine Irraggiungibile. Dipinti e Disegni di Carlo Michelstaedter*, edited by Antonella Gallarotti, 15-52. Gorizia: Edizioni della Laguna, 1992.

———. 'Leopardi e Michelstaedter tra Autenticità e Inautenticità.' In *Italiana*, edited by Albert N. Mancini, Paolo Giordano and Pier Raimondo Baldini, 219-27. New York: American Association of Teachers of Italian, 1986.

———. 'Michelstaedter tra 'Persuasione' e 'Rettorica'.' *Italica* 63, no. 4 (1986): 346-60.

Blanchot, Maurice, *The Literary Space.* Lincoln: University of Nebraska Press, 1982.

Bloomfield, Morton, W. 'A Grammatical Approach to Personification Allegory.' *Modern Philology* 60, no. 3 (1963): 161-71.

Bo, Carlo. *L'Eredità di Leopardi e Altri Saggi.* Firenze: Vallecchi, 1964.

Bonafin, Massimo. 'Appunti sull'Intertestualità Parodica.' In *Intertestualità*, edited by Massimo Bonafin, 21-8. Genova: Il Melangolo, 1986.

Brianese, Giorgio. 'Essere per il Nulla. Note su Michelstaedter e Heidegger.' *Studi Goriziani* LIX (1984): 7-44.

———. 'Il Silenzio e i Richiami. Per una Rilettura de 'I figli del Mare' di Carlo Michelstaedter.' *Studi Goriziani*, no. 65 (1987): 7-22.

———. *L'Arco e il Destino. Interpretazione di Michelstaedter.* Abano Terme (Padova): Aldo Francisi Editore, 1985.

———. 'Michelstaedter e Greci. Appunti per un Confronto.' *Studi Goriziani* 72 (1990): 23-48.

Bridgeman, Teresa. 'On the 'Likeness' of Similes and Metaphors (With Special Reference to Alfred Jarry's 'Les Jours et les Nuits')' *The Modern Language Review* 91, no. 1 (1996): 65-77.

Brisson, Luc. *Plato the Myth Maker.* Chicago: University of Chicago Press, 1998.

———. 'The Role of Myth in Plato and its Prolongations in Antiquity.' *The European Legacy* 12, no. 2 (2007): 141-58.

Bibliography

Brose, Margaret. 'Leopardi's 'L'Infinito' and the Language of the Romantic Sublime.' *Poetics Today* 4, no. 1 (1983): 47-71.

Cacciari, Massimo. 'Interpretazione di Michelstaedter.' *Rivista di Estetica* XXVI, no. 22 (1986): 21-36.

———. 'La Lotta 'su' Platone.' In *Eredità di Carlo Michelstaedter*, edited by Silvio Cumpeta and Angela Michelis, 93-106. Udine: Forum, 2002.

———. 'Leopardi Platonicus?' *Con-tratto* I, no. 1 (1992): 143-53.

Camerino, Giuseppe Antonio. 'L'Impossibile Cura della Vita e della Società. Affinità di Michelstaedter con Svevo e la Cultura Absburgica.' In *Dialoghi Intorno a Michelstaedter*, edited by Sergio Campailla, 59-74. Gorizia: Biblioteca Statale Isontina, 1987.

———. *La Persuasione e i Simboli. Michelstaedter e Slataper.* Milano: Istituto Propaganda Libraria, 1993.

Campailla, Sergio. *A Ferri Corti con la Vita.* Gorizia: Arti Grafiche Campestrini, 1981.

———. 'Espressionismo e Filosofia della Contestazione in Michelstaedter.' In *Scrittori Giuliani*, 103-31. Bologna: Pàtron, 1980.

———. 'Il Terzo Regno.' In *Poesie*, 9-31. Milano: Adelphi, 1994.

———. 'Le Prime Interpretazioni di Michelstaedter (1910-1916).' *Cultura e Scuola*, no. 114 (1990): 17-26.

———. 'Michelstaedter Lettore di Ibsen.' *Lettere Italiane* XXVI, no. 1 (1974): 46-63.

———. 'Postille Leopardiane di Michelstaedter.' *Studi e Problemi di Critica Testuale*, no. 7 (1973): 242-52.

———. *Quaderno Bibliografico su Carlo Michelstaedter.* Genova: Università degli Studi, 1976.

Carchia, Gianni. 'Linguaggio e Mistica in Carlo Michelstaedter.' *Rivista di Estetica* 9 (1981): 126-32.

Cariolato, Alfonso, and Enrico Fongaro. 'Figure dell'Infigurabile.' In *Parmenide ed Eraclito. Empedocle*, 80-92. Milano: SE, 2003.

Caruth, Cathy. 'The Force of Examples. Kant's Symbols.' In *Unruly Examples. On the Rhetoric of Exemplarity*, edited by Alexander Gelley, 277-302. Stanford: Stanford University Press, 1995.

Cavaglion, Alberto. *Otto Weininger in Italia.* Roma: Carucci Editore, 1982.

Cecchi, Emilio. *Taccuini.* Vol. VI. Milano: Mondadori, 1976.

Cerruti, Marco. *Michelstaedter.* Milano: Mursia, 1967.

Chatman, Seymour. 'Parody and Style.' *Poetics Today* 22, no. 1 (2001): 25-39.

Cinquetti, Nicola. *Michelstaedter. Il Nulla e la Folle Speranza.* Padova: Messaggero, 2002.

Connery, Brian A., and Kirik Combe. 'Introduction.' In *Theorizing Satire. Essays in Literary Criticism*, edited by Brian A. Connery and Kirik Combe. New York: St Martin Press, 1995.

Cooper, David E. *Metaphor.* Oxford: Basil Blackwell, 1986.

Costantini, Alessandro. 'Il Testo Letterario e l'Enunciazione (Appunti per una Teoria Semiotica).' *Strumenti Critici* 46 (1981): 442-57.

Couliano, Ioan P. *The Tree of Gnosis: Gnostic Mythology from Early Christianity to Modern Nihilism.* San Francisco: Harpercollins, 1992.

Cumpeta, Silvio, and Angela Michelis, eds. *Eredità di Carlo Michelstaedter.* Udine: Forum, 2002.

Davidson, Donald. 'Truth and Meaning.' *Synthèse* 17 (1967): 304-23.

———. 'What Metaphors Mean.' In *On Metaphor*, edited by Sheldon Sacks, 29-45. Chicago: The University of Chicago Press, 1979.

De Man, Paul. *Aesthetic Ideology.* Minneapolis, London: University of Minnesota Press, 1996.

————. *Allegories of Reading*. New Haven, London: Yale University Press, 1979.

————. *Blindness & Insight: Essays in the Rhetoric of Contemporary Criticism*. New York: Oxford University Press, 1971.

————. *The Rhetoric of Romanticism*. New York: Columbia University Press, 1984.

————. 'The Rhetoric of Temporality.' In *Interpretation. Theory and Practice*, edited by Charles Singleton, 173-209. Baltimore: John Hopkins Press, 1969.

De Mauro, Tullio, ed. *Grande Dizionario Italiano dell'Uso*. Torino: Utet, 1999-2000

Debenedetti, Giacomo. 'Michelstaedter.' In *Saggi*, 141-55. Milano: Mondadori, 1999.

Deleuze, Gilles. *Difference and Repetition*. London, New York: Continuum, 2004.

————. *Nietzsche and Philosophy*. London, New York: Continuum, 2006.

Demichele, Carmela. 'La Via Luminosa.' In *Il Maestro del Deserto Carlo Michelstaedter*, edited by Antonia Acciani, 75-88. Bari: Progedit, 2005.

Depew, David J., Russel Scott Valentino, and Cinzia Sartini Blum. 'Introduction: Carlo Michelstaedter's Persuasion and Rhetoric.' In *Persuasion and Rhetoric*, IX-XXVII. New Haven, London: Yale University Press, 2004.

Derrida, Jacques. 'White Mythology: Metaphor in the Text of Philosophy.' *New Literary History* 6, no. 1 (1974): 5-74.

Devtag, Antonio. *Michelstaedter. La Grande Trasgressione*: Piccolo Teatro 'Città di Gorizia', December 9-10, 1981.

Diepeveen, Leonard. *Changing Voices. The Modern Quoting Poem*. Ann Arbour: University of Michigan Press, 1993.

Eco, Umberto. *Semiotica e Filosofia del Linguaggio*. Torino: Einaudi, 1974.

————. 'The Theory of Signs and the Role of the Reader.' *The Bulletin of the Midwest Modern Language Association* 14, no. 1 (1981): 35-45.

Ferroni, Giulio. *Storia della Letteratura Italiana. Il Novecento*. Torino: Einaudi, 1991.

Foucault, Michel. 'Nietzsche, Genealogy, History.' In *The Foucault Reader*, edited by Paul Rabinow, 76-100. New York: Pantheon Books, 1984.

Freadman, Anne. *The Machinery of Talk: Charles Peirce and the Sign Hypothesis*. Stanford: Stanford University Press, 2004.

Frege, Gottlob. *The Frege Reader*. Edited by Michael Beaney. Oxford; Malden, MA: Blackwell Publishers, 1997.

Fryre, Northrop. *Anatomy of Criticism: Four Essays*. Princeton: Princeton University Press, 1957.

Gadamer, Hans Georg. *Truth and Method*. New York: Crossroad, 1982.

Gallarotti, Antonella. 'Ricordare Attraverso la Carta: Carlo Michelstaedter.' In *La Speranza: Attraverso l'Ebraismo Goriziano*, 87-104. Monfalcone: Edizioni della Laguna, 1991.

————, ed. *L'Immagine Irraggiungibile. Dipinti e Disegni di Carlo Michelstaedter*. Gorizia: Edizioni della Laguna, 1992.

Garcia Pignide, Lucile. 'Michelstaedter: Un Punto di Vista Psicanalitico.' In *Eredità di Carlo Michelstaedter*, edited by Silvio Cumpeta and Angela Michelis, 135-40. Udine: Forum, 2002.

Gasché, Rodolphe. 'Deconstruction as Criticism.' *Glyph*, no. 6 (1979): 177-215.

Gearhart, Suzanne. 'Philosophy Before Literature: Deconstruction, Historicity, and the Work of Paul De Man.' *Diacritics* 13, no. 4 (1983): 63-81.

Gelley, Alexander. 'Introduction.' In *Unruly Examples. On the Rhetoric of Exemplarity*, edited by Alexander Gelley, 1-24. Stanford: Stanford University Press, 1995.

———. 'The Pragmatics of Exemplary Narrative.' In *Unruly Examples. On the Rhetoric of Exemplarity*, edited by Alexander Gelley, 142-61. Stanford: Stanford University Press, 1995.

Genette, Gerard. *Palimpsests: Literature in the Second Degree*. Lincoln: University of Nebraska Press, 1997.

———. *Paratexts. Thresholds of Interpretation*. Translated by Jane E. Lewin. Cambridge, New York, Oakleigh: Cambridge University Press, 1997.

Gentile, Giovanni. 'Recensione a Carlo Michelstaedter, La Persuasione e la Rettorica.' *La Critica* XX, no. 4 (1922): 332-36.

Giordano, M. G. 'Il Pensiero e l'Arte di Carlo Michelstaedter.' In *Sotto il Segno di Michelstaedter*, edited by T. Iermanno. Cosenza: Edizioni Periferia, 1994.

Godbout, Jacques T. *The World of the Gift*. Montreal & Kingston, London, Ithaca: McGill-Queen's University Press, 1998.

Goldmann, Lucien. *Towards a Sociology of the Novel*. London: Tavistock Publications Ltd., 1975.

Gomperz, Theodor. *Greek Thinkers: A History of Ancient Philosophy*. London: Murray, 1901-12.

Gould, Timothy. 'The Audience of Originality: Kant and Wordsworth on the Reception of Genius.' In *Essays in Kant's Aesthetics*, edited by Ted Cohen and Paul Guyer, 179-93. Chicago & London: The University of Chicago Press, 1982.

Hannoosh, Michele. 'The Reflexive Function of Parody.' *Comparative Literature* 41, no. 2 (1989): 113-27.

Harrison, Thomas. *1910. The Emancipation of Dissonance*. Berkeley, Los Angeles, London: University of California Press, 1996.

———. 'The Michelstaedter Enigma.' *Differentia: Review of Italian Thought*, no. 8-9 Spring/Autumn (1999): 125-41.

Havelock, Eric A. 'The Linguistic Task of the Presocratics.' In *Language and Thought in Early Greek Philosophy*, edited by Kevin Robb. La Salle: Hegeler Institute, 1983.

Householder, Fred W. 'Parodia.' *Journal of Classical Philology* 39, no. 1 (1944): 1-9.

Howland, Jacob. 'Plato and Kirkegaard: two Philosophical Stories.' *The European Legacy* 12, no. 2 (2007): 173-85.

Hutcheon, Linda. *A Theory of Parody*. New York, London: Methuen, 1985.

Iwin, William. 'What is an Allusion?' *The Journal of Aesthetics and Art Criticism* 59, no. 3 (2001): 287-97.

Jonas, Hans. *Gnosis und Spätantiker Geist*. 2 vols. Göttingen: Vandenhoeck & Ruprecht, 1992.

———. 'Myth and Mysticism: a Study of Objectification and Interiorization in Religious Thought.' *The Journal of Religion* 19, no. 1 (1969): 315-29.

———. *The Gnostic Religion : the Message of the Alien God and the Beginnings of Christianity*. Boston: Beacon Press, 1963.

Kanduth, Erika. 'Dal Tu all'Io nella Poesia di Carlo Michelstaedter.' In *Eredità di Carlo Michelstaedter*, edited by Silvio Cumpeta and Angela Michelis, 125-34. Udine: Forum, 2002.

Kant, Immanuel. *Critique of Judgement*. Translated by J. H. Bernard. Mineola, New York: Dover Publications, 2005.

Kaufmann, Wanda Ostrowska. *The Anthropology of Wisdom Literature*. Westport: Bergin & Garvey, 1996.

Kelber, Werner H. 'In the Beginning Were the Words: The Apotheosis and Narrative Displacement of the Logos.' *Journal of the American Academy of Religion* 58, no. 1 (1990): 69-98.

Klossowski, Pierre. *Nietzsche, il Politeismo e la Parodia*. Milano: SE, 1999.

La Rocca, Claudio. 'Esistenzialismo e Nichilismo. Luporini e Michelstaedter.' *Belfagor* LIV, no. 322 (1999): 521-38.

Lang, Berel. *The Anatomy of Philosophical Style: Literary Philosophy and the Philosophy of Literature*. Oxford, Cambridge: Blackwell, 1990.

Lansing, Richard H. *From Image to Idea: A Study of the Simile in Dante's «Commedia»*. Ravenna: Longo Editore, 1977.

Leopardi, Giacomo. *Tutte le Poesie e Tutte le Prose*. Edited by Lucio Felici and Emanuele Trevi. Rome: Newton & Compton, 1997.

———. *Zibaldone*. Edited by Lucio Felici. Roma: Newton & Compton, 1997.

Levin, Samuel R. 'Allegorical Language.' In *Allegory, Myth and Symbol*, edited by Morton Bloomfield, W., 23-38. Cambridge, London: Harvard University Press, 1981.

Ligi, Livio. *Il Teatro in Rivolta. Futurismo, Grottesco, Pirandello e Pirandellismo*. Milano: Mursia, 1976.

Lloyd, David. 'Kant's Examples.' In *Unruly Examples. On The Rhetoric of Exemplarity*, edited by Alexander Gelley, 255-76. Stanford: Stanford University Press, 1995.

Lonardi, Gilberto. '«Alter Ridebat... Flebat Alter»: A Proposito di Democrito/Eraclito in Leopardi.' In *Il Riso Leopardiano. Comico, Satira, Parodia. Atti del IX Convegno Internazionale di Studi Leopardiani*, 97-105. Firenze: Leo S. Olschki Editore, 1995.

Lukács, Georg. *Soul and Form*. Translated by Anna Bostock. London: Merlin Press, 1974.

———. *The Theory of the Novel*. London: Merlin Press, 1971.

Lukács, György. *L'Anima e le Forme*. Translated by Sergio Bologna. Milano: SE, 2002.

Lyons, John D. *The Rhetoric of Example in Early Modern France and Italy*. Princeton: Princeton University Press, 1989.

Magris, Claudio. *L'Anello di Clarisse*. Torino: Einaudi, 1984.

———. *Un Altro Mare*. Milano: Garzanti, 2003.

Marcheschi, Daniela. 'La Persuasione o il Dileguare dell'Illusione del Tempo. Note a Carlo Michelstaedter.' *Letteratura Italiana Contemporanea*, no. 10 (1983): 17-38.

Margolis, Joseph. 'Notes on the Logic of Simile, Metaphor and Analogy.' *American Speec* 32, no. 3 (1957): 186-89.

Martin, Warner. *Philosophical Finesse: Studies in the Art of Rational Persuasion*. Oxford, New York: Clarendon and Oxford University Press, 1989.

Mauss, Marcel. *The Gift: The Form and Reason for Exchange in Archaic Societies*. London: Routledge, 1990.

Mengaldo, Pier Vincenzo, ed. *Poeti Italiani del Novecento*. Milano: Mondadori, 1978.

Merola, Nicola, ed. *Ricerche sul Moderno*. Soveria Mannelli: Rubettino, 2005.

Michelis, Angela. *Carlo Michelstaedter, il Coraggio dell'Impossibile*. Roma: Città Nuova, 1997.

Michelstaedter, Carlo. *Il Prediletto Punto d'Appoggio della Dialettica Socratica e Altri Scritti*. Edited by Gianandrea Franchi. Milano: Mimesis, 2000.

———. *La Persuasione e la Rettorica*. Edited by Sergio Campailla. Milano: Adelphi, 1982.

———. *Opere*. Edited by Gaetano Chiavacci. Firenze: Sansoni, 1958.

———. *Parmenide ed Eraclito. Empedocle*. Milano: SE, 2003.

———. *Persuasion and Rhetoric*. Translated by Russel Scott Valentino, Cinzia Sartini Blum and

David J. Depew. New Haven, London: Yale University Press, 2004.
———. *Sfugge la Vita. Taccuini e Appunti*. Edited by Angela Michelis. Torino: Nino Aragno Editore, 2004.
Monai, Fulvio. 'Michelstaedter Anticipatore in Arte dell'Espressionismo.' In *Dialoghi Intorno a Michelstaedter*, edited by Sergio Campailla, 159-75. Gorizia: Biblioteca Statale Isontina, 1987.
Morson, G.M., and C. Emerson. 'Extracts from a Heteroglossary.' In *Dialogue and Critical Discourse: Language, Culture, Critical Theory*, edited by M. Macovski, 256-72. New York: Oxford University Press, 1997.
Mortara Garavelli, Bice. *Manuale di Retorica*. Milano: Bompiani, 2002.
Muzzioli, Francesco. 'Il Vociano Michelstaedter.' *Alfabeta*, no. 57 (1984).
———. 'L'Antagonismo di Michelstaedter.' In *Ricerche sul Moderno. Terza Edizione*, edited by Nicola Merola, 309-15. Soveria Mannelli: Rubettino, 2005.
———. *Michelstaedter*. Lecce: Milella, 1987.

Negri, Antimo. 'Il Riso di Nietzsche e il Riso di Leopardi.' In *Il Riso Leopardiano. Comico, Satira, Parodia. Atti del IX Convegno Internazionale di Studi Leopardiani*, 65-86. Firenze: Leo S. Olschki Editore, 1998.
Nietzsche, Friedrich Wilhelm. *The Gay Science*. Cambridge, New York: Cambridge University Press, 2001.
———. 'On the Genealogy of Morals.' In *Basic Writings of Nietzsche*. New York: Modern Library Edition, 1992.
Nimis, Stephen A. *Narrative Semiotics in the Epic Tradition*. Bloomington, Indianapolis: Indiana University Press, 1987.

Paganelli, Fabiola. 'Il Sorriso Tragico di Carlo Michelstaedter.' In *'Quel Libro Senza Uguali'. Le Operette Morali e il Novecento Italiano*, edited by Novella Bellucci and Andrea Cortellessa, 53-67. Roma: Bulzoni, 2000.
Papini, Giovanni. 'Un Suicidio Metafisico.' In *Tutte le Opere*, 817-22. Milano: Mondadori, 1961.
Parmenides of Elea. *Fragments*. Translated by David Gallop. Edited by David Gallop. Toronto, Buffalo, London: University of Toronto Press, 1984.
Pastore, Federico. *La Conoscenza come Azione. Saggi su Lukács*. Milano: Marzorati, 1980.
Penner, Terry. 'Socrates and the Early Dialogues.' In *The Cambridge Companion to Plato*, edited by Richard Kraut, 121-69. Cambridge: Cambridge University Press, 1992.
Perelman, Chaïm, and Lucie Olbrechts-Tyteca. *Trattato dell'Argomantazione. La Nuova Retorica*. Torino: Einaudi, 1966.
Perna, Valerio. 'Dal Libro alla Parola.' In *Il Maestro del Deserto Carlo Michelstaedter*, edited by Antonia Acciani, 61-74. Bari: Progedit, 2005.
Pieri, Piero. *La Differenza Ebraica. Ebraismo e Grecità in Michelstaedter*. Bologna: Cappelli, 1984.
———. 'Per una Dialettica Storica del Silenzio. La 'Vergogna' del Filosofo e l'Autoinganno dello Scrittore.' In *Eredità di Carlo Michelstaedter*, edited by Silvio Cumpeta and Angela Michelis, 225-35. Udine: Forum, 2002.
Pirandello, Luigi. 'Pirandello Parla di Pirandello.' *Termini* 2 (1936): 22.
Piromalli, Antonio. *Michelstaedter*. Firenze: La Nuova Italia, 1968.
Platone. *Tutti gli Scritti*. Edited by Giovanni Reale. Milano: Rusconi, 1997.
Preziosi, Luigi. 'Una Giovinezza Spezzata (Echi Leopardiani in Michelstaedter).' *Studi Goriziani*, no. 66 (1987): 81-96.

Prezzolini, Giuseppe. *L'Arte di Persuadere*. Edited by Alberto Asor Rosa. Napoli: Liguori, 1991.

Quintilian. *The Institutio Oratoria of Quintilian*. Translated by H. E. Butler. London: Heineman, 1969-77.

Quispel, Gilles. 'Gnosticism and the New Testament.' *Vigiliae Christianae* 19, no. 2 (1965): 65-85.

———. 'Hermes Trismegistus and the Origins of Gnosticism.' *Vigiliae Christianae* 46, no. 1 (1992): 1-19.

Ranke, Joachim. 'Il Pensiero di Carlo Michelstaedter. Un Contributo allo Studio dell'Esistenzialismo Italiano.' *Giornale Critico della Filosofia Italiana*, no. 4 (1962): 518-39.

Raschini, Maria Adelaide. *Carlo Michelstaedter*. Milano: Marzorati, 1965.

———. *Michelstaedter*. Venezia: Marsilio, 2000.

———. 'Rilettura di Michelstaedter.' In *Dialoghi Intorno a Michelstaedter*, edited by Sergio Campailla, 89-96. Gorizia: Biblioteca Statale Isontina, 1987.

Reale, Giovanni. *Per una Nuova Interpretazione di Platone. Rilettura della Metafisica dei Grandi Dialoghi alla Luce delle 'Dottrine non Scritte'*. Milano: Vita e Pensiero, 1991.

———. *Storia della Filosofia Antica*. 3 vols. Vol. 1. Milano: Vita e Pensiero, 1976.

———. *Storia della Filosofia Antica*. 3 vols. Vol. 2. Milano: Vita e Pensiero, 1976.

Rée, Jonathan. *Philosophical Tales: An Essay on Philosophy and Literature*. London, New York: Methuen, 1987.

Richards, I. A. *The Philosophy of Rhetoric*. Oxford: Oxford University Press, 1936.

Ricoeur, Paul. *The Rule of Metaphor: Multi-Disciplinary Studies of the Creation of Meaning in Language*. London: Routledge & Kegan Paul, 1978.

Rose, Margaret A. *Parody: Ancient, Modern and Postmodern*. Cambridge: Cambridge University Press, 1993.

———. *Parody//Metafiction*. London: Croom Helm, 1979.

Sanò, Laura. *Le Ragioni del Nulla. Il Pensiero Tragico nella Filosofia Italiana tra Ottocento e Novecento*. Troina: Città Aperta 2005.

Sarri, Francesco. *Socrate e la Nascita del Concetto Occidentale di Anima*. Milano: Vita e Pensiero, 1997.

Schelling, Friedrich Wilhelm Joseph von. *The Philosophy of Art*. Edited by Douglas W. Stott. Minneapolis: University of Minnesota Press, 1989.

Schopenhauer, Arthur. *Parerga and Paralipomena. Short Philosophical Essays*. Translated by E. F. J. Payne. II vols. Oxford: Clarendon Press, 1974.

———. *The World as Will and Representation*. Translated by E. F. J. Payne. 2 vols. New York: Dover Publication Inc., 1969.

Secchieri, F. *Con Leggerezza Apparente. Etica e Ironia nelle 'Operette Morali'*. Modena: Mucchi, 1992.

Semeraro, Licia. *Lo Svuotamento del Futuro. Note su Michelstaedter*. Lecce: Milella, 1986.

Severino, Emanuele. *Il Nulla e la Poesia. Alla Fine dell'Età della Tecnica: Leopardi*. Milano: Rizzoli, 2005.

Sibley, Gay. 'Satura from Quintillan to Joe Bob Briggs: A New Look at an Old Word'. In *Theorizing Satire. Essays in Literary Criticism*, edited by Brian A. Connery and Kirik Combe. New York: St Martin Press, 1995.

Soskice, Janet Martin. *Metaphor and Religious Language*. Oxford: Clarendon Press, 1985.

Speliots, Evanthia. 'Image, Myth and Dialectic in Plato.' *The European Legacy* 12, no. 2 (2007): 221-23.

Stella, Vittorio. 'La Riflessione sull'Arte in Michelstaedter.' In *Dialoghi Intorno a Michelstaedter*, edited by Sergio Campailla, 137-58. Gorizia: Biblioteca Satale Isontina, 1987.

Stirner, Max. *The Ego and Its Own*. Cambridge: Cambridge University Press, 1995.

Strappini, Lucia, Claudia Micocci, and Alberto Abruzzese, eds. *La Classe dei Colti. Intellettuali e Società nel Primo Novecento Italiano*. Bari: Laterza, 1970.

Suleiman, Susan Rubin. *Authoritarian Fiction: The Ideological Novel as Literary Genre*. New York: Columbia University Press, 1983.

Szondi, Peter. *An Essay on the Tragic*. Stanford: Stanford University Press, 2002.

Taviani, Giovanna. 'Attualità di Michelstaedter.' In *Ricerche sul Moderno. Terza Serie*, edited by Nicola Merola, 317-21. Soveria Mannelli: Rubbettino, 2005.

———. 'Lettura (Attuale) di 'La Persuasione e la Rettorica' di Carlo Michelstaedter.' *Annali della Facoltà di Lettere e Filosofia*, no. 17 (1996): 207-18.

———. *Michelstaedter*. Palermo: Palumbo, 2002.

Tihanov, Galin. *The Master and the Slave: Lukàcs, Bakhtin, and the Ideas of Their Time*. Oxford: Clarendon, 2000.

Todorov, Tzvetan. *Theories of the Symbol*. Ithaca: Cornell University Press, 1982.

Turner, John D. 'The Gnostic Sethians and Middle Platonism: Interpretations of the Timaeus and Parmenides.' *Vigiliae Christianae* 60 (2006): 9-64.

Vasiliou, Iakovos. 'Conditional Irony in the Socratic Dialogues.' *The Classical Quarterly, New Series* 49, no. 2 (1999): 456-72.

Vattimo, Gianni. *Nietzsche*. Bari: Laterza, 1985.

Waldstein, Michael. 'Hans Jonas' Construct 'Gnosticism': Analysis and Critique.' *Journal of Early Christian Studies* 8, no. 3 (2000): 341-72.

Weininger, Otto. *Sex and Character*. New York: AMS Press, 1975.

Williams, Michael Allen. *Rethinking Gnosticism: an Argument for Dismantling a Dubious Category*. Princeton: Princeton University Press, 1996.

Wittgenstein, Ludwig. *Tractatus Logico-Philosophicus e Quaderni 1914-16*. Translated by Amedeo G. Conte. Torino: Einaudi, 1995.

Zappen, James P. *The Rebirth of Dialogue: Bakhtin, Socrates, and the Rhetorical Tradition*. Albany: State University of New York Press, 2004.

Lightning Source UK Ltd.
Milton Keynes UK
03 March 2011

168598UK00001B/34/P